Trouble

Trouble

A Memoir

Marise Gaughan

monoray

First published in Great Britain in 2022 by Monoray,
an imprint of Octopus Publishing Group Ltd
Carmelite House
50 Victoria Embankment
London EC4Y 0DZ
www.octopusbooks.co.uk

An Hachette UK Company
www.hachette.co.uk

Distributed in the US by Hachette Book Group
1290 Avenue of the Americas
4th and 5th Floors
New York, NY 10104

Distributed in Canada by Canadian Manda Group
664 Annette St.
Toronto, Ontario, Canada M6S 2C8

ISBN (Hardback) 978 1 91318 398 1
ISBN (Paperback) 978 1 80096 001 5

A CIP catalogue record for this book is available from the British Library.

Printed and bound in UK

1 3 5 7 9 10 8 6 4 2

This FSC® label means that materials used for the product
have been responsibly sourced

For no one

AUTHOR'S NOTE

Human beings are notoriously unreliable witnesses, but this book is my life, as witnessed by me. Names, places and descriptions have been changed, to protect the privacy of people who didn't agree to be written about.

A further disclaimer: This is not a play-by-play of everything that has ever happened to me, but rather a story, of a father and a daughter. And I write this story as a twenty-nine-year-old woman, looking back, so the memories I write as fact may not actually be that. They are how I remember them, through the fuzzy lens of someone who has made it out the other side. When I think back, on my father and my destruction, I remember each moment principally through the emotions I felt, not always the specific details. As much as we want the clarity of things to be black and white, they exist as bookends, with the true story contained within.

CONTENTS

CONTENTS

Somebody gets into trouble, then gets out of it again.
People love that story. They never get sick of it.

Kurt Vonnegut

ONE

DISNEYLAND

1

When I think back, to everything that happened before now, the memories that come easiest are all the firsts. I lay them out in front of me, like Post-its of my life, trying to decide which one is most important; which one I can point to and say, *AHA, this is it!* The first time my father broke my heart. That one is the clearest to me. It's the one I've pulled off so many times that the sticky back has long since faded away. But this story starts before then. It starts when he just pulled at it a little bit; when nothing was broken, and everything could still be fixed. When this story begins, as I grew up in Dublin in the 1990s, I thought it would end somewhere else.

I am eight, and my dad comes into my bedroom early one Saturday morning. Well, early for him. It's 10am and he rarely rises before noon. He is in a dressing gown and from the loose way he's tied it I can see he doesn't have anything on underneath. Gross. *You know how much I love you,* he coos at me, sitting much too close. I scoot away. *Yea, Dad, sure.* Please don't hug me please don't hug me. He does, and I feel his breath on my head. It's smothering me. *I won't drink again, I promise you. Look at me.* I hate looking at him. *I swear on your life I won't drink again; I love you too much.* I nod, and reluctantly laugh. *Okay, you win, Dad. I love you too.* He raises his arms in celebration and I laugh again as he starts reciting, *One small step for man… You know I met Buzz Aldrin, don't you? Bought me a fish pie and we played blackjack.*

I nod, because he's told me a variation of this story a hundred times before. Sometimes it's blackjack, sometimes it's roulette, sometimes they leave the casino and go fishing. I'm eight years old, and I think my dad is the most interesting man to exist, even if the stories don't always add up. Even if his drinking gives me the same feeling in my stomach as being on the top of a roller coaster, right before it drops. None of that matters now, though, because he's quit for good this time. He loves me too much. He leaves my room and I bask in my value. I'm the reason he's stopped drinking! My brother will be so jealous.

Downstairs, an hour later, I instinctively sniff the empty glass beside the kitchen sink. My heart drops. It's vodka. I scrub the glass, rinsing it over and over again with Fairy liquid. If I can wash away the alcohol, it means it didn't really exist in the first place. If I can erase the stain of this lie, it means my dad was telling the truth.

My father was an alcoholic. Not the type of alcoholic where you only realize it after the fact – I didn't have to put together the jigsaw of addiction, slowly realizing what he was, piece by piece. It was presented to me clearly from a young age. *Dad is an alcoholic. That's why he doesn't drink.* He first went to rehab when he was twenty-seven, a year after he married my mum, and spent most of his life from then in sobriety. Alcoholism was just this adult word presented to me, more of an identity for my father than a thing I regularly experienced.

I knew it made him different to other dads. That he didn't go down the pub every Friday night, or order a beer during dinner, instead asking for two Cokes in a pint glass. Addiction was something that only belonged to my father, that only existed within the four walls of our home, which is why we never talked about it to other people. I pretended to my friends that he drank. *Oh yes, my dad drank beer and watched the big football match last week, oh yes, my normal dad does very normal dad stuff, thank you very much.*

I dry off the glass and place it back in the cabinet. *Oh yes, my dad has really quit drinking this time. Oh yes, my dad is back to normal dad, thank you very much.*

2

That night, he can't get the keys in the door, so the loud banging wakes me up. From my bed I hear him stumble in the door. I get up and sit on the stairs, my head peering through the banisters at the dark hall beneath me, listening to him and my mum fighting in the kitchen. I don't know what exactly is wrong. Just that something is wrong. There is a feeling in my stomach. Like butterflies, but bad butterflies. Moths. Trying to nibble away at my body, from the inside out. I think about running downstairs to warn my parents, in case the moths escape me and try to get inside them, but I am glued to the stairs. So I just sit here, listening to words I don't understand, in tones that make the moths dance harder. My brother, who is four, comes out of the room we share, holding his favourite teddy bear, and I quickly bring him back to bed. I don't want him to be around whatever this is. If I can just absorb it all, everything will be okay.

When I come home from school that Friday, my mum sits me down. *Dad has gone away for a few months*, she says. *To a place that will make him better. It's called rehab.* She hands me a brand-new Barbie doll. I scream in excitement. This is my first Barbie of my very own. *Let's send Dad away every year*, I tell my mum, stroking my Barbie's hair. We go to visit him a month later. My brother and I sit on the sprawling lawn, playing with my Barbie, while my parents speak on a bench beside us. The sun is shining and the grass is so green. I'm pretty sure I could play on this lawn for the rest of my life.

Daddy is getting better, my mum tells me on the car ride home. Oh, I like the sound of that! I look out the window behind me as we drive away, sad to leave the nice lawn and my new, getting better dad. *Why can't we stay here too?* I know the answer as soon as I ask. This isn't a place for kids. Kids don't need to get better.

When he was allowed back home, when he signed his release forms and was given back his wallet and the laces in his shoes, the clinic counsellors advised my father to attend a meeting a day for the first ninety days. He showed up to one, on day one, and didn't stay until the end. My father didn't believe in Alcoholics Anonymous. *Not for me*, he announced gleefully, whenever it was mentioned. *The day I volunteer to go into a room full of men, to moan for an hour about alcohol, is the day I shoot my brains out! Some people need their hand held while getting off drink, and some of us aren't little bitches.* He was so proud of himself for doing it alone, like he was slaughtering a cow himself instead of buying packaged mince in Tesco. I never understood his aversion to meetings. *There's a reason so many people go to AA. They're supposed to help you when you have the urge to drink*, I would later try to reason with him. *When I have the urge to drink, I'm already drinking*, was his response. So, a week before my ninth birthday, he drank again.

3

Our family, minus Dad, has spent the past five days with Mum's relatives in Meath. My dad's absence isn't unusual. He is sporadic in his attendance of family events and school meetings and sports competitions. *Family minus Dad* is our typical RSVP. *Working* is the usual excuse we give, and I wonder how much work someone can do in bed, with the curtains drawn. When he did show up, he'd be so much fun to be around – making everyone laugh, the centre of attention – that any grudges would be quickly forgotten.

Still, I miss him when he's not around. And I know he misses me. *When you are away from me, I feel like a limb is missing,* he once told me, *that's how much I love you*. On the car ride home, I count down the minutes until we are back in our house, until I am back with him. *Give the countdown a rest*, my mother says, clearly agitated. *Concentrate on the road, not me*, I yell back. I imagine my father, sitting in our hallway, his foot hanging off his leg, waiting for my return. It feels like a race against time; we need to get back before he's left with just a stump. *Step on the gas*, I shout, and my mother rolls her eyes. *I hate a back-seat driver. Pipe down, and play I spy with your brother*. I ignore her, and instead stare out the window, watching the rain drip down, trying to guess which drop will win. I make a pact with myself – if I pick the winner, it means Dad will be okay. I sigh, relieved, when I watch my raindrop cross the finish line.

Mum pulls into our driveway, and I jump out of the car before she's turned off the ignition. I walk into a cold house, with my mother and brother trailing me, and call out for my dad. No answer. I sense a shift in Mum's mood. As a rule, I don't understand my mother, because she is quiet and distant and nothing like me, but sometimes I can feel her. She rushes upstairs, and I am right on her back, knowing some shit is about to go down. I am excited. I gear up to take my dad's side. My brother is my mother's child, but I belong to my father. Children are like parents: we love both equally, of course, but there's always a favourite. We walk into the bedroom, and there he is, naked in bed, with vomit on the floor beside him. My excitement turns to nausea. Oh shit. I want to look away, but my eyes stay glued to him. The moths are back, stirring inside of me. I look to my mum, willing her to solve this. She is always the problem solver, especially when the problem is my dad. *You fucking idiot*, she says, spitting out the words at him, and he slurs back, eyes rolling to the back of his head. She walks out of the room. It's just me and him now. *I hate you!* I'm surprised at my own words, at how easily they pour out of me, at how much I believe them to be true. He says nothing, rolling over to hang his head off the bed. Through the sheet I can see a small wet circle growing around his crotch.

I tell my dad I hate him, and take it back as soon as I am alone. In my bedroom, I get down on my knees and pray. *Dear God, please take back what I said. I love him, I love him, I love him.* Tears fall down my face. *Something bad took over me when I looked at him, it might have been the devil, but please, God, please know I love him.* I squeeze my hands together in prayer, hoping that means something; that God can see how serious I am. *Please, God, please, just bring my normal dad back to me.* I lean down and bite one praying hand, until it hurts, until there is a red jagged outline left on my skin, a physical sign so God knows I am serious. I know I am praying for both of us.

My mother comes into my bedroom, a burning cake outstretched in her hands. *Happy birthday to you*, she sings. *Go away*, I tell her. She ignores me, and keeps singing out of key. *Oh my God, Mum, you can't sing to save your life*, I moan, and she continues to ignore me. *Make a wish*, she instructs, when she has stopped making my ears bleed. *But make sure the wish is just for you.* I begrudgingly close my eyes and blow out the candles. *Hip, hip, hooray*, she shouts. When I don't respond, she sits down on the bed beside me. *Look, I know this isn't a good birthday. But you have a whole lifetime of birthdays ahead of you. And if this is the worst one, that means, for the rest of your life, it will only get better.* I mull over her words. *That's a good point, actually. I didn't think of it like that.* She's forgotten to bring any cutlery, so I stick my hand in the cake and bring it to my mouth. *Come on, Marise*, she yells, *think of the duvet!* I flick a piece of chocolate onto her blouse. *Maybe that's my birthday wish! You ever think of that?* She looks at me, then grins. I watch her scoop up a piece, and smush it right into my sheets. I gasp, then laugh, and she laughs, and now we're both laughing, staring at the chocolate stain on my bed.

He continues to drink for another two weeks, empty bottles of vodka collecting in the kitchen, as I avoid him, as he avoids me, until one day he retreats to his bedroom and stays there. That's always how it goes with his drinking. He decides to take that first drink, and he decides to take the last. All that power, to destroy and rebuild, is contained within him. My only role is being a witness to it all.

He stays in his bedroom, sweating and screaming, until the following Saturday. During that week, his moans ring through the house, and I increase the volume on the TV when I hear them, until the Rugrats have drowned him out. *Detoxing*, Mum says, adding another word to my vocabulary that I don't really understand. I slot it next to *sober, addiction, alcoholism* and *rehab*, then cover those words with a thick sheet. *Just don't bother him. Leave him alone.* I nod, staring at the television, surprised that she thinks I need to be told that. *Isn't Angelica so funny?* I flatly ask, without looking at her. My mum smiles. *She sure is. She reminds me of you.*

When he comes out, on day seven, he's back to normal dad. He walks into the living room when I'm watching cartoons. He sits down on the couch, and I ignore the heat building up inside my body. *I won't ever drink again*, he tells me softly. I reach over and grab his hand, not looking away from the TV. Even though I've heard those words countless times, I still believe them. I know he means it this time. I give his hand a squeeze. *I'm right here, Dad. I've always been right here.*

4

Give a thing and take it back,
God will ask you where is that,
you will say you do not know,
and catch a chain and down you go.

I am sitting in class, hunched over a piece of paper, drawing six lines so I can make a cool-looking S, when my best friend Aoife says this to Rachel. Rachel had given her a pencil earlier that morning, and was now asking for it back. I look up, over at Rachel, and chime in. *She's right! You'll go to Hell if you take it back!* Rachel solemnly nods, letting Aoife keep the pencil. There are some facts you just can't ignore. And Hell is number one on the list.

Because I go to a Catholic school, and live in a Catholic country, and am a Catholic, I know pretty much everything there is to know about God. He is the most powerful thing in the world. He lives in the sky, next door to Santa. When it rains, it means He's taking a shower, or else you've killed an ant and He's crying. God cries when any of His creations are murdered, and He doesn't miss even an ant-killing because He's always keeping an eye on us. From up there in the sky, He can see everything we do. He is always watching us, and can even listen to our thoughts. God loves me, because He loves everyone, but He's deeply upset at all of us, because His only son had to die for us. He wanted us to do good, and instead we keep sinning, and He let his only son die for *this*? So, He's a little bit angry at us, and is itching for a slice of revenge. His main punishment is Hell. I have nightmares about Hell on a regular basis. The devil is always poking me with a hot stick, and the only other people there are Hitler and serial killers and Protestants. I am starving hungry, but the only food available to eat is shepherd's pie, which is maybe my least favourite food on the planet.

In the playground, we talk in whispered tones about Hell. *You're there for eternity, which I heard was one hundred years*, Rachel says, and my eyes nearly explode from my head. *That is so long!* The gravity of the situation makes us drop our heads, staring at the gravel. We are all terrified of ending up there.

The only time Hell nightmares were replaced was last spring, when we found out about nuclear explosions, and that there was a nuclear plant over in England, and if there was an explosion and the wind was blowing west, we'd all die. We didn't sleep for a week straight. I took to listening to the radio every night, waiting for an announcement of disaster. Aoife cried every time she saw a dark cloud in the sky. Around the same time, the government sent packets to every home, that consisted of an iodine tablet and a pamphlet on what to do if there was a nuclear explosion. That proved to me it wasn't just childish fear; it was a very real and credible threat. If adults were scared too, it meant it was real.

I asked my dad for advice on what we should do when it happened. *Well,* he said, *we'd probably have an hour or two from knowing about it until it kills us. I think I'd crack open a bottle, tell everyone I love that I love them, and call everyone I've fallen out with.* He paused for effect, then finished, *So I could die in peace.* I was aghast. *You wouldn't try to save yourself?* He laughed a knowing laugh. *Kiddo, there's no saving any of us when that happens. You die accepting it, or you die in denial. Either way you're dead on the ground.* I heard my mother giving out to him that evening as I cried in my bedroom, terrified of our impending doom.

I woke up the next morning, determined. *I need an envelope and a stamp,* I told my mother. I sat down at the kitchen table and wrote a letter to Tony Blair, using my brand-new gel pens. Each page got a different colour, and they were scented too! I was sure they would convey a sense of gravity to the British Prime Minister. In cherry red and grape purple, I gave an impassioned plea to close Sellafield plant. *It is really not fair that you could kill people in a different country, just because of how the wind blows.* His secretary responded a few weeks later, and my mother screamed in delight when the postman came. *A letter for Miss Marise Gaughan,* she shouted up the stairs, waving it in the air. *A very important letter for a Miss Marise Gaughan.*

I wanted to wait until Dad was home from work to open it, but I was afraid he'd get jealous. He might tell me, *That's weird, I just got off the phone with George Bush earlier*, and he'd make my letter less important. I decided to open it without him. *Only because it might be time sensitive*, I told my mum, *I shouldn't keep Tony Blair waiting*. My mum agreed with me. *I think that's smart; we'll just tell your dad about it later. This is your letter, and your moment.* I looked up at her when she said that, and dropped the letter on the table. I grabbed her waist and hugged her. *Thank you, Mum. This is your idea, so you'll tell Dad it was your idea?* She nodded, and I sat back down at the table and tore the envelope open as my mother paced the kitchen. *A letter from the Prime Minister of fecking Britain! I've never heard of someone getting such a letter. You are so smart and confident*, she told me. *Mum, stop it! You're making me so nervous*, I said, but secretly hoped she'd keep going. *Read it out loud*, she instructed. *Thank you for taking the time to write to the Prime Minister. He appreciates hearing from you and will consider your thoughts.* I placed the paper down on the table, in shock. Tears fell down my cheeks. I handed my mother the letter, so she could read it for herself. *I've done it, Mum*, I choked out, through my tears. *He's going to close Sellafield.*

Now I have solved the threat of nuclear disaster, I just need to get my dad into Heaven, and then I'll really be able to sleep at night. See, my dad is destined for Hell, and that worries me greatly. There are 950,000 reasons why you could go to Hell, and one of them is if you don't go to mass. Family minus Dad goes every week. I scream in resistance each Sunday morning. *But whhhhhhhyyyyy?* I wail, shoving my feet into too-tight black shoes. *Because God wants you to*, Mum always tells me. *He suffered for us; don't you think you can suffer a bit back?* When I ask her why Dad gets to stay home and I have to go, she mumbles something about him being exempt. *He has a doctor's note letting him off,* she tells me, batting me away with a towel, applying her lipstick in the bathroom mirror. That explanation checks out. My father loves the doctor's office more than any other place in the world. He visits Dr Roache religiously, and is on first-name basis with Gerry. Every time he sees him, he comes home with a new prescription, and I watch him popping all his different pills as he sits in his underwear in his bed. Pharmacy receipts line the top of the fridge, hundreds of them, and when I find them while searching for hidden sweets, I feel I've discovered a terrible secret, even though it's a secret I already knew.

It still makes me jealous, seeing my dad asleep in bed while we trudge off every Sunday morning, wearing itchy trousers and too-polished shoes, because there's nothing I hate more than mass. Mass goes on far too long, and the priests talk so low I can't make out what they're saying. Wouldn't make much of a difference if I could, though, because they just repeat the same five things they do every Sunday. They're not like the priests on TV shows, who tell interesting stories and bang their fists in passion, and everyone stands up and shakes their asses shouting HALLELUJAH. *Those aren't real priests,* my mother says dismissively, *that's just Hollywood. Real priests don't sing songs, but they do notice if you don't show up to mass, and they pass that on to God. And you don't want to make God mad, do you?* I grudgingly shake my head.

My mother doesn't seem to care that my dad is going to Hell, which strikes me as odd because she really, really cares about God. She blesses herself every time we pass by a church, and lights a candle when someone is sick. She keeps holy water in her purse, and splashes us with it when we go on long car rides. When one of us has been really bold, she goes to mass an extra time that week, praying for our troubled soul. She says stuff like *It's God's plan; when your time is up, it's up* when someone dies unexpectedly. During mass, she knows exactly when to sit, and stand, and sit back down, and then kneel. She doesn't have to look around her to copy everyone else, like I do. She just *knows* it. Like it's written in her bones. I've been to mass approximately three thousand times, and the standing-sitting-kneeling dance is still as hard as the choreography to Steps' '5, 6, 7, 8' (I spent an afternoon trying to learn that dance with my friends, but gave up in a huff when my brain refused to remember all the different hip swaps).

I figure my mother is just more blessed than me, and when I tell her that she giggles in glee. *I remember thinking the exact same about my mother,* she says to me, *and I bet your daughter will think the same about you.* I make a face when she says that, disgusted at her train of thought. Her mother is the coldest woman I've ever met. When we show up to her house, she's always baking some ham to oblivion, and never seems happy to see us. In the entire time I've known her, she's never asked me a single question about myself. She stays with us for a week every year, and it's my least favourite week of the year. I am forced to bring her to daily mass, and last year, during one of those never-ending seven days, some mix of love and duty filled my body as we walked home and I grabbed her hand. She pulled back so quickly it was like I was the devil himself, scorching her with his evil coal. *What do you think you're doing?* she hissed at me.

I look up at my mum in the kitchen. I love her, sure, but I don't want to belong to her heritage. *I am not your daughter, though, not in that way. I belong to Dad.* I point to the freckle on my nose, as confirmation. *I know you both created me, but I am made from him.* Mum rolls her eyes when I say this. *Okay, you're right, you know it all. You're only your father's daughter, I guess I don't exist at all.*

5

Sarah Louise lives ten doors down from me, and she is a girl who is just changing into a woman. I know that because my mother has told me so. *She doesn't want to play your kid games anymore because she's outgrown that girl phase, so please leave her alone.* Last summer Sarah Louise played hopscotch with me, but now she has massive knockers, and every time I see her walk down the road, her schoolbag hanging off her shoulder, I take off towards her. I run myself into her chest, then theatrically bounce back. *Your boozas are so big!* I scream, holding my eye, like she has socked it with her juicy boobs, and she always gets embarrassed, quietly telling me to *piss off, please.* If Sarah Louise was just a girl, she'd be laughing with me. But she is now pretty much a woman, according to my mum, so she is ashamed by her own body, and unable to laugh at herself.

That's what happens when you become a woman. You become mortified at the space you take up, and try to fold into yourself. I know this because I study my mum and her friends. They wear so much make-up I can't make out what their faces really look like, and they cover their legs in the summer because they're embarrassed by the veins that run through them. My mum has a long scar up her arm, from the wrist to the elbow, with twenty-two little scars against it, so it looks like she has loads of tiny Xs all down her arm. She got it in a car accident when she was a teenager, and never gives me more information than that. I am obsessed with her scar. I think it's the coolest thing in the world. *You're so lucky,* I tell her, *to have something so badass on you.* She always pulls down her sweater sleeves. *Leave me alone. It's not badass; it's embarrassing.* She has a perfect square scar on her left cheek, from the same car accident, and that one bothers her even more. When I lean over and trace my finger against it, she jumps up, away from me. *Stop it! Stop looking at how ugly I am.*

My mother is embarrassed about every part of her. I can't make head nor tail of it. When I grab her boobs, out of jealousy, wanting desperately what she has, she moans at me, *They are so saggy, I know. Get away from me. Stop making fun of me.* I stare at her. The distance between us is so far it makes me think she's from another planet. *Are you kidding me? They're amazing!* Boobs are the coolest thing in the world to me, and I can't wait to have my own. Sometimes I sellotape balls of toilet roll to my chest to feel like I have them. I pose in front of the mirror, my hands cupping my chest. *You're goooorgeous*, I purr out.

I am nine years old, with no boobs and no embarrassment, so am certainly not a woman. Then I discover something else, something that surpasses even my desire for a bra. When I first find my clit, I think I am the Christopher Columbus of female pleasure, because I have never heard anyone talking about it, and if every girl has one surely they'd be shouting off the rooftops about how good it felt? As a prudent measure, I decide to keep my clit to myself. When no one is watching, I rub it against furniture to give myself a good feeling. I've seen my dog, Bingo, do something similar. Poor Bingo only has three legs, because two years ago a traveller's dog attacked him on the local GAA football pitch and he had to get it chopped off. But his horniness wasn't amputated with his back leg. If anything, the leg was just holding him back. Once free of that extra weight, he humped anything he could get his three paws around. I always screamed and hit him when he defiled my teddy bears, but now I understand. He knew that good feeling. In the beginning, I rub myself against any surface that is within my reach – the leg of the chair, the side of the couch, the corner of my bed, but I quickly learn the best way to feel really good is through my pillow. It's soft enough not to hurt, but solid enough to grip and ride. I put the pillow between my legs and hump until that lovely feeling explodes within me, then fluff it back up and place it on my bed, running downstairs to watch 'Rugrats'.

That secret special feeling is my favourite thing in the whole world, but my next favourite is reading. My mum brings me to the library every week and I take out as many books as I am allowed. Seven with a children's library card. I have one finished by the time my mum parks our car in the driveway. I run up the stairs and get into my bed, opening a new one, flicking through each page until I am dizzy. My mother comes into my bedroom at nine o'clock each night to turn off my light. Tells me to go to sleep. *The books will still be there in the morning. You get cranky when you've stayed up too late.* Most nights I sneak my lamp back on once she goes downstairs. Each half an hour, I remove the pane of glass from the lamp and stick it to my condensed window to cool down. When my mum comes upstairs to go to sleep around eleven, she stops in at my room and touches the glass of my lamp to check if I've been reading. It's cold, so she kisses my forehead and quietly leaves the room. I turn it back on and keep going. The next morning, she has to drag me out of bed for school.

I love almost all the books I check out. *They're all so brilliant,* I earnestly tell the librarian when I return them. *Do you have any more of Judy Blume, though? She just might be my favourite.* I love the young women characters she creates, with complexities I didn't know girls were even allowed to have. I really love the Americanness of her descriptions. Shopping malls! School dances! Sidewalks! Give me it all. The librarian smiles and checks her computer. *You're in luck! There's a copy of 'Iggie's House' we just got in.*

One afternoon, my librarian accidentally lets me check out 'Forever', Judy Blume's young-adult book. The difference between children's books and young adults is usually either an eating disorder or sex. I get lucky with 'Forever'. It's not about a girl and her weighing scales. It's about two eighteen-year-olds who fall in love, and have sex, and nothing bad happens to them for it. There's one passage that describes the night they first do it. It's three sentences. The words 'breast' and 'thrust' are contained in those three sentences.

The first time I read it, I feel like I have discovered the meaning of the universe. I see a rainbow above my head; an orchestra is playing, children are dancing. I dart my eyes around the living room, making sure no one has eyes on me, no one's seen what I've just read, and slowly turn over the corner of the page, marking my place. I lunge up the stairs, taking two at a time, my heart ready to break through my chest. There is an excitement that is running through my bones as I slam my bedroom door closed. *Oh my God, oh my God, ohmygodoh.* I slide my wine cords down my legs in a quick shimmy and throw the Groovy Chick duvet off my bed. I open the book back up, my fingers shaking with adrenaline. I stick my wrecked pillow between my legs and reread those three lines over and over again, humping it until I come. *Oh God, ohgod, oh.* I go back to those sentences so much over the next month that the page curls and the ink starts to smudge.

I decide one day to share it with my friends, by having a reading on my front lawn. I know I should keep it inside of me, but I can't help myself – I am ready to burst with the weight of this superpower. I convince myself that I'm thinking altruistically; I want everyone to feel the magic I do when I read it. I am willing to sacrifice myself for the greater good. A girl on our street, Hannah, gave me a taste of her slush puppy a few months ago, and slush puppies are now my favourite drink, so I want to return the favour. I'm not sure how they'll react, even though I'm hopeful for a positive response, so I feign half indifference. *Isn't this just...wild?* I say with hesitation, looking up from the book and out to my friends. Ellen looks down at the ground, and Amy up at the sky, and Hannah is inspecting her palm so intently she might be predicting her future. Aisling is biting her nails and Niamh is sucking her thumb. The only one looking at me is my best friend, Aoife. Her eyes are wide, and she slides her hand across her neck quickly, telling me, *Abort, abort!*

I instantly realize what a massive mistake this has been. *Save me*, I frantically mouth to Aoife. She nods and clears her throat. *Let's play rounders?* I feel the tension break as everyone quickly nods and disperses from my driveway. I throw my book under the rose bush and follow them up the road, my cheeks hot with shame. *Maybe Judy Blume is too American for my friends to really understand?* I think to myself as I hit the tennis ball across the green. *Or maybe I'm a superhero?* As I watch the ball fly over my friends, sailing across the field until it bounces onto the road, I realize what absolute horseshit that is. Girls can't even be superheroes. I run across the field as hard as I can, passing one base and another, my breath thumping my chest. *Or maybe I'm just a freak?*

6

On the back pages of my mother's newspaper, there are ads for sex hotlines. Girls with big lips, mouths gaping open, promising a good time, baby, if you call this number. I tear out my favourite girl and stare at her picture while I hump my pillow. One evening, I go into my parents' bedroom. There is a telephone on a chest of drawers beside the bed. This is the private telephone. The one in the hall is for my mum to catch up with her friends, or organize playdates for me and my brother. The one in the bedroom is for her to call her sisters, in shushed tones, when my dad hasn't come home that night. As much as I strain my ear against her door, I can never make out the words she is saying. It's the private telephone, for conversations we don't want other people to hear.

I dial the number on the page. My hands are shaking. *Hello, sexy,* I hear the other end breathe out, and I immediately hang up. That's enough to make me come into oblivion for a while. I call back the number a few weeks later. I listen a little longer this time, and it's an automated message. *Press one if you want to talk to a girl, you bad boy.* I never press one, instead listening to the introduction message over and over again, feeling a tingle in my body. Soon, I am calling the number every day. I will myself to press one.

On a rainy Tuesday, when the TV is playing a rerun of 'Rugrats' I've seen five times already, I sneak up to my parents' bedroom and pick up the phone. When I hear the same girl repeat her speech, I count down from five, and press one. My heart is ready to burst through my chest, but I hold the phone close to my ear. I hear a honey voice, and believe it's the girl from the picture. *Hey, big boy, how are you today?* she asks. *I'm good, how are you?* I answer back, my child voice high and uneven. *Woah, what?* she responds, and her voice isn't like honey anymore. I quickly hang up, and don't call back. I throw away that piece of paper so I can never be tempted again. I know I've pushed it too far. I can't even admit to it during Confession that Sunday. *God, forgive me for I have sinned. I have fought with my brother and taken the Lord's name in vain.*

Ten Hail Marys, the priest tells me.

Oh Mary, mother of God. I know God only really hires men, so you're the only one who might understand. From one girl virgin to another, have you ever had urges that make you both alive and wishing you were dead at the same time? How do you make it go away? What if you don't want it to leave?

A month later, my mother sits me down. She has a phone bill in her hand. *Have you been calling…some numbers?* she asks. *There are charges here for £140.* If I can't confess to God, I'm certainly not confessing to her. *I called a competition on Nickelodeon. The prize was tickets to Disney World, so I called a lot. I'm so sorry.* My mum has no choice but to believe her nine-year-old daughter just wanted a trip to Disney World, even though she called the number herself to check. Sometimes you have to believe the words someone tells you, even if you know they are lying. You hope if you believe hard enough, you can will it into truth.

7

We visit my granny in Mayo four times a year. Even though she's my father's mother, he usually only joins us on one of the trips. For the rest of them, it is Family minus Dad. It's much more fun when he's with us, so I'm glad he's sitting in the passenger seat for this one. As my mother drives out of our estate, he reaches around and grabs my ankle. *Listen to this joke,* his voice bellows. *A three-legged dog walks into a Western bar.* I scream and kick his hand away. *No, I hate this joke. No, Dad, noooo.* He takes off his seatbelt and turns around. *And he says, I want to know the man who shot my paw!* He makes a gun with his hands, and shoots me. I shriek with laughter. *You know I hate that stupid joke!* My mum theatrically sighs. *Lower the energy please, I have a long drive ahead of me and I can't deal with the two of you screeching.* My dad ignores her. *The man who shot my paw! Shot my paw! My paw!!!* He bends over in laughter, slapping his knee, which makes me laugh even more.

It takes us five hours to get to granny's house, and I get car sick before we've even left Dublin. My dad is already snoring, having rolled back his chair so much he's basically horizontal, and my knees are crushed. My mother tut tut tuts as she turns onto the motorway. *Typical Dad, leaving me to deal with you two by myself.* I stick out my tongue, and then get queasy. My mother has a plastic bag in the glovebox, ready for my barfing. She shoves it in my lap when I start to spit on the car floor. *Stop doing that, it's disgusting! Use the bag.* I yack in it, emptying up my stomach, and two hours later, when we stop for sandwiches in a hotel by the Shannon, I am famished. I horse the bread into my mouth. *This tastes amazing!* My mother snatches the packet of crisps from my hands. *Pace yourself! We've another three hours to go. And I've run out of plastic bags.* My dad dismisses her. *Let her eat what she wants!* He hands me his packet of crisps. *You know I always have your back*, he says, winking. I lean over to hug him. *I'm so glad you're here*, I whisper, shoving the crisps into my mouth.

Granny Mary lives in a run-down cottage, right beside the Atlantic Ocean, and has a TV with only three channels, and none of those channels have cartoons. They have the news, and mass, and people speaking Irish. It's the most boring TV I've ever encountered. When we pull up onto her driveway, me and my brother run from the car and bypass the house, heading straight through the overgrown grass to the water, throwing off all our clothes on the way down. We hear our dad scream at us in encouragement, his voice getting more distant with each step we take. *That's it, kids, be as free as the wind!* We jump into the freezing cold waves, laughing.

*

In my granny's kitchen, there is a framed photo of Jesus, nailed to the cross. Blood dripping from his wrists and his ankles. A crown of thorns atop his head. The image flickers as I move across the room. Jesus's eyes follow me, as I sit at the table, and go to the fridge, and stand by the window. Me and my brother jump around the kitchen, laughing as the eyes never leave us. It's magic. *He is always watching us!* We scream in excitement, clapping in applause, like it's a Penn and Teller show in Vegas.

It feels less like magic when I am alone in the kitchen. It gives me the creeps. I spend less time there, to avoid Him. I eat my dinner in the living room, in front of the fire, yelling conversation at my deaf granny, trying to hide my annoyance as she asks, *What?* for the eighth time in a row. I grab yogurts from the fridge without pausing to check the flavour. I try to trick the trick, jumping as quick as I can across the room, hoping the mechanics of the picture can't keep up with my lightning speed. He always follows me. Even when I leave the room, I feel His dying eyes burning through me, following me everywhere I go. Jesus, poor Jesus with His bloody head and wrists and ankles; poor Jesus who died for our horrible sins, can see every bad thing I do. *But He died for this*, I try and rationalize to myself, as I quietly hump my granny's pillow. *He knew how bad people really are. That's why He's sad and covered in blood. People have always been so bad, it's human nature. He knew that.*

And then I come.

8

After five days of boring TV, when my granny has slipped me and my brother a tenner each, I wave at her through the rear window of the car, her body becoming smaller and smaller, until there's none of her left. Instead of the usual five-hour journey home, we drive across to Galway and check into a run-down motel. My parents insist on Irish holidays every year, and I don't realize it's because we're broke, so I think there's some patriotism at play. When all my friends spend two weeks in Majorca, coming home with tanned skins and braids in their hair, I smile and judge. *We like to keep the money in the country. My dad says it's anti-Irish to have a holiday abroad, but I'm glad you had a good time diving into a pool.*

The next morning, my dad tickles me awake. *We're going on an adventure,* he tells me, *just you and me, kid.* I squeal in excitement. Adventures with my dad are always my favourite part of holidays. We've ridden roller coasters together, and eaten mussels, and shouted at passers-by over our hotel balcony. *Please help me, this man has kidnapped me!* I yelled down, my dad roaring with laughter. *You're my best friend,* he sometimes told me during those adventures. I didn't say anything back, because he wasn't my best friend. The two Aoifes are my best friends. I have at home Aoife and in school Aoife. It's easy when your two best friends share a name. You don't have to pick. My dad is my dad, and dads can't be best friends. My dad doesn't really have any friends, though, so I know it's not that special that I'm his best one. My mum has her sisters, and the girls she works with, and the other mums she goes on walks with three times a week. *Men are loners; they're okay not being that close to anyone,* my mother tells me when I ask her about it, *and anyway he does have friends, Marise. He has friends.* But she can't name any of them for me when I ask.

We leave my mother and brother at the dump of a motel. *What do you think they'll do today?* I ask my dad in the car. *Probably something boring,* he replies, and I laugh. *Yea, I bet!* We drive to Renvyle Hotel, thirty miles outside the city of

Galway. *This is where I used to work, when I was in my early twenties.* It has an outdoor swimming pool. In Ireland! *It's like selling scarves in the desert,* my mum says when I tell her about it the next day.

I jump into the pool, shivering, while my dad catches up with old friends. That's how he introduces them. *These were my friends way back.* I study their faces, trying to make sense of the man my father used to be. A person who had friends. The staff bring chicken wings and chips to me at the pool, and a new bottle of Coke every time I finish one. *Your dad was so crazy back in the day,* they tell me, laughing, *the stuff he used to get up to.* They don't expand on it further, and I don't ask, because I know my dad will tell me the stories himself when we are back in the car. My dad never babies me, or keeps secrets, the way my mum does. *This is adult stuff,* she always says, but my dad says there's no such thing as adult stuff, it's just human stuff, and he tells me everything my mum won't.

When I have dried off my body from the pool, when he has said goodbye to the ghosts of his past, we drive around the town of Connemara, eating ice creams that are melting all over our hands. My dad sees a sign for an art gallery and puts on the brakes. He winks as he parks the car. We walk in, and the gallery is just one woman with thirty paintings on the walls. She has thick grey hair and is wearing a shawl. *Notions,* my mum would say, if she was here.

My dad steps into the room and comes to life. *I'm an art dealer, I own some great pieces from Greece and Morocco.* I look at him for another wink, but it seems like I am not in on this joke. He buys a painting for £300, and I get a little nervous, knowing my mum will be furious at him. My dad can sense my worry, because he's very good at understanding me. *Magic money,* he says to me, winking. That's what he calls using his credit card. *You don't really have to pay this stuff back,* he tells me when I am a bit older. *I have five different credit cards and thousands of debt, and I'll just call them up eventually and say I'm going to pay back a tenth of it, and they'll agree. It's all about negotiating, baby.*

In the gallery, he asks me if I want anything. There is a tiny painting my eyes linger over. It's full of my favourite colours: purple and pink streaks against a baby-blue background. *That was the only time the northern lights were visible here in Galway*, the shawl woman tells me. *She will have it!* he yells. I jump up and down on the spot. *This is crazy, Daddy.* We pack them into the car and start talking in bad French accents. *Ma-tha will be mi-sing us, we muhst goh homme*, I say to him, but he waves me off, turning the car off the road and toward a restaurant. *Baby, we're art dealers, so we're gonna eat like kings.*

My dad orders first, and I copy him. The salmon. I've never tasted anything like it. It is drenched in butter, and lemon, with a pinch of pepper. *This is the best thing I'll ever eat*, I tell my dad confidently. I don't know that someday I will eat tacos, with meat marinated in chilli seasoning, extra salsa, on the side of a street in LA with my best friend, both of us drunk. Or that I'll go to Michelin-starred restaurants in Amsterdam, and not need to look at the price, stuffing my face with caviar and lobster and lamb. Or that I'll have a bowl of chilli in a diner owned by my boyfriend's uncle, after an ice hockey game, with my foam hand beside me, and I'll ask for seconds because *Holy shit, this is the best thing I've ever tasted, and excuse me, but what are these green spicy things on top, and can I have some of them to go?* I don't know any of that aged ten, so this is the best meal I've ever had.

Shoving mouthfuls of that fish into me, across from the person I love most, I've never felt more like I matter. I am my dad's daughter and wife and business partner all in one. When the bill comes, he slides it over to me. *I assume you'll take care of this,* he says, smiling. I nod, *Of course, it's my treat.* He gets up to use the bathroom, and slips me some magic money. I pay, typing his birthday into the keypad, adding a ten per cent tip because I read somewhere you do that. He comes back to the table and thanks me profusely. I laugh. *It's your money, Daddy,* I say, breaking the spell. *This money doesn't belong to anyone. We're just using it for right now. Some day when I am old and can't walk, we'll use the money you have, and it will be just the same.*

You're not my best friend, I tell him on the way back to the hotel, *because I already have two best friends. But you're the best dad ever.*

I'll take that, he says, beaming, and leans over to kiss my head.

9

It is three weeks before our trip to Disneyland Paris, which will be my first time on an aeroplane. Me and my brother have been especially bold during the two weeks leading up to this. We've been fighting in mass. *Like animals,* my mother comments as she drives us home. *Pure wild animals*, she says, shaking her head, *and in the house of the Lord.* Usually, the hint of God's wrath calms us down, but there is something in the air that makes us think, *Let's burn the whole thing to the ground.* Nothing my mother says resonates with us. When a burned-out car shows up on our road one day, my brother, on my dare, goes up to it and licks it. That's her final straw. My mum is at her wits' end with us, so she tells us. *Please, do something,* I hear her beg my dad one night. My ears perk up at those words. My mother never asks my dad to do anything.

The next day he comes home and pours a million pounds on to my brother's bed. I see the notes fly through the air, at least fifty of them, and scream in delight. *Have we won the lotto?* I ask him. *No*, he tells me, with his serious face on. His serious face is so rarely used it takes me a few seconds to recognize it. *Quite the opposite, actually. I went down to the travel agent and got a refund on our trip to Disneyland. We're not going anymore, because you've both been so bold. Here's all the money we got back. I think we'll buy a dishwasher instead.* Our faces fall. *Maybe two*, he adds. *You're joking, right?* I ask, waiting for the release of seriousness he always gives me. *I'm not. You think because I'm your friend I can't be a parent too? But I can.* He laughs when he says this. *I can be a proper father. And we're not going to Disneyland.* I look over at my mother, silently begging her to undermine him, but she just smiles. *Your father is right.* 'Your father is right' are words I've never heard from her, so I know she means serious business. *I hate you both*, I scream, pulling my brother's arm as I run out of the room. *We've really messed up this time*, he tells me, and I reply, *But it's more your fault, for licking that burned car.*

We both cry ourselves to sleep that night. The next morning, when I have accepted our fate, I corner my mother in the kitchen. *I'll never misbehave again, I swear on God. Please just don't take anything else away from me, and I'll be good for the rest of my life.*

Five days before we had been due to fly to Paris, my dad gathers us in his bedroom, his fat belly exposed over the duvet as he sits in his bed. *It was all a trick*, he says gleefully. *We're still going!* My jaw drops. I look at my brother and see tears forming in his eyes. *A lesson*, I hear my mother shout from the landing. *Not a trick, a lesson.* My dad ignores her, standing up on the bed. He reaches for both our hands to pull us up. We dance on the bed, my father screaming a Johnny Cash song. Me and my brother sway along, silent, still in shock.

When Disneyland comes, it's all the sweeter now we know we clawed it back. The first day, me and my brother are armed with our autograph books. My mother takes pictures as we pose by fountains, giving the peace sign. We hold open the park map, deciding which ride to go on next. *This is like I dream*, I tell my mum, and she squeezes my hand. My dad follows us around the park, always a few steps behind. He complains the entire morning we are there. *Too much walking*, he says. *My bad back is acting up.* He makes us sit down on every bench we see. *Please*, I hear my mother whisper to him. *Please don't ruin their trip.* I look away when she says this, embarrassed at her desperation. Out of the corner of my eye, I think I see him nod.

That afternoon, he is a different person. He rides every roller coaster I want to, and screams alongside me as we hurl through the air. He buys us all Mickey Mouse ears and slush puppies. He makes me laugh as we wait in the long queue. When we board Space Mountain, the biggest ride in the park, he squeezes my hand when my legs start to shake and says, *Think how good this is about to be!* I squeeze back. *It's already really good, Dad.*

After the second day, my dad takes to his bed. He stays in it the next morning, as we brush our teeth and put sunscreen on our noses. *Come on, Dad, get dressed*, I urge him. *The bus will be here in five minutes to take us over to the park, so you have to hurry.*

I'll follow you over, he tells me. We don't see him again until we return from the park. He's sitting in his underwear, eating room service. *Dad*, I scream, and run towards him, jumping up onto his belly. *It was so much fun and there was fireworks and I saw Donald Duck and he bopped my head and signed my book.* I look over at his empty silver tray and feel a knot form in my stomach. *But we're supposed to go down for dinner now. Apparently, Mickey Mouse might show up.* He laughs and pats his belly. *You know I can always have two dinners, kid*, and bounces up out of the bed. On the way to the lift, I jump on his back, and he bucks me, pretending to be a bull. Both of us laugh as he does it. *But wait, Dad, your bad back*, I suddenly remember, jumping down from him with guilt. *Ah, it feels a lot better now*, he tells me forgivingly. *How convenient*, I hear my mother say.

The next morning, I listen as my mother's words rise into the air, while I lie in bed with my eyes closed. *You're missing out*, she tells him. I think of the roller coasters and the teacups and Minnie Mouse. She is right, he is. *You're missing out on memories with them*, I hear her continue. *These are the moments you won't ever get back.*

My dad stays in bed until we are packing our suitcases the next day. *What an amazing trip*, I tell him on the bus to the airport, my autograph book full of scribbles sitting on my legs. *I'm really glad you brought us on it.* He smiles and pats my leg, without looking at me. *You know I'd do anything for you, kiddo.*

You missed out on some really fun stuff, though, I say, leafing through my autograph book. *Oh shut up*, he snaps at me. I look over at him. *You shut up.*

You're so annoying.

Well, you're a loser.

We continue to argue. *I hate you*, I hiss. *I wish you weren't my fucking daughter*, he replies.

I storm across the aisle, and punch my brother in the arm. *Change seats with me.* I dramatically plop down beside my mum. *I'm not talking to Dad anymore. He just told me he wished I wasn't his daughter.* My mother sighs. *And I suppose you weren't to blame at all for this fight?*

I nod. *Exactly. I wasn't.*

She rolls her eyes. *You know he doesn't mean what he said. He can be so childish sometimes. But you know he loves you.* I reluctantly nod, and walk back over to my brother. *Change back.* I sit in silence beside my father, waiting for him to make the first move. When he doesn't, I swallow my pride and cut into the dead air. *Just take it back, please.* I hear my voice crack as I speak. He looks over at me, and his face softens. *Fine, I take it back. Now you take yours back.* I do, and by the end of the bus ride, we're laughing about the time he thought my mother's boss was going to murder him, so he showed up to his house with a knife in his jacket pocket. When we get to the airport, my mother pulls me aside. *Are you all right?* I look at her like she has ten heads. *I'm fine, go away.*

On the plane back to Dublin, me and my dad are laughing so hard the rows around us stare. I feel my mother's gaze on me. I ignore it. *Everyone is jealous of us,* he tells me, and I nod. *They wish they had our craic.*

When the plane lands and my dad stands up to take down our bags, I stare at him. I'm not stupid; I am almost eleven years old, so I can see he is a flawed adult, but I also know he loves me very much. I am ten and three quarters, and I think that is enough.

10

The school year we all turn eleven, something changes. A shift in the paradigm. We all get mobile phones for our Confirmation, a physical gift to signify our leap into adulthood. We use these vessels from God to text boys, *what you up to? write back x,* and to text each other, *which boy do you fancy? wb x.* The change is palpable. God is out. Boys are in.

Me and Aoife celebrate the birthday of Leonardo DiCaprio by sneaking biscuits from our homes every night and depositing them in a shared Ziploc bag. *In two months' time, we'll have enough to have a party*, we tell each other. By the time Leo's birthday rolls around, the biscuits have turned to mush. We still eat them, letting the soft dough break up in our mouths, as we talk about how attractive he is. *Someday when I am an adult, I will meet him and he'll plant a kiss right on my face.* We both squeal at that possibility.

At the same time, Christina Aguilera releases her song 'Dirty'. *Too dirty to clean my act up*, we all scream at lunchtime, trying to copy how her hips move. We position our bodies so the boys in the school attached to ours can see our sexy moves from their yard one hundred metres away. *If you ain't dirty, you ain't here to paaaaarty.* We flick our hair as we sing, not looking at the other yard, but hoping they are looking at us. Everything we do is now for them.

It is finally acceptable to admit you have desire, but only if that desire is for a boy. I feel a bit trapped by these parameters. No matter how much I try to move my hips seductively, none of these boys like me. They make fun of me, and prank-call me on my brand new Nokia 3210. *Hello, is this Marise?* I hear from my phone. I quickly say yes. *You're so gross and ugly*, I hear, now with extra voices, all laughing. I hang up the phone with tears in my eyes.

I rewrite history in my diary every night. *Darragh flirted with me today, and I flirted back!* I scribble out. *I think he might ask to be my boyfriend.* I draw hearts around boyfriend. Darragh is the heartthrob of our class, because his voice has broken and he has barely any acne on his angular face. Darragh has never even looked at me, but I know to fancy him, because everyone else fancies him. When I get my prank calls, I convince myself he isn't there with them. He is busy, reading a book or volunteering to help the needy. Darragh, with his deep voice and sharp jaw, is certainly above them all.

Still, I'm not picky. When my phone rings and I hear, *You're a fucking freak*, I forgive them all instantly. I want, desperately, for one of them to accept me. For one to call me up after the prank call, telling me they love me. It doesn't even matter who it is; I'd prefer it to be Darragh, but I'd take any of them. But my big romance never happens. Instead, anytime I am around them, I feel less than. I tuck my hair behind my ears and suck in my stomach, staring at the ground when they speak, hoping it will just swallow me whole. The only time I feel comfortable is around girls. But girls can't be a fairy-tale story. Romance includes just two people, a boy and a girl, and I am here, waiting, but my prince refuses to show up.

I want so badly to have a boyfriend. But instead, all I have is girls. And girls don't really count.

11

Sam wasn't my friend, not exactly. I didn't get to pick her. She was the daughter of my speech and drama teacher, a woman my mother liked because she drove me home every Tuesday after class, so I had to be friends with Sam even though I didn't like her so much. When I went on playdates to her house, her mum would let her stop at the petrol station and buy whatever amount of pick-and-mix she wanted. She was so spoiled like that, and it made me not like her. I didn't like people who got everything they wanted. My favourite characters in books were always full of unmet desire, of constant wanting. If you're just given pick-and-mix sweets any time you want them, there's no way you can ever be an interesting person. You need some unfulfilment to be a fun person to be around. She was also sort of fat, probably from all the pick-and-mix. I didn't like that about her either. *Have you thought about playing any sports?* I'd ask her, trying to be helpful.

A month after my eleventh birthday, I am sleeping over at her house. Her parents are away, so her older brother Kevin is babysitting. Six months earlier, at some weird Halloween party her mother threw when we all had to dress up as a Shakespearean character, I got in trouble for screaming *KEVIN'S A VIRGIN* as loud as I could when the fireworks went off, so now Kevin stays in his room when I am over, playing computer games. Sam and I watch 'American Pie', a DVD we find in her sitting room, and scream and laugh, in complete shock at what we are seeing on screen. We eat as many sweets as we can in her kitchen, and drink a full two-litre bottle of Coke. We are so hyper, laughing hysterically on the kitchen floor at any stupid thing. We go upstairs around midnight, and we're both too wired to get to sleep, so we lie in her bed, talking. I've never thought she had anything interesting to say, but tonight is different. Somehow my body is right next to hers, and I feel a kind of energy coming from her, or maybe it's just coming from me, but it's there, between us. I don't think, and reach my hand over and brush against her breast.

Because she is a bit fat, she has boobs. She doesn't push me away, so I squeeze. I am so turned on – this is like a real-life sex hotline. We remove all our clothes, and start to climb over each other's bodies, half laughing, rubbing against each other. I start to scissor her, rubbing my vagina against her and God it feels so good I think my body is about to burst open. *Oww, that hurts,* she says after a few minutes, *I don't like that.*

Yea, me neither, I quickly agree.

I grab my pyjama bottoms and shove my legs into them, turning over so I'm against the wall. I pretend to snore so she thinks I'm asleep. I can't actually sleep for hours, because I'm replaying over and over again the feeling of her body against me, and the rush inside me it created. *Hail Mary, mother of God. Make this disgusting desire inside me go away.*

The next morning, when we wake up, we avoid eye contact. *God, I was so hyper last night, I don't remember anything that happened*, I tell her into my bowl of cereal. She says nothing, and I know we are in agreement. Whatever happened didn't really happen. When my mum collects me, she asks me if I had a good time. *Sam is annoying*, I tell her. *She's not my friend, and I'm not sleeping over there again, and you can't make me.*

But it doesn't end there. Six months later, we are down in her holiday home in Cork, after spending the day jumping in the waves of the sea. There were boys at the beach, and we flirted with them in the sea. Giggling at any dumb thing they said, shrieking when they splashed us.

But that was then, and this is now. We're both lying in tiny bunkbeds, just me and her in this small space, and I can hear her breathing if I concentrate enough. That alone is giving me that tingly feeling I both hate and love so much. *Come up to my bed*, she says, in such a whisper I can't be sure it really happened. I ignore her, and pretend to snore, my heart racing and my eyes open. I think of the boys at the beach, and the tingly feeling goes away. *I'm not gay*, I tell myself. In fact, girls can't even be gay. That word is reserved for whispers about men, like my weird self-confessed bachelor cousin Matty, or for punchlines on TV shows my dad laughs at. I am not gay, it's just boys don't pay me any attention, or are mean to me when they do. I am not gay; I just called that girl on the hotline because there were no men in the adverts. I took what sexuality was offered, which always is a woman's. I am not gay, but I do eventually climb up to her top bunk, the darkness hiding her face, as I grab every part of her.

12

When you're a girl who has impure thoughts about another girl, you better find a way to destroy them, or else you'll end up burning in Hell forever. Girls aren't supposed to have sexual desires toward anyone, never mind another innocent girl, so you better buck up or accept your destiny with the devil. Even though God had lost centre stage with me and my friends, we weren't so heathen to think Hell just stopped existing because it wasn't in vogue anymore. The fire pits were still burning away, in the background, waiting to accept the worst of us.

I am determined not to end up there. At eleven, I know I am old enough to be tried as an adult, in the court of God. I build up an arsenal of hobbies, to distract myself from my grubby thoughts. Gymnastics, and swimming, and speech and drama. I show up to an audition for the film 'Evelyn' and, after I've recited my lines, the director cruelly barks, *More like all speech and no drama!* I cry on the car ride home. *I'm not cut out for acting, I quit.* My mother tuts in the driver seat. *Did you not see Colin Farrell walk in? He had his head shaved, but it was definitely him. If you had just been more natural...*

She doesn't really mind when I quit something, though, because something else always pops up in its place. Tennis, and debating, and Spanish lessons. I am always kept busy. My mother is delighted at my eagerness. After school, she puts our favourite gameshow, 'Countdown', on the TV, and I am ready with my pen and paper. We concentrate on the random nine letters Carol Vorderman has placed on the board, so the contestants can try to make the biggest word out of them. *I have a five-letter one!* I announce with glee. *Well, I got a seven-letter one, so try a bit harder*, she responds.

She signs me up to the local running club. I hate running. I like racing, and I love winning, but I hate the training for the race, day after day, the miles I have to pound on the cement as my ears burn with the cold and I get a stitch in my side. I complain to my friend Cliodhna as she runs beside me. To distract ourselves, we talk about boys we want to kiss. We make a list of the top five mouths we want against us. Neither of us has been kissed yet, not really, which makes it all the more tantalizing. I think of Sam's lips against mine. *Girls don't count*, I remind myself. We go through the list every second day, on our runs, cutting out boys and moving others up the list. We make fun of our coaches to pass the time, each of us trying to outdo the other with the dumb shit we say. *I bet he cries after sex, and his wife has to wipe away his dumb tears.*

I bet he gives her a blow job!

We laugh, even though we know laughing is taking up energy that we need to finish these five miles. We still laugh.

Our coach Terry travels alongside us, driving his van at seven miles an hour, other cars beeping him impatiently. He's been doing this ever since he found out we were taking a shortcut that cut off two miles. He was so furious when he caught us. *You idiots are your own worst enemy; you're only cheating yourselves.* Any time Terry gets mad, and we're always making him mad, he spits all over himself. If we laugh it just makes him madder. *I want the news not the weather*, I tell him once. My mum finds out I've said this and makes me call over to his house later that night, with a bouquet of stupid flowers, to apologize. I hate saying sorry when I don't mean it, so I start to cry. He accepts the flowers with a grimace. Terry doesn't like tears.

When the going gets tough, the tough get going, he yells out his window every Tuesday, Thursday and Saturday, in the comfort of his van while it pisses down outside. We roll our eyes and continue talking. *Ross has gotten cute, so I'm moving him up my list.* We hear the tyres screech in the rain as we laugh. *Wake up, girls*, he screams out. *Anything worth having is going to hurt like fuck to get.*

13

I give every hobby in my orbit the college try, but I soon realize my vocation is poetry. I compose my first poem, a classic three stanza describing how much I love my pals, lyrically titled 'Friends Forever', and my dad tells me I'm a genius. *Just like Yeats, but much better.* I nod, not knowing who Yeats is, and keep writing. As long as my father likes it, I want to keep doing it. I type up my poems on the computer in class and print them out. I place each one in a clear plastic pocket, and carry around my folder of poetry under my arm. I write poems about breakfast cereals, and the Special Olympics, and being on the cusp of getting my period, but my favourite poems to write are for dead people.

My cousin died suddenly last Christmas, when he was twenty years old. I didn't know him, but I cried when I saw his open casket. Seeing death so upfront. I write a poem for him. It rhymes, so I know it's good. I rob a stanza from a mass card I got from my granny. Plagiarism wasn't a word I learned until I was a teenager. I take other creative liberties; I create a long illness he was suffering from, instead of his real-life sudden death. It is easier to rhyme that way. I read it out to my dog once I'm finished.

*We mourned and mourned for days, but something
    pulled us through,
We knew that you were happy, and out of pain too.*

A life and a death, neatly wrapped up in five verses. My dog licks my toes in appreciation.

The poem gets a great reception. One of my aunts loves it so much she frames it, and it takes centre stage on her mantelpiece. I write another one when a girl in the class above me dies. Cancer. Only twelve years old. My mother knows her mother, so we go to the funeral.

*God has proven to the world that he only takes the
    best,
Because on the 9th of December you were laid down
    to rest.*

I sit back in my bed and admire my work. I think I can make a business out of this: writing a poem for someone when they die, and selling it to their grieving family members. I present my business plan to my mother. I need her help with it. I need her to give me numbers in her phonebook when the people die. Ideally, I'd have her making the calls too, because people are more likely to buy a poem if an adult is selling it. She is ironing when I make my pitch, offering her a 20 per cent cut for doing almost nothing. She sets down the steaming iron, so it makes a little bounce on the ironing board. *That is insensitive and ridiculous. You really only think about yourself, don't you? Absolutely not. You will do that over my dead body.*

I wish, I hiss back, grabbing my stack of papers and storming out. An artist, halted by red tape. *This is why Van Gogh chopped off his ear!* I scream from the stairs.

I slam shut my bedroom door, and sit down at my desk. I write out the dedication for the book I'm sure to have by fourteen. *To my father, who always believed in me.* It's a slight towards my mum, for not helping me with my business idea, so I want her to feel awful when my poems become a blockbuster hit. When I show it to my dad that night, he cries. *This means everything to me.* I look down at the floor, mortified at his excess emotion. I wanted him to like it, but not this much. *Why can't you ever be cool?* I ask. *Why do you have to overdo everything?* He slaps the page from my hand, and we watch it fall to the floor. *Don't be a bitch*, he tells me. *I can feel what I want. I feel things more than other people do, that's not a sin. And you're my daughter, so fight it all you want, but you're the exact same.* I lean down and pick up the page, smoothing it out. *You're right, Dad*, I tell him, feeling bad for hurting his feelings. *Sometimes, I think we're the exact same person.* He lights up at that. *Keep writing these poems – they're better than any other poem that has ever existed!*

14

My dad was a great storyteller. It didn't seem to matter that most of it was lies. When I was twelve he showed me a photo of him and Mikhail Gorbachev. *Gorbachev was very important to history*, I told my friends in the playground during lunch. *He was like a good Stalin. And he thought my dad was funny. They're going to make a documentary together.* I didn't realize that Gorbachev was quite shiny in the photo, almost like he was made of wax. That the photo was of my dad in Madame

Tussauds. I was twelve, and accepted what he said. I couldn't wait for the documentary.

Dad lied the way other people told the truth. The lies slipped out of him like poetry. He lied like someone was going to end up on the cross because of it. Dad didn't tell lies, lies told Dad. They held his mouth and forced themselves out, tumbling head-first onto his chin. He lied about what he had done, and what he was going to do. He lied about who he knew, and how well he knew them. He lied about how much he had, and how much he made, and how often he had broken his leg.

Lying is in our DNA, I decided once I realized my dad was a liar. Irish people have had to lie to survive. We lied to the British, so they wouldn't shoot us. We lied about who was in our homes, and the last time we saw our IRA cousins. We lied about saying mass, and teaching class, and the language we spoke behind closed doors. We weren't born into existence as liars, but we were forced into it, as a response to oppression. Even guerrilla warfare, the Irish's favourite type of fisticuffs, is a lying type of fighting; peace until it isn't.

If the English had never invaded us, my father would never have lied, I decided. Look, I know blaming the English for my father's lying is far-fetched and insane, but I was a twelve-year-old girl watching her father's truth unravel as I pulled the thread, turning over and over until there was nothing left of it.

15

Dad's lying was a symptom of his madness. That's what my mother would tell me. *You know your father is cracked; you have to take anything he says with a pinch of salt.* I rolled my eyes when she said that. *Well, you're married to him. You chose him. If he's crazy, that surely makes you crazy by association.*

I loved to argue with my mother, trying to run circles around her as she did the same to me. But sometimes she sidestepped me and threw an unexpected punch right in my face. *There was a time he wasn't this way, you know*, she said softly. *I loved that man. I'll never stop loving that man.* I looked away from her, my cheeks hot with embarrassment on her behalf. The tension in the air made me queasy, so I quickly changed the subject. *Want to play 'Countdown'?* She nodded, relieved. *Yes, turn it on, and I'll go get the pens.*

Dad might have been mad, but his madness was often very fun. He'd wake me up in the middle of the night to write down a dream he had. *You'll write the book, and we'll make millions!* He was always coming up with get-rich ideas, so he could escape his dead-end bartending job. He needed something less manual, he'd tell me. He had broken his back a few years earlier, falling through a trap door into a basement. He kept the crutches and used them when other illnesses flared up. *Some day I will burn those stupid crutches*, my mother said to me. *So your father can learn to walk on his own two feet.* I shot her a filthy stare. *That is so typical you. You are too boring to understand his genius.* I was regurgitating words he had fed to me, but that didn't make them less true. Every genius who has ever existed seemed mad to other people, so he always told me. It's pretty much a requirement. Dad was mad, but only because he was special – he was different to everyone else. *People find that threatening*, he told me, and I nodded.

Dad was a genius, which meant he always had wild ideas, but he had so much enthusiasm for them that I'd buy into it too. He invested all his savings into a device for taxi drivers that would give passengers internet access during the ride. He would take my brother out of school on days there were trading fairs, and have him recite the sales pitch at makeshift booths in sports halls around Dublin. Passers-by took leaflets from a nine-year-old boy with a bleached-blond mohawk, and smiled as he stuttered through his words. The pair of them never made a single sale, but that didn't deter my dad. He hatched a deal with the local electronics store, buying fifty 47-inch TVs to give away, for free, to anyone who bought the device. *You haven't worked out the profit margin*, my mother screamed at him when he arrived home with five TVs in the car and told her he had to make another ten trips to collect the rest. *This will cost you money. And why the hell are you giving out free 47-inch TVs when we don't even have a 47-inch TV?* My dad brushed off her anger. *It's business, you wouldn't understand. I've been number crunching and big-picture thinking.*

He easily offloaded the free TVs, but couldn't get a single contract signed, and then Wi-Fi was introduced the next year, so the business went bust. *No harm*, he told me, *I wasn't into all that paperwork anyway.* I was always finding paperwork in car doors and under his bed, often with stains that made the ink run off the page. One day, bored while he was driving, I read a page. *Hey, why is my name on this?* I asked him, seeing Marise Gaughan printed and a squiggle next to it. *Oh, I had to make you a director of the company, can't remember why.* I squinted at the squiggle. *Is that my signature? That's illegal, you can't forge my signature!* My dad waved me away. *Oh, grow up, people do it all the time. I made you, I made the hand that can write a signature, so really I'm entitled to use it from time to time. You would have a different attitude if I had sold it for millions, let me tell you. You'd be kissing my feet in appreciation then!*

A few months later, he made a film about a man from a

small town in Mayo, whose big claim to fame was having a lot of illegitimate children. Dad paid for five hundred DVDs to be made and sold two. Then there was the comedy DVD, where he dressed in drag and recorded himself giving advice as an agony aunt. That was another five hundred DVDs (*An investment!* he told my mother). He would make me laugh so much when he'd practise his sales pitch on me.

I wish I could just remember the scams and crazy ideas; the excitement of having a dad a bit off the hinges. I wish I could remember them without any cloud hanging over me. But mental illness isn't just the fun, crazy, wild shit. Mental illness is senseless, and draining, and relentless. It is an incredibly ugly thing that can engulf you without you realizing it. My father spent so many years fighting the urge to drink, he didn't notice that there was another demon in the room, slowly eating away at him.

When mental illness goes unchecked for that length of time, it can eventually destroy the person you love. And it happens so gradually you can never put your finger on it. Slowly, without you realizing, until suddenly, they're gone.

16

Trying to pinpoint when my dad got sick is futile; it wasn't a switch, when he was okay one day and then suddenly wasn't. Some madness works like that, but often it is more elusive. My dad was always a bit crazy, and I loved his craziness, how he was so unlike every other adult I knew. His craziness lit up rooms, and made everyone howl with laughter. So when he fell into deeper depths of madness, alarm bells didn't instantly ring. He was just being himself, albeit a bit more than normal. The only time I felt alarmed was when I saw him empty. But back then, I didn't know that was the beginning of the end.

I am twelve and a half years old. Some days after school, my dad brings me into the bar where he works so I can write my poems on the computer in the back office. He gives me a bowl of mint chocolate chip ice cream as I sit at the bar afterwards, watching him pour pints. *This one is about the Special Olympics, will I read it to you?* He puts down his towel and leans forward across the bar. *Absolutely, I'm all ears.*

When I'm finished, he pours me a glass of Coke. *That's the best poem I've ever heard, darling. You're really gonna be something special someday. In fact, you already are.* I nod along, and lift my bowl to my mouth to slurp down the melted ice cream. *This is my favourite dessert in the world, I think. How do you always know that?* I take a spoon of it and pour it on the bar, swirling it around with my finger, picking out the chocolate chips and flicking them at him. *Because knowing you is my favourite thing to do*, he tells me. *Someday, the whole world will know you, and I'll have to book a meeting to get to see you!* I laugh. *Probably, but I'll always let you skip the queue.* He smiles when I say that. *You know, I'm not sure how long I'll get to live. I know, deep down, that I am not meant to get old. But I really hope I get to live long enough to see you get the things I know you're meant for.* I look up at him, puzzled. I know not everyone gets to be old; my cousin Paul, and my uncle Joe, and second cousin once removed Sarah, and my classmate Stephanie, they all died before then. But my dad cannot possibly know that he'll get cancer, or a brain tumour, or a seizure, so how is he so sure? *You could get old*, I tell him, gently, like I am breaking bad news. His head goes out of my view, fumbling beneath the bar. He surfaces with another scoop of ice cream for me, and plops it into my bowl. I squeal in delight, quickly forgetting what we've just been talking about.

Less than a year later, he is fired from that pub. He spends his days sitting on the couch, in his dressing gown, without the TV on. My mother tells me that Dad is sick. *Sadness can sometimes be a sickness*, she warns me. *I don't understand it, and I hope you never understand it either.* We avoid the sitting room, afraid we'll catch it too.

Some days I feel brave, and peek in the room to check on him. He smiles when he sees me, but it never reaches his eyes. I know my normal dad has gone missing, and this person staring back at me isn't a stranger I recognize. This isn't drunk dad; it's someone else.

They accused me of drinking on the job, he tells me one day, while looking at the wall. *I never drank on the job, ever.* Neither of us pretend to believe that, but I also know he isn't drunk right now. When I look at his eyes, they aren't glazed over, like they would be if he was drinking. Instead, they are empty. I've never once wished to see my dad's drunk eyes, but right now I pray for them. When I look at this hollow person in front of me, it terrifies me so much that I wish he had a vodka in his hand instead. *Who are you?* I think, *and what have you done with the person I know?* I climb into his lap, even though, at thirteen, I'm too big for that stuff now, and rub his belly. *I love you, Dad*, I whisper into his chest. *Please come back to me.*

TWO

FLAMMABLE

1

I am fourteen. It's the night before my business studies mock exams, sometime in February when the nights are still long and it rains every day. For the past two years I have been a straight-from-Hell nightmare of a child. *Disruptive*, my class reports say. *Needs to learn to control herself.* When you don't understand the whirlpool of emotions inside you, anger is the easiest one to pull out. There are weekly meetings to discuss my behaviour. My teachers point to my test scores as an example of my potential. *We want to help you.* I sit, slumped down in the chair with my arms crossed, shooting them daggers. I don't see anyone that needs help.

Only my mother shows up to these meetings. Only my mother listens earnestly to the same things my teachers have said the week before. Only my mother grips the steering wheel tightly as she asks me to *please, get your shit together.* My father, he's busy. He is asleep when these meetings happen. He is looking the other way when I throw textbooks across the kitchen. When I scream *I hate you*, it's to my mother, because she is the only one left. My dad has already walked out of the room.

Dad isn't the enemy, though. He collects me from hockey practice and makes my friends laugh by cursing in front of them. He shows up to my school, unannounced, and lets me skip Irish class so we can have a long carvery lunch. He sneaks bags of sweets into my room at night. *Don't tell your mother, but I know you love sugar. And what's so bad with indulging in something you love?* My dad gets me, because I am a carbon copy of him. We are made from the same stuff, so he always says. And he's been sober for the past four years. He hasn't been my enemy in a long time.

I am fourteen, and I am studying, because I still do very well at school, despite my behaviour problems. During the Christmas exams, I easily finished the maths paper. The questions seemed like a joke. *How could anyone not know this? How stupid do they think we are?* I spent the next hour looking around the exam hall, my eyes catching a girl in my class called Shauna. I wasn't friends with Shauna, but I knew about her. I had heard her name roll off the tongues of boys. That was the biggest currency. To have a boy talk about you. *Hot, slut, frigid, bitch.* It didn't matter what they said, just that they had you in their mouths.

I looked down at my finished paper, and then over again at her. Her blonde hair somehow glistened in the dark exam hallway. Beautiful Shauna, with her straight teeth and big tits. Beautiful Shauna, who all the boys wanted to fuck. Her lips were puckered in concentration. Her brows furrowed, like she had to take a shit. I kept staring. I knew Shauna was thick. She didn't find the very easy questions easy. These second-year maths exams were her Everest, and she was getting frostbite. *Why do you care?* I thought to myself. *If I looked like you, none of this would matter.* As soon as the words entered my brain, I felt embarrassed. It wasn't very feminist of me. But it was true. If I looked like her, I wouldn't give a shit about this. But I didn't, so I did.

I am fourteen, studying for an exam I know I'll get an A in, and my father walks down into the kitchen, drunk, and pours himself a vodka. He hasn't been my dad in seven days. He's fallen down at the same hurdle he's easily jumped over for four straight years. I have been waiting for this day. Every time he had come home during the past four years, when he would struggle to get his keys in the door, I would bolt up in my bed. *It's back*, I'd think, walking out to the landing. Relief filled through my body when I saw my normal dad staring back at me. Now the timer has been restarted again.

It's just me and him in the kitchen. I put down my pencil. *Why are you so pathetic?* He ignores me, finishing his vodka in three quick gulps. He pours another. I walk up behind him and slap the drink from his shaking hand. Glass shatters on the kitchen tiles. *Fuck you*, he snarls.

Am I just imagining that? Does anyone really snarl? Or do we just create villains out of people to make us feel better?

I watch him as he pours another drink. He holds the cup high as he walks out of the kitchen, trying to lose me. I follow him from room to room. *You sad, loser cunt. I hate you, do you know that?* My voice is calm. It's just a fact. *I hate you I hate you I hate you.* I'm almost singing it. *Shut up, you fucking bitch!* He runs up the stairs, his dressing gown exposing his naked body as he moves. I watch him lose his drink as he takes each step, precious liquid bouncing off the glass and splashing on to the carpet. I smile. *You're a loser*, I shout after him. I sit back down at the kitchen table, thinking about what I'll say to him next. How much more biting it will be. How it will finally make him listen.

An hour later, I hear my dad call my name. *What the fuck now?* I stomp up the stairs, taking two at a time. I wish my dad would hit me, like the alcoholics I see in movies. I wish I could have a concrete reason to hate him, some big AHA moment, that I can point to and say, *This is it!* Instead, I just hate him because I love him. That's barely hate at all.

I walk into his room. The curtains are drawn and the lights are out and he's in his underwear on top of the bed, his fat belly hiding his face. Sometimes as a kid I would rub his belly, pretending there was a baby inside. *Oh, I can feel it kick!* There's a hot, thick smell in the room. Not for the first time, I feel suffocated. *What. Do. You. Want?* He tells me to grab a pen and paper, he needs me to write something down. As annoyed as I am, I comply. I am still his daughter. He starts calling out words that don't mean anything to me. *805488567 with AIB bank, to your mother. The house, you and your brother. Anything left to a dog charity.*

I look up at him, confused. *Wait, what? Why are you telling me to write that?*

It's my will. I want to have a will. I don't laugh at the absurdity of me writing his living will and testament on the back of a receipt for the weekly shop. I don't shut him down for his over-the-top dramatics. His words are slurred, and not in a usual drunk way. He's speaking like he's paralysed. Spit drools down his chin. The colour of his face reminds me of my cousin Paul, at his open casket after he died. An unnatural pudgy paleness. He is drenched in his own sweat, and even though I'm on the other side of the room, I can tell it's cold.

There's something else happening in this room that I am unaware of. I don't know what compels me, what undercurrent is dancing through the stiff hot air, in between me and my father, but I run over to him and hug him. I wrap my arms tightly around his belly, leaning my head on his chest. I hear his heart beat. As a kid, I'd listen to that same sound for hours, until I drifted to sleep.

I am crying now, huge heaving sobs. *I love you I love you I love you*, I gasp out, like it's the last words I'll ever say. Like it's the last words he'll ever hear. It's strange; my body knew before my mind did. My legs ran to him and my arms hugged him and my mouth let out *I love you*. My body felt my dad's desire to die before my mind understood.

I want to die, he tells me. I am frozen. Every part of me has stopped working. I am an outsider observing this; it's a book I am reading. I am watching me, listening to him. I am not part of this. This is not real. *I will die*, he follows up. *I've taken enough pills to kill myself, and I am going to die tonight.*

This is not real. This is not. This is. Oh my fucking God this is this is this is my dad is going to fucking die no no what what do I no fuck no fuck.

I am going to die, he says, almost proudly. I want to punch him in the face and stick my fingers down his throat, so he can throw up his death. I want to run out of the house and forget it is happening. I want him to die. I want him to live. *Are you joking?* I ask him, over and over again. *I'm about to call an ambulance, so tell me if you're joking. Tell me. Are you joking, please?* He just writhes around the bed, moaning. I go to dial 9, and then I pause. Is it 999 or 911? They both sound right. I panic and dial 991, then quickly hang up. Definitely not that.

I blink, and my mother and brother are now in the room. My brother starts to cry, silent tears rolling down his cheeks. My mum says nothing, but takes the phone from my hand. She dials 999. She calls my dad a *fucking idiot*, which is jarring because she hardly ever curses. He doesn't like that. He sees himself as a tragic victim, not an idiot. He's a martyr, dying for a cause we can never understand.

He shifts up a gear, getting abusive. He shouts terrible things at us, that we can barely make out. He's better than us. We don't deserve him. He wants to die, he reminds us. *I know, but please don't, Dad*. I stand in the hot bedroom until red lights flash through the window, and there's an urgent knock on the door, and the ambulance takes my dying father away. I beg them to save him. I cry and plead, *PLEASE SAVE MY DAD. PLEASE.* They don't say anything to me, instead concentrating on him. My mother shoos me into the kitchen and closes the door, telling me to keep it down; the neighbours will hear. Me and my brother sit side by side at the kitchen table. He is still my little brother, even if he has leg hair now and spits on the ground when I talk to him. Even if he gets Player of the Year plaques, for his GAA skills, and even if he ignores me when he sees me when he's out with his friends, he is still my baby brother. We hug each other for the first time in years. It feels unnatural, and I want to make fun of it, but I can't. I might have robbed my brother of his father. The least I can do is hold him as it happens.

Mum walks into the kitchen, breaking the spell. *They've taken him to the hospital. Nothing more we can do now.* Her calmness relaxes me. *I'm going to have to go out to the nosy neighbours now and make up something, Jesus Christ. You two go to bed, you have school in the morning.*

I go to protest, but she swats me away. *If you think you're missing your test because of this, you have another thing coming. Your life isn't on pause because of this, so get to bed.*

2

I sit my business studies exam the next day, wondering if my dad is alive. I answer all the questions easily. My friends are messing by the lockers afterwards. Saoirse pulls at my hair. I slam her against the locker, hard. *What the fuck is your problem?* she asks. *You! You are my problem.* She massages her arm as I put the next period's books into my bag. *Don't be a bitch. You want some of my banana?* She sticks the banana under my nose, and I hit it out of her hand. *Grow up*, I yell, power-walking to my next class.

I get changed into my shorts before last period, because even though my dad might be dead, it's still Wednesday, and every Wednesday I practise sprints on the college track with my running club. I love Wednesdays, because I get to leave school half an hour early to make practice. Skipping Spanish, my least favourite class. Hablar, hablo; who fucking cares? I pace the bus stop, slapping away images of my cousin dead in his casket, images of my dad dying in his bed. I put my hand out to wave down the 75 bus, like I've done for the past 126 Wednesdays. The driver doesn't look at me as I feed the fare into the machine. The coins drop down the metal chute, as they always do. Life doesn't pause for death. Tuesdays keep turning into Wednesdays, no matter what any of us do.

My spikes sink into the spongy rubber as I run, my chest pushing forward against the wind. Each breath of air I take is just enough to keep going. I hear the thump thump thump of my feet. A melody. My eyes are focused straight in front of me. I see the finish line, and I push my arms forward. I dip my body as I cross it, then collapse on the orange track, gasping for breath. My friend Cliodhna sprays me with water, and I laugh. I wrestle her on to the grass, and we keep laughing as we rub mud on to each other's faces, until our coach screams at us to stop. *Get back here, girls! We've another three sprints to do.* I race alongside her for each 200 metres, both of us wanting to win. She's my competition for those thirty seconds. As soon as we cross the finish line, we stop caring. She's back to being my friend. It really is that black and white. We try to trip each other up as we jog back to the start line, hysterically laughing as we do stupid voices, just like we always do. For a moment, I've forgotten a Wednesday could be anything other than this.

Home from running practice that evening, I toss my bag onto the floor and sit down at the kitchen table. My mother is sitting in my father's chair, staring at the wall. *Is he dead?* I ask. She reaches her hand across and places it over mine. A squeeze. *No. They released him a couple of hours ago. I don't know where he is.* We both sit in silence, knowing exactly where he is. In some dark pub, picking right back up where he left off. I hear the clock ticking from the wall behind me. The sound growing louder as each second passes. What now? Where do we go from here? *Are you hungry?* she asks. I laugh. *Actually yea, I'm starving.* The world, it keeps fucking turning.

He comes home later that evening, stinking of booze. None of us speak to him. He is a ghost, still alive but haunting us all the same. After a week, he goes into his room and sweats and screams for six days, then comes out sober. Back to normal dad. We never mention what he did, to him or to each other. The secret of my father remains locked within our home.

My business studies teacher hands me the results to my mocks the following week: I get the highest grade in the class. *And my dad was dying*, I think to myself, proud. I laugh with my friends, and go to running practice three times a week. I win races, and drink at the weekends so I can kiss boys, and then afterwards make fun of those boys. But every single night when I go to sleep, I think about how I almost killed my father, and wonder what kind of person can do that to someone they love. I hope no one I ever meet finds out my terrible secret.

My real secret isn't that I almost killed my father. That is a secret, but I don't know how real it actually is. My actions that night made him want to die, and I guess I'm lucky he didn't, that I caught him just in time. Except he called my name, making sure I caught him in time, so maybe he didn't really want to die. Maybe he just wanted to punish me for pushing him to that place, a place with no other exit but that.

But, when I peel back the layers, underneath that horrible secret, of pushing my father into death, there is another. A secret I cannot rationalize, no matter how hard I try. I can't push it off to him, or anyone else. It's all me. This secret is the truth. And the truth is that when I came home the next day, and asked my mum if he was dead, a big part of me wanted the answer to be yes.

3

In April, I quit running. It is two days before a big race. I am running some practice sprints against a girl I am faster than. She beats me in one race. On the second one, I feel her ready to pass me by, and I feign a muscle pull. I can't accept losing to her. I fall down on the track, screaming in agony. My coach, Terry's wife, runs over, and massages my thigh. *I am injured*, I tell her, and hobble off the track. My mother has been watching it all from her car, and helps me into it. She looks at me from the mirror as she drives. *I am fucking injured*, I shout from the back seat. She shakes her head. *You forgot what leg was sore, and limped on the wrong one as you walked to the car.* I glare at her from the back seat. *I am really hurt, you bitch.* I watch her change gear. *It's okay to lose,* she begins. I interrupt her. *No, it isn't – you only bring me to McDonald's if I win!* She sighs. *Yes, I prefer if you win. But it's okay to lose. The only thing that is not okay is to quit because you're losing.* Her eyes stare at me from the mirror. *You did this in the class race when you were ten. You pretended your ankle gave way because Rebecca was passing you by. You can't give up because you don't want to lose. You have to cross that finish line and accept the result. This is more important than just a race, Marise. This is about deciding what type of person you want to be. You don't want to be a coward.* I roll my eyes and decide to never run again.

When I get home, once my dad has woken up, I tell him what happened. He rubs my leg and disregards everything my mother said. *No one wants to fade into oblivion,* he tells me. *It is better to get out while you're still hot; when everyone can miss your name. There's no shame in that.*

4

When May comes, I am in religion class and Mr Cummins is talking about alcoholism. I give Mr Cummins a hard time because he's made the cardinal sin of being a male teacher in an all-girls school. *Absolute perv,* I say twenty times a day. *Are you sure your real name isn't Mr CummING?* Mr Cummins has tried really hard to help me, but you can't help people who don't know there's something wrong. You can't tell someone their house is on fire if they can't see any smoke – you'll just seem like a mad pervert. So it goes.

He is describing alcoholism, and he tells us most alcoholics go back to drinking. It's just a fact. After class I confront him. *As usual you can't tell us anything correct, not all of them drink again, you absolute idiot.* Before he can respond or admonish me, I burst out crying. *Please tell me not all of them do.* He knows, somehow; this man who I have been so unforgivably horrible to for the past three years just knows exactly what I mean, so he doesn't ask any questions. *You're right,* he says softly, *I was wrong: not all of them do.*

5

By the time June rolls through, the weekly disciplinary meetings have disintegrated, switching from preventative to punishment. My teachers no longer require a parent there, so my mum stops showing up. *You're going to do whatever you want to do,* she tells me, *so what's the point in me being there?*

I smile. *How classic you! Ignoring what is slapping you in your face.* Since that night in February, we have grown even further apart. I blame her for everything my dad did, because I need someone to be culpable, and he's certainly not the cause of my pain.

Look at your potential, my headmistress tells me, holding up a recent exam, narrowing my life to a grade on a piece of paper. *Who cares?* I respond.

This meeting is about Mr Delaney. I called him a paedophile because he looks like a paedophile, and all the girls called him a paedophile, but then I had to try to one-up everyone else, and told all my friends that I had caught him looking up a girl's skirt.

These are serious allegations, my headmistress begins. *No, no, hold up, I was joking, I made it up. He's obviously not really a paedo, I was just having a laugh.* My headmistress stares at me. *That's not funny.* Except it is funny to call your male teacher a paedo when you are fourteen – I wouldn't have made the damn joke if I didn't think people would laugh. But that's strike one.

Is there anything happening at home? they ask.

Oh, you'd love that, I spit back. *But no, nothing bad has happened at home.*

I don't feel like I'm lying. My father's suicide attempt feels like a dream I had imagined, for attention. *Everything is fine at home*, I reiterate. It's easy to forget about something when you are pretending it didn't really happen.

This meeting is because I stole a letter from Miss Birmingham's desk that had her address on it, and said I was going to come by that night and throw a brick through her window. Miss Birmingham, who gave me an A in every essay I turned in, who told me I had a gift, that my writing was very good even though my behaviour wasn't, that was the same Miss Birmingham I loved to terrorize. I didn't have any vendetta against her. In fact, I liked her, because she told me I was special, but I also hated the weakness I saw in her. She was so meek she let me lift a letter from her desk and all she did in response was beg, *Please, no, give it back*. Except, it turned out, she wasn't meek enough not to report the threat. *I was joking*, I insist, and my headmistress reminds me, yet again, that I am not funny. Strike two.

We want to help you, my principal says. *Just give us something, please*. I stare back, giving nothing.

Today's meeting is because I stole Miss Jones's chair. Miss Jones has a wooden hip and got a lovely special swirly chair to sit in because of it, and I refused to give it back to her even when she begged me to have some decency. I swivelled around in her decadent throne and said, *What are you talking about? I don't have your chair. You need to get new glasses, Miss.* And then she ran out of the room crying. Strike three.

This isn't going to work out, my principal tells me. *We have tried to meet you halfway, but you won't even give us that.*

This fourth-strike meeting is over the PE coach, who was out on sick leave, so she had her very hot son take over her classes. He had blond hair and fat muscles and was young enough we all could imagine him being our boyfriend. I pretended my thigh hurt me and he deep-heated it, because I was the best runner in the school and he needed me to compete the following week. *Higher,* I told him as he sprayed me, *you need to go higher up my leg.* He got flustered. *Can you please stop it? This isn't nice, what you're doing.* When he drove me to the competition the next week, I opened up his glove box and leafed through the documents I found. He leaned over to grab the papers from me. *Stop it! You should respect me.* I licked my lips. *I like it when you get angry.*

I nod. They are right. They've given me more strikes than I deserve, and I still haven't got my shit together. I'm not even sure what my shit is, never mind being able to scoop it up into a neat little box.

I think it's best if you leave this school. We're not expelling you, so it won't be on your record. But we're at a dead end here, so this seems like the only solution.

That seems fair, I say, ending our last meeting on that cordial note.

Truth be told, I've been feeling trapped, in a box of my own making, so when they tell me I have to leave, I feel relieved. I don't like who I am becoming, and I don't have the strength to stop it, so I feel grateful to get a reset button. To begin again.

6

After the last day of classes, when a whole summer is stretched in front of me, before I start again at a new school, my dad drives me over to my friend Sarah's house. *Don't do drugs!* he yells out the window, and I laugh. In my bag I have a water bottle filled with vodka from his cabinet. My mum only drinks wine and Bacardi, so I am safe to siphon out Smirnoff or Jameson from the bottles, topping them up each time with water. It is the perfect crime, and one I do every few weeks. The dad who notices the vodka tastes like water isn't the dad who gives a shit about me stealing it. He isn't the dad who gives a shit about me at all.

We blare music in Sarah's room, and scream at our friends as they come in the door, throwing ourselves around each other. My mother hates how I interact with my friends. *Shrieking to say hello. Long hugs goodbye, like you're going off to war. All so dramatic.* She's so old she's forgotten how good girlhood feels. We all dance in Sarah's bedroom, mouthing along to Gwen Stefani. *Few times I've been around that track, so it's not just gonna happen like that.* This isn't the type of dancing we'll do in a few hours, when there are boys watching and we become self-conscious, swaying our hips carefully and licking our lips because we read in a magazine that that was sexy. In this bedroom, without any audience, we are wild, screaming from the tops of our lungs, holding hairbrushes as microphones.

Teenage girls are bitches. I hear that from TV shows, and

adults, and boys our age. The first time I was called a bitch, I was five years old and the Mexican kid on our road, Alejandro, muttered it at me when I wouldn't let him piss in my front garden. That's a thing little boys like to do. Whip out their tiny willies and let it all go. Alejandro called me a bitch because I wouldn't let him piss like my dog, Bingo. I told my mum and she told his mum, and he arrived at my door the next day with a chocolate bunny, even though, get this, it wasn't even Easter! So I forgave him. I knew his dad was mean to him, and he was just passing on some of the mean. He didn't even know what the word meant, just that it was a bad word.

Bitch was a curse word, but it was the most acceptable one. *Fuck* would get you grounded for two weeks, but *bitch* just got you a dirty stare. The first time I learned the word *cunt*, I was eleven, and my friend Annie told me it meant vagina. My mum was getting dressed in front of me, and she took off her belt and it accidentally hit me in the, well... *Ow, my cunt*, I yelled. My mother went pale, and then bright red. She screamed at me for twenty minutes straight. I immediately retired the word from my vocabulary.

Bitch stayed, though. Bitch bitch bitch. I'm a bitch, you're a bitch, we are bitches. If someone called you a bitch, you took a big deep breath in and hit them back with *A bitch is a dog a dog barks bark is a tree trees are nature and nature is beautiful, SO THANK YOU FOR THE COMPLIMENT.* You were a bitch if you did something bad to someone else, but it was fleeting. No one stayed a bitch for more than a minute or two, but then teenage girls came along, and I turned into one, and I learned what bitches we were just for existing.

Please curl my hair, I beg Sarah. *I really want to look hot.* It will take her forty minutes, but she agrees and heats up her hair straightener. She tenderly pulls each curl from the hot iron, teasing it and spraying it in hairspray. I hear the delicious crunch while she does it. *Ah, the sound of beauty*, I think. All six of us cram on to her bed, deciding on outfits and making each other laugh. *Teenage girls are vapid and stupid and cruel*, I hear from the same TV, and adults, and boys who call us bitches. And so what? I can solve every maths part on 'Countdown', and recite all fifty states of America in less than a minute, and name every minister in the government, but that stuff doesn't make me feel alive, not like these girls do. If that is being vapid and stupid and cruel, give me all of its juiciness, piled high on a plate. I'll devour it and ask for seconds. *Be generous with the spray, so they stay in*, I tell her. *Make me fucking flammable.*

We spread out our make-up on the bed, picking and choosing from all the products. Despite our different skin tones, we all use the same foundation, painting layers on our faces with a brush. I look at my face in the mirror and see the streaks of orange across it. I can't make myself look like the girls in magazines, no matter how hard I try. I throw the brush on the floor, and rub my face with my hands. I only really like blush anyway. I apply circle after circle of hot pink on my cheek, while the other girls do mascara and eyeshadow and lipstick. Fiona grabs the palette from my hands. *Girl, you have enough.* I look in the mirror, admiring my fuchsia cheeks. *Oh come on, just one more!* She laughs and hands me the palette. *But just let me blend it, okay?* She rubs her fingers softly on my face. If teenage girls are bitches, I want to be a bitch for the rest of my life.

We get dressed, and undressed, and dressed again. Hmming and hawing in front of the mirror. I put on a baby-blue crop top, so my very adult belly button is exposed. *Super sexy*, Ciara tells me. I pull a tiny skirt over my thighs. It's from the holiday section of Primark. It's bright turquoise and the same material as a swimsuit. *So sexy*, I think, as I rub the stretchy nylon in my hands. The skirt barely covers my ass, and if I jump everyone will be able to see the birthmark on my left cheek. So I put on a thong underneath, and make a plan to jump all over the dance floor.

Less is more, I tell my friends, *I think I read that in 'Cosmo'.* I slip my feet into white wedges that are two sizes too big for me, and stumble around the room like a baby giraffe. I feel positively divine. *Glitter!* Saoirse shouts, and we all scream in excitement. Powders and sprays and lotions are passed around the room and slathered over every bit of skin we have on show, until we all resemble slimy, beautiful seals. We sip from our water bottles on our walk to Becks. Becks is a sketchy underage disco, inside the hall of a rugby club. It's a place where fourteen-year-olds strap naggins of vodka to their legs that they then drink in the toilet once they get in, and then go give wanks on the dance floor. Undercover tabloid reporters run exposés on Becks every couple of years. *Young women defiled on dance floor,* the headlines read. *Do you know what your kids are getting up to?* We've been going to Becks for the past two years. At fifteen we're almost too old for it, so this is our last one. Next year we'll get fake IDs and go to real nightclubs, but for now we're still kids, technically.

One of the bouncers, Ronnie, is a known celebrity among us girls, and I'm 90 per cent sure he's a creepy pervert. He is anywhere between forty and eighty-five, and he stands at the door, letting his favourite girls skip the queue, placing his hand on their exposed midriff to guide them in. When, later, I watched 'Dazed and Confused' in college, I shrieked at the Matthew McConaughey character. The best thing about high-school girls... *That's fucking Ronnie!* Except Ronnie doesn't look like Matthew McConaughey, or have his Hollywood charm. Ronnie is an ugly old man with a little power, who uses his power to touch the shoulders of fourteen-year-old girls, drunk on Smirnoff Ices.

Once inside, already buzzed on my vodka and a WKD Blue that Sarah shared with me on the walk down, me and my friends run to the toilet to down the rest of our drinks. It takes us twenty minutes to walk a few feet from the entrance to the bathroom, pushing past boys in Ralph Lauren t-shirts, collars popped. There must be four hundred teenagers crammed in here, and at least two hundred and fifty of them are boys. I squeeze Sarah's hand. *That's good odds*, I scream in her ear. Sweat drips off the dark walls as we all file out of the toilets, holding each other's hands in a chain. We smoke cigarettes outside, falling over our kitten heels and laughing hysterically. The vodka hits me once I step out into the cold autumn air, and I'm struggling to see straight. I lean on Ciara's shoulder as I puff. *You're not even inhaling*, says one of the cool girls. I call her a dumb *bitch* and blow smoke in her face.

On the dance floor, I kiss anyone who asks me, and don't stop any spotty-faced boy who roughly shoves his finger in my knickers. *Don't mess up my glitter*, I whisper into their ears, falling on top of them, propped up only by their finger inside me. I run back to my friends in between each one. *I think he fucking scratched my vagina,* I yell, fanning my face with my bag. We laugh and dance to Rihanna, sweat dripping off our bodies, hugging each other tight as the lights flash to the music. *I love you*, we slur into each other's ears. Three of us cram into the toilet cubicle over and over again throughout the night, taking turns to pee, hovering our asses over the piss on the toilet seat. *You're the best. No, you fucking are.* Saoirse fixes my hair in the mirror. I rub lipstick off her teeth. *More pretty now.* We walk back to the dance floor, linking arms so we feel more secure. The floor is wet, but sticky, so sometimes we slip, but never fall. *I love you all*, one of the girls says, and we scream and raise our hands, touching our sweaty palms together. Drunk on the vodka, and each other.

My dad collects me at midnight. I see his car pull up when I have bread stuffed in my face. Someone told us that bread sobers you up, so there is a crowd of drunk teenagers eating loaves of bread outside the gas station next door. I hug the girls goodbye. My wedges are in my hand. I don't remember taking them off. I run across the forecourt to my father. I can't find the door handle to open the car. *Dih you gehih removed, you bashturd?* I yell. My dad opens the door for me, and makes fun of me for being drunk. He's not mad, of course. *I'll stop by the chipper on the way home, we can share a battered sausage.* I start to cry. *How doed you know scatly what I wanned?* He slaps his steering wheel. *I wish I had my video recorder; this is priceless. Hey, have I ever told you about the three-legged dog that walks into a Western bar?* We both burst into laughter, tears falling down our faces as we chuckle away in the car. No one makes me laugh like my dad. He doesn't even have to be telling me a joke.

7

When I start my new school, my mother makes me lunch every day. Piece of fruit, sandwich, granola bar. I spend every lunchtime eating my food in the bathroom stall. Putting toilet paper down on my seat, then opening my paper bag. I listen to the sound of piss hitting the ceramic bowl next to me as I chew down my tuna. During those hour breaks, that stretch on to infinity, I often cry. I feel so lonely. When sobs escape me, I stuff toilet paper in my mouth, afraid another girl will hear my desperation as she takes a leak. But I don't need to be so worried. I am invisible to everyone around me.

I try to keep in touch with my old friends, but I'm bad with my phone, and a part of me believes that, to start afresh, I need to shed myself of everything I used to be. So by October I'm no longer in contact with them. I wait for the influx of new friends, but they don't come. At my new school, everyone already has their friend group, and no one seems interested in adding me to theirs. I had thought I wanted a new beginning, but now, faced with one, it scares me. I can't just be alone with myself. I need a new hobby to distract me from my thoughts.

I ask for a Bible for Christmas. My mum gets me a paperback edition in which they talk in the King's English, and I don't have a clue what they're saying. I sellotape up the cover so it won't rip, and carry it around with me. I try to read from the beginning, but there's that part when Lot fucks his daughters that I'm not so sure on, so I skip to the New Testament. I underline sentences that sound good. There's a lot of them. Even if you're not religious, the New Testament has a lot of good lines to live by. If you take out the religion from the Bible, it makes a lot more sense.

In February, I sit down my parents for a grand announcement. *I am becoming a Protestant.* I hear my mother gasp. *Why, Marise?* she wails. *Why, of all things, a Protestant? A Protestant. God forgive you. Your poor grandad, if he knew. God rest his soul. A Protestant!*

I think I am a Buddhist actually, my dad says, with a straight face. *Oh fuck off. Stop trying to outdo me.* He lets out a deep sigh. *I don't know why you need to be so full of hatred, especially when you know I have cancer.*

I catch my mother rolling her eyes. Dad's list of fake illnesses grows longer by the day. He also suffers from seizures and has diabetes. Sometimes, he gets the two confused. A month ago, I came home with my brother and mum, after collecting my brother from the local police station. I pressed my ear against the interview-room door and heard, *Underage… drugs,* until a police officer shooed me away. On the drive home, during a red light, Mum swivelled around to face my brother. *Get ready, because your father will punish you so bad.* I side-eyed my brother. Mum was out of her depth. I don't think she even believed what she had said.

We walked into the house and, once the door shut, heard a loud thump thump thump upstairs. We all ran up the stairs, and Dad was having a seizure, on the bathroom floor. I started to scream, but my brother shushed me. He knew what to do. Apparently, it had happened before. When they were in the car together, my dad driving. My brother had to turn the steering wheel, to make sure they didn't crash. *It's his diabetes. He needs his medication,* my brother said, and reached into Dad's pocket and took out what looked like a pack of Altoids. He opened them up. They were empty. What now? My brother knew the answer to this, too. *Get a chocolate bar. It's his blood sugar.* Dad was still flailing around the bathroom floor. I stuck a Snickers in his mouth and immediately he recovered. *What a miracle,* he said to us from the floor. We forgot all about my brother's mishap with the law, so overjoyed were we with my diabetic/epileptic father's recovery. He was always very creative in his ways to avoid responsibility.

His cancer was the latest block in his pyramid of bullshit. Cancer of the spine that was so nuanced the doctors weren't able to find it on any scan they did. *Modern medicine leaves a lot to be desired,* he said, dismissing his clear test results. *I know it's there; I can feel it in my gut.*

My mum theatrically grabs her head, still reeling from my Protestant conversion. *Please, both of you, give it a rest. I'm getting weak. I'm actually physically weak.* My father wanders out of the room, annoyed he isn't getting more attention. During his last few steps, he adopts a limp. He turns to face me at the door. *I accept your spiritual journey. Being this close to death, I can see the…* My mother kicks shut the door, making me giggle. *I'm sorry, I can't listen to him. I cannot deal with both a cancer patient and a Protestant under the one roof.*

Well, you better learn to deal with it, I tell her sternly. *I am a Protestant now. It's my choice, and you have to accept it. Isn't that our family motto? Accept it all.*

I am sure my mother knows what I'm alluding to, but she doesn't take the bait. *Oh calm down! You don't need to be so dramatic, Marise. My life motto is an easy life, but do you think I get that?* I roll my eyes. My mother is always talking about wanting an easy life. It's in her nature, she tells me. *Not my nature,* I tell her proudly, and she agrees. An easy life is at odds with her not easy husband and not easy daughter, but she keeps wanting it, all the same.

She agrees to drive me to the Protestant church every Sunday, but makes it clear she's doing so under duress, and if I say one word about it to her family, she'll make me walk the five miles. I meet with the de facto priest and his wife after mass each week, having a cup of coffee as we discuss Matthew, Mark and co. In Catholicism, you are taught to be afraid of God. He's an all-encompassing, power-wielding fanatic: always watching you, ready to punish you for any misstep. With Protestants, God seems more like a friend. He's there to make you feel good. *I think I could get used to your God,* I say to the Protestant priests. *Our God,* they say, smiling as they correct me.

I'm not having sex before marriage, I tell my mum in the kitchen, as she makes my dinner. She side-eyes me. *It's not about marriage. You should save sex for someone you love, who respects you.* My mother is deeply practical in a way that bores me to death.

It's for religious reasons, I'll have you know. I hold up my Bible to drive home the point.

It's always some extreme with you, isn't it? Why can you never just be? I finger my Bible. *No sex,* I repeat. *I am abstaining.* She stirs around the chicken in the pan. *You are your father's daughter all right. You definitely didn't come from me.*

Since his suicide attempt, those words – *your father's daughter* – annoy me. *Maybe I came from neither of you. You ever think of that? Maybe I'm a direct line from Mary herself.* Mum laughs. *Protestants don't believe in Mary.* That was news to me. *Yea, I know,* I say defensively. *Was just trying to relate.*

She adds a packet of sauce to her chicken. *That's full of sugar,* I tell her. *You should try making something from scratch.* She sticks out her tongue. *Maybe Jesus can feed you instead.* I nod, and shove a piece of chicken into my mouth. *See, you're getting it now. I'm divine.*

I take out my Bible every day during lunch, my highlighter in hand, ready to bright-yellow the passages that are important. No one cool stays in the classroom for lunch. Anyone who has friends leaves once the bell hits one. They go to the shops, or to each other's houses. Maybe they get fingered in bushes by the boys who go to school down the road. I don't know; I'm never invited. I just know that all the cool girls leave. It's only the rejects left. Girls I'd never talk to, but am okay talking at. *Anyone want to be saved by Jesus Christ?* The other girls ignore me, staring into their lunch. You can ignore someone and still be listening. And I know they're listening to me. I'm only religious if there's an audience. I know I only exist if people are looking at me.

Now I have Jesus on my side, I no longer eat my sandwiches in the bathroom stall. I munch down on my apple in the open. *He died for our sins, girls. Is there anything more holy than that?* No one answers me, but that was never the point. The point is that they're listening. I can't fade away into nothing if I have eyes on me. I stand up from my desk, flicking my hair so it falls over my shoulder, and throw my apple core in the bin, knowing they are watching. *Jeremiah 29:11, girls. God has hope for us all.*

A few months later, I read 'The God Delusion', a book that dismantles religion with the type of snobby sloppiness a teenager just eats right up. *God's not real*, I tell my mum when she's making me French toast one morning. *Oh God forgive you*, she says, handing me a plate of eggy toast. *Don't need his forgiveness, because I don't believe in him. I'm an atheist now.* I slowly roll the word off of my tongue, savouring each syllable. *Wait, hold on, so that means you're not Protestant anymore?* I solemnly shake my head. She lets out a laugh. *Oh thank God! You've finally come to your senses!* I shoot her daggers. *I am an atheist*, I repeat. *So long as you're not a bloody Protestant. There's hope for you yet, my girl.* I theatrically throw my tattered Bible in the bin, to try and prove my point, but she ignores me, dancing around the kitchen. *Four months of driving you to that place every week, and now I am finally free. My Protestant daughter is no more!*

If I am being honest with myself, I am relieved too. I was getting sick of getting up early every Sunday morning, sick of trying to find meaning in the same words on a page. Not believing in something is so much easier to do.

8

That following summer, when I am sixteen, we are getting ready for a family holiday to Barcelona. Part of some football trip for my twelve-year-old brother and his teammates. I was surprised when my mum booked tickets for all of us, because my parents don't like football. They love GAA, the Irish football. English football is too boring for my mum to watch, and too unpatriotic for my dad to enjoy. But my mum thinks it will be good for us to go away together. *You're sixteen now,* she tells me while we're packing our suitcases, *this might be the last opportunity for us to go away as a family.* I know once me and my brother outgrow family holidays, it will mean my mother won't get another one. Dad barely agrees when his kids are involved, and I know he loves us so much more than he does his wife. Right now, this is Dad giving it his all, and it's barely anything. I feel a pang of guilt, knowing what is in store for my mum, and knowing how much less of a life it will be than she deserves. *When I have a job and am rich,* I tell her while we're packing, *I promise I'll take you on a holiday, just me and you.* She puts down a shirt of my dad's on the bed. *I'd really love that, Marise. We could lay on a beach and get tans, and drink cocktails and eat nice food… Oh, I think that would be lovely.* I smile at her. *It's a plan.*

In Barcelona, there are fifteen other families on this trip, but we don't really interact with them. We eat dinner beside them, but don't actually talk. It's jarring. In the elevator of our hotel, one of the other mothers asks me if I am German, and doesn't believe me when I tell her no. She has lipstick on her teeth. She kinda looks like a horse. *These people are stupid*, I complain to my mum over breakfast. She shushes me while eating a hard-boiled egg. *Just figure out a way to enjoy yourself, please.* I walk over to my dad. He's eating breakfast at a different table, separate from us. For no other reason than he's my dad, and he's odd sometimes. *That woman does look like a horse*, he says. *She's a slut.* I sit down with him. *She fucking is!*

When my mum brings my brother to soccer practice, getting on the bus with all the other parents, me and my dad stay behind in the hotel. He buys me cocktails in the hotel bar as we people-watch. We imagine perverse backstories for anyone we see. *That woman over there, she's drinking red wine because she has sex with her dog, and the Merlot reminds her of his red dick*, one of us says, and then the other tries to outdo it with something worse. *She's trying to get over the love of her life, who was a horse. He kicked her in the teeth when she tried to kiss him, so she can't eat solids anymore.*

We laugh, and I usually love to laugh with my dad, but his laughter feels hollow now. I know what that means, but I ignore it. We're on holiday, and my dad may be an alcoholic, but he's given up for good, and even though I've heard that sentence before, I know it's true this time. Even if he hasn't said it, I know he's sorry for trying to die. On the third night, after ordering me two piña coladas, he tells me he has an urge to drink. He is finding it hard to say no. I tell him to shut up. I am not his parent, or his sponsor. I am his child, and I definitely don't have the answers. *You can't do this to me*, I tell him, *you can't expect me to solve you. It's not my problem.* He lets out a sigh, and orders me another drink. *You have no idea the pain I feel. You're too selfish to think about me.*

The waiter interrupts him, placing a massive piña colada with a pink umbrella onto the table. *Gracias*, we both say. *Haha, jinx*, I tell him, and he laughs. *See?* he says. *We're just the fucking same. Me and you are made from the same thing, and that's why it hurts me extra when you can't understand how hard things are for me.* I stir my drink with my flimsy umbrella. *I don't like it here either, okay? But it's important to Robert, and it's important to Mum, and I love her, I guess.* I cough when I say that, embarrassed to admit it. *Of course, I love you more.* I look up at my dad when I say that, and he is smiling, so I continue. *I don't like this place either, Dad, I promise. But shouldn't we just suck it up, so the people we love can have a good time and not worry about us? I'm sure Mum doesn't love driving me to my friends' houses every weekend, or making you your dinner every night, but she just does it, and I think we should just do this back, just to be fair.*

I look up at him again, and his expression has changed. I don't know when it changed, so I'm not sure what words to take back. His eyes are black, and I look down at the table, unable to meet them. *You fucking know your mother is simple. She does enjoy that shit. It is so much harder to be me, and you're a bitch, just like her, if you can't see that.* I stand up from my chair, so hard my cocktail shakes on the table, and stare directly into his eyes. *Fuck you, Dad, fuck you for taking something fun and making it horrible. Why can't you be normal?* I slap my hands on the table. *Why can't you be a normal dad? I am not your fucking friend, I am your child, and you are putting too much on me, you absolute prick. If you want to drink, fucking drink. I'm not your sponsor, I don't need the play-by-play of how you are feeling. Do whatever you want to do and don't involve me in it. Please just grow the fuck up.* I walk away from him, shaking. *Fuck you, fuck you.* I hear the words, but I am not sure who is saying them.

Where's your father? my mum asks, when she gets back from the practice and sees me sitting on my bed, alone. I panic, and cover for him. *He's gone searching for a cigar shop that the receptionist told him about. He might be a while.* We are all in bed, not sleeping, when he stumbles in at 2am. I am consumed with guilt as I hear him vomit all night in the shared bathroom. I don't tell my mum that I could have stopped it.

My mother's alarm goes off at 6am, and we get up immediately. None of us have slept, besides my dad, who is passed out on the bathroom floor. I kick him awake, and we pack and leave the room. *This is my fault*, my brother whispers to me on the bus to the airport. *He would never have drunk if he didn't have to come on this stupid trip.* My brother isn't even thirteen, but my dad is already robbing him of things he loves. *He would have drunk anyway*, I tell him, punching him in the shoulder. *Dad is the most selfish person to ever exist. He was always going to do whatever he wanted.* My brother looks unconvinced. *It's not your fault*, I say softly, but he is already looking out the window and doesn't hear me.

On the plane home my dad is across the aisle from me. He orders two vodkas and a Coke from the flight attendant. The Coke is just for show. He pours the two vodkas into a plastic glass, and I stare at him. If I could kill him with my eyes, he would keel over on top of the tray before he could even take a sip. I say every voodoo prayer I can imagine to make it happen. Instead, he takes the plastic cup to his mouth, then pauses. Maybe it's working. He looks over at me, meeting my gaze. I don't look away. Neither does he. We are at a stand-off. *Dear God, please...* He interrupts my prayer by lifting his cup to his lips and drinking, without breaking eye contact with me.

I watch him down his vodka; I see the hostility in his eyes and I finally understand that terrible people exist, and sometimes they're the people you love. Before, I always thought he would redeem himself – and he would, albeit temporarily. So I would forgive him, even when he didn't ask for forgiveness. But watching him down that drink, staring into my eyes, I realize he will never give enough of a shit about me to stop thinking about himself for one fucking minute. *He's dead to me*, I say to the space in front of me, and lean back my head on the aeroplane seat to stop the tears falling.

9

When we get home, he drinks for another few days, then detoxes. A week later, he is back to normal dad. He tries to hug me, on day one of being normal dad, but I push him away. *We're not going back to that*, I tell him. He nods and walks away, and we don't speak for eight months after that. Eight months is a long time when you live in a three-bedroom semi-detached house. There's not enough room to escape someone else when you share the same bathroom. You have to be strong-willed to ignore someone that long. But I am. When I walk into the kitchen, and he is sitting at the table, I walk right back out. When my mother tries to orchestrate meetings, all three of us trapped in her car, I look down at my phone, bored. I pretend he doesn't exist when he's half a foot away from me. I know if I say one word to him, it will be to forgive him, and I don't want to forgive someone who doesn't see all they've done wrong. I look the other way when I meet him on the stairs. The silence pierces through my brain. *Just forgive him,* my mother begs, *I want things to go back to normal. Fuck you*, I spit out at her. *Fuck you for ever thinking this was normal.*

After eight long months of deafening silence, I write Dad a letter. If we aren't going to talk about our feelings, I will write them down. You can't pretend you forget a letter like you can a conversation. Writing it down makes it real. The words spill out of me before I have a chance to catch them and dilute them. I stare at the sentences in front of me, reading them back like I'm a witness to it all. I remove myself from them. *This person is very angry,* I think as I fold over the letter, *but this person is not me.*

This girl is angry that her father tried to kill himself and her family didn't say a fucking word about it for a year afterwards. She is angry that her dad's addiction was always skirted over in hushed tones, since she was five years old, so she never really understood what it was. She is angry at her mother, for enabling his behaviour and not protecting her. Even though she would have told her to fuck off if she had tried. She is angry at the shame of having an alcoholic father. That he can't go down to the pub on a Friday and have a few beers, like normal dads do. She is angry that she is embarrassed by him, that she looks at him fighting the hardest battle many have to face and thinks, *Pathetic*. She is angry that he puts so much on her shoulders. Like she is responsible for his shortcomings. *This poor, stupid girl*, I think, looking at my reflection in the mirror.

I walk down the stairs, the letter burning in my hand. I wish I had written about the pain pulsing through me. Instead, I call him weak, evil, a cunt. I let him know how much I wish I wasn't made from him. I tell him if I ever end up like him, I will kill myself. *I will never do to my child what you have done to me. If I realize I am exactly like you, I will kill myself, and save innocent people the pain of loving me. I will never be as selfish as you.*

I throw the letter at him in the conservatory, past midnight, when he is smoking a cigar, watching the same Elvis documentary he has seen fifty times. I run up the stairs and shut my bedroom door, terrified of what will happen, but glad I am moving the needle forward, from playing pretend to what really is. I sit on my bed, shaking, looking out my window into the conservatory, wondering if he even cares enough to read it.

Looking back, I wish I could have saved him from that letter. I wish that, once I'd written it, I'd torn it up into twenty pieces, impossible to put back together, because God knows my nosy mother would have tried. I wish I didn't have to hurt my father to show him that he had hurt me.

He comes up to my room an hour later. He is angry now too. *How could you say these words? How could you hurt me like this?* I am silent. *You're a selfish piece of shit*, I repeat over and over in my head. He starts to cry. I've seen my dad cry much more than my mother. *Men don't cry*, I hear people say, and I side-eye them. Which men? Usually he cries to make other people feel bad, but this time is different. It feels different. *He is realizing something*, I convince myself. He doesn't say much, just sits at the edge of my bed and tries to push out words, but they get caught in his throat. He reaches his arms out instead, and I crawl into them, our cheeks side by side, not sure whose tears belong to whom.

Maybe he is realizing, for the first time, that his problems aren't his own. That there is a cause and effect to everything we do. That I have absorbed his fuck-ups. Maybe, but he doesn't say anything. And the next morning, as it always is in our house, it is like it has never happened. The letter breaks the silence between us, and my mother is happy because we're being civil to each other, but it doesn't do enough. It doesn't make him fix what he has broken. So, I close the door to my father, with an ease I find both comforting and terrifying.

10

Even during my brief foray into religion, even when my dad dipped back into a vodka bottle, I still had desire dripping through my body. My want never left me, even when I tried to replace it with Jesus. I imagined the Protestant priest spreading my legs during our talks, kneeling down and tasting my pussy. I fantasized about my religion teacher fucking me in my uniform, my knee-high socks raised in the air. I humped my pillow when I thought about them, and then, once I came, was immediately disgusted with myself. I knew there was something wrong with me, because a girl wasn't supposed to be this horny. Girls were supposed to be good. And good girls didn't think such nasty thoughts.

When I found a folder of pictures on the family computer, covertly labelled 'boobs', I immediately ratted out my brother. *He's got thirty-five images of women's breasts saved to the computer we all use*, I shouted at my mum. She awkwardly laughed. *Gross. I will ground him, don't worry, that's really not okay he did that. But boys will be boys...*

Boys were allowed to be pervs, because it was written in their DNA. They couldn't help themselves. They were driven by desire, unlike girls, who just reacted to it. It was the biggest divider I could see in the genders. If a girl did something sexual, she certainly didn't orchestrate it; it just happened to her. Even my 'mature' friends, the girls who sucked boys' dicks, only did it because the boys begged them to, because they were pressured into it. Girls didn't instigate things, they just responded. But I also knew I wanted to instigate something, to have someone touch my body, because I was desperate for it to be touched. I didn't even care who did it, I just wanted to feel a hand against me. And I knew that wasn't normal for a girl, so I felt hot shame anytime I thought about it. I knew my perverseness was masculine, and that horrified me. I fantasized about someone coming along and cutting it right out of me, leaving me a bloody wreck, but pure. I wanted, desperately, for someone to take what I felt, to rip it straight from my stomach and hold it in their hands, so it would then belong to them.

When I get a part-time job in a book store at sixteen, I shamelessly flirt with my manager. He is twenty-eight, with that nerdy hot look I just eat right up. A bony body and a face made of angles, with thick-rimmed glasses sitting on top of his big nose. He rolls up the sleeves on his white shirt every shift, and I positively die. *What a fucking stud*, I think, as he separates the newspapers into the racks. He lets me stock the card section every time we're on shift together, which is the easiest section to do because no one buys greeting cards anymore, so I add two plus two and deduce he's secretly in love with me.

My Lolita, he sometimes calls me, and I blush. I haven't read the book, but I know it's about a teenage girl and a grown man, and they fuck each other, so I'm sure he is flirting with me. *I could be your Lolita*, I tell him a few weeks later, looking down at the floor as we stock the shelves. He laughs. *You're too young to be this intense. You need to take it down a peg or two*. My cheeks burn with embarrassment. He is allowed to call me his Lolita, but it's not cool for me to say it back. The bridge between what men can feel and what I am allowed to feel is a mile apart.

During one shift, he hands me a book titled 'Annie John'. *This is about lesbians, but it's also much more than just that*. I freeze. *Why are you giving me this?* I ask. *Because you like reading, and it's a good book*. I breathe out, relieved. *I don't care about lesbians. I don't want to know about women fucking women*. I emphasize the fucking, to make him think about fucking me. He laughs. *Why do you have to be so forceful? You have to learn to relax*. Despite his stupid lesbian book, which I never read, I still fantasize about our passionate affair, unable to keep our hands off each other in the stockroom, him brought to his knees with desire. I imagine him exploding in my mouth and then, right after it, proposing to me. I think about how good that would feel, for someone to want me that much.

When I buy a copy of 'Lolita', I make sure to hunt him down, asking him to give me the employee discount on it. He scans his badge without making eye contact.

Later that night, I come thinking about him, and I feel relieved. Even though I know I shouldn't have this burning desire, I feel a bit better that it's directed towards a man. I know, once I finally have sex, the man, whoever he is, will take hold of it, owning it, and I will be the helpless girl, just accepting the horribleness men are programmed to feel. Once it really happens, I won't have to feel bad about my desire. All I'll have to do is accept. And what a relief that will be, to just accept.

11

I spend a year and a half trying to flog my virginity to any man who looks twice at me. I wear short skirts and curl my hair, before pinning it back in pigtails. I bat my eyes and say words that would make my mother blush. Every man that even holds the door for me, I try to strike up conversation with. I know I'm coming across desperate, but I am desperate. None of them take the bait, and I start to wonder if the bait is rotten. If maybe I'll never be able to offload my filthy thoughts to someone else.

It takes a full eighteen months before someone bites, and when they do it's a massive let-down. I am seventeen, and have just started university. It's the night of my Debs, and I am on the bus, which is gunning down the motorway, the driver desperate to drop us back at our former school and get rid of us. I have found hotness this summer; my braces have been removed, my hair highlighted, and birth control (prescribed for painful periods) has made my tits grow a size. Fake tan hosed onto my naked body, by a friend of my cousin who owns a spray gun. Make-up expertly applied by a girl at the Mac counter, layer after layer, and one more layer after that, for luck, so when she shows me her work in the mirror, I can hardly recognize myself. *Gorgeous*, she says, and I agree, counting the degrees of separation from myself and pretty. I am wearing a white dress from the clearance section of a wedding store. A dress I chose with my mother after trips to eight different shops. There is vomit all down the front of it, from me spewing my guts on the hour-long bus ride home.

My date is a boy who broke down crying in an Urban Outfitters changing room three weeks ago, telling me he was gay. We had been dating for five weeks before that, and I liked hanging out with him, even though he was overly masculine and had polar-opposite interests to me. We hung out in his living room mostly: he would watch a basketball game and scream at the TV, and I would read a Lionel Shriver book and ask him to *shut up, please*. During the breaks he would come over and kiss me. I liked him kissing me, but I really liked the distance between us in between the kisses. It was comforting.

I didn't like him all the time, though. I didn't like him the night he talked about a guy in his class who had come out as gay and called him a *fucking fag*. I screamed and threw the remote at his face when he said it. It wasn't even the word he said, but the way he said it. He spit it out like it was poison. But I let it slide, because I really wanted him to be my first boyfriend. A big part of any relationship is accepting things that make your skin crawl. I knew that because I knew my parents. My mother made a steak for my dad when he was stone drunk, shouting about her being a whore, and they had recently celebrated twenty years together. Love was rooted in acceptance, for better or worse, and, more often than not, it was worse.

TROUBLE

As I stood over him in the Urban Outfitters changing room, as he knelt on the wooden floor and I ran my fingers through his hair, I thought of that night. It now made much more sense. He wasn't angry at the guy in his class; he was angry at himself. It made me like him a little more. But then I looked down at him, weak and helpless, getting wet patches on my t-shirt, and felt a power I didn't know what to do with, and it made me resent him. *There's something wrong with me*, he said in between sobs, grabbing my waist with his hands. *There's something wrong with all of us*, I told him, trying to wriggle myself free from his grasp. *At least you know what yours is.*

On the bus home from the Debs, we are both too drunk to remember all the befores. We hold hands as I stick my head out the tiny window, gulping cold air into my lungs. *You're my best friend*, he slurs into my ear, and I squeeze his hand. *Same, same*, I say back. Our friends whoop at us from their seats. They don't know about the gayness, so think we're still dating. *Get it, man*, one guy I've always despised shouts. Get it, man. I guess tonight means more to them than it does to us.

When the bus drops us all off at our former school an hour later, we will walk the mile to his house and take ten minutes to turn his key in the door. We will quietly walk up the narrow stairs, and lie in his single bed. My head will still be spinning from the tequila shots. I will pull my vomit-streaked dress over my head and climb back into the bed in my underwear. I will lean my almost naked body against his almost naked body, and he will pull me closer to him. His dick will grow hard, and he'll grab my hand to feel it. *Maybe I'm not gay*, he'll tell me, and I'll climb on top of him, that *maybe* being enough for me.

It won't be like the books and movies have promised; it is neither explosive nor painful. It won't be like I imagined; he won't take control of me, won't rip away my want from inside of me. The next morning, there will be no blood on the sheets, and I'll barely remember it happening, except for visions that will flash through my head of looking away from him, at his bedroom door slightly ajar, and wondering if his parents could hear. Or the power I felt rush through me as he came inside of me, and the tears falling down my cheeks, as my dirty desire flooded back into me. Or of afterwards, both of us naked, with my head on his chest, and him telling me, *Actually, now I'm sure I am gay.*

I'll remember that.

I'll remember how inconsequential it all seemed. How detached you can feel from someone who has been inside of you. At how different the action of his penis entering my vagina played in both of our minds. How at the very moment he said, *Now I'm sure I am gay,* I thought, *Thank God, now I'm definitely straight.* And how good that felt. Like I was transferring my gayness to him. Like it was now his problem, and I was the outsider, patting his head as he cried beneath me.

12

When I graduated university, I moved to Chicago. I got a job with a salary, and fell in love. With enough distance from the life I used to live, I felt comfortable. I forgot to respond to a lot of my father's emails. He sent long rambling messages that didn't make much sense. It was easy to click delete. Sometimes, he would send emails on behalf of Bingo. *The old man is an alcoholic and never bothers to give me a slice of ham anymore, and I'm itching to go ride the neighbourhood bitches. I think I got one up the duff. She told me she was on the pill, I'm not ready to be a dad, fuck, I only have three legs.* They made me laugh out loud at work when I read them, but when my co-workers asked me what was so funny, I pulled up an 'Onion' article. I didn't ever mention him to other people. If you stop talking about a person for long enough, they eventually disappear. That's what I thought at twenty.

When I was a child, I had blonde curly hair. My mum used to tell me, *There was a little girl who had a little curl, right in the middle of her forehead. When she was good, she was very, very good, but when she was bad, she was horrid.* She'd always say it when I was in trouble, and it would still make me giggle. *I'm the little girl! I have the curl!* When my dad was good, he was very, very good. And when he was bad, he was horrid. How do you marry those two opposing people? My dad was my hero, and my villain. I loved him, and it was a burden. It was magic some of the time, but most times it was a burden. It was a relief to give up on him.

I'm twenty-one years old now, walking through arrivals at Dublin airport, after a year away, and my dad is waiting for me. He jumps on top of me with excitement, smothering me with kisses. *I've missed you so fucking much, kid.* I laugh and shake him off. *I'm tired, let's go home.* We walk to the car park, and he can't remember where he left the car. We search for an hour and a half and can't find it. I grow angry. *Just fucking remember.* He starts to cry. *I'm sorry, I was just so excited to see you, I forgot where I left it.* I wipe away his tears while avoiding eye contact. My child father. The security guard has to look through his cameras to find it.

A few months later, he helps me move into my apartment in Dublin, an hour away from my parents' house. He watches me lug box after box from the car to my new bedroom. *I'd love to help, but you know I've a bad back*, he says, leaning against the bonnet. I smile, and hug him with one hand. *See you around, Dad.* He holds me longer than he needs to. *Please just don't disappear*, he whispers in my hair. I prise his arms from me. *I am right here, Dad, relax. I'll always be right here.*

Every few months, we meet for dinner. We eat mussels and crab, and talk in stilted conversation. What was once second nature is now a foreign language. In between those meals, he calls me up, moaning about his latest illness. *Have you ever heard of Lyme disease? Because I'm certain I have it.* I always roll my eyes. Sometimes, he texts to say he's close by; can he call in for a coffee? Most times I decline, but sometimes I say yes. *Bring me some chocolate.* He arrives at my house with three plastic bags full of sweets. *I couldn't decide what you wanted, and I fucking love you, so I bought the whole shelf.* I laugh and put the kettle on. My crazy dad.

I'm twenty-two and we are celebrating Christmas together. This is the first year without our three-legged dog Bingo. *I miss him so much*, my dad tells me through tears. *He was just a dog*, I try to reason with him. We have Christmas dinner with my mum's family, eating turkey and gravy and Brussels sprouts, and my dad spends the entire evening sitting in the other room, on his iPad, earphones in. *Oh crazy, eccentric Dad*, we say, while looking down at our plates.

Dad's fabricated illnesses have become terminal. He tells me he thinks his cancer is back, and it's inoperable this time. He's losing feeling in his legs, and wants to buy a wheelchair. When my phone buzzes, I read his text. *You better get your eulogy ready. I've been doing some research online, and I'm 99 per cent sure I have ALS.* My mother and I wonder if he really has a tumour now: he's become so difficult to talk to and is acting like a stranger. My vibrant, mad father is gone. He's just solemnly mad now. We try to sit him down, to get through to him, but it never works. You can't help someone who doesn't think they need help. It's a mantra I tell myself over and over again, to forgive myself for idly watching him slip away.

I am in London on a work trip. I can expense my food, so I feel very grown up. I am twenty-three, and it's 16th April, and I Instagram a photo of me eating a breakfast burrito with kale juice. *It's a goooood day, how can anything go wrong?* I write as a caption. My dad calls me and I look down at my phone and ignore it. I can't deal with him now. I don't want to deal with him now. I look down at 'Dad' flashing up on the screen and I silence it and finish my burrito. It's a good day, how can anything go wrong?

I get a flight home the next afternoon, a taxi to my apartment in Dublin, then video call my boyfriend in Chicago. Our relationship is messy, like any relationship between people too young to understand what love means. We've been together since I was twenty, and long-distance for two years. I loved him before he loved me, and I dragged him into that love, kicking and screaming. But here we are: in love. We talk about our separate lives, away from each other. *I miss you*, I say to the screen.

My brother calls me when I'm on Skype. Which is weird, because I didn't know he even had my number. *Dad's missing. Haven't seen him in three days.* So? Our dad is nuts. Who knows what he is up to, but he'll be back. *He called me yesterday*, I tell my brother, to put him at ease. *He called me and I ignored it, but I'll call him back now, all right?*

Dad's drinking again, he tells me. I feel my heart sink. It's the three worst words that exist in the English language. Dad's drinking again, and now I'm eight, wanting to hold my baby brother and block his ears. Dad's drinking again, and I'm nine, screaming that I hate him. Dad's drinking again, and I'm fourteen, writing the answers to my exam and wondering if he's dead. Dad's drinking again, Dad's drinking again, Dad's drinking again. I am every age I've ever been, stuck in a white room and the walls are quickly closing in on me. I inhale! Inhale! Inhale! But there is not enough air in the world to stop me drowning in his defects.

My boyfriend sees my body stiffen up, so I click 'end call'. He can't see me like this. He doesn't know my dad is nuts. *Bad signal*, I quickly email him. I've been protecting the secret of my father my whole life. I can't let it unravel now. I keep talking to my brother. This is the longest conversation we've had in ten years. We make jokes. We ignore the panic rising up between us. We act uncaring. *I think he's finally done it this time*, my brother says casually. I laugh and tell him to relax. *Dad loves himself too much to...*

My brother sees fluorescent yellow through the pane of glass in the door. *It's the police, Marise. They're here.* There's no emotion in his voice. We both exhale. It feels like we have been holding our breath our whole lives for this moment. I was never sure what exactly that moment was, but now it's here, of course it is this. It was always going to be this. *Keep me on the phone, don't hang up. Please.* I hear a distant voice speak. *Are you the next of kin to Thomas Gaughan?*

13

They found his body in the Dublin canal that evening. I feel...
nothing. I walk into my kitchen, ignoring my roommate, Levi,
who is sitting at the table shoving oatmeal into his mouth.
Why anyone would eat oatmeal at 7pm is a mystery to me, but
Germans are always odd. I chop up a wilting watermelon on the
counter. The sharp knife cuts into the hard rind easily. *It's crazy
how something can seem so indestructible, but be so easily
destroyed*, I tell him, not looking away from the pink flesh in
front of me. He nods. *If you have the right tool, anything can be
reduced to just its parts.* Germans are very practical like that.
They can take a metaphor and trim it into a literal meaning. It's
pretty much written in their DNA.

Levi asks me how my day has been. *My dad has killed
himself*, I tell him, with the same tone as *We're out of milk*.
I eat a wedge of watermelon as he stares at me. *I'll be gone for a
couple of days. Make sure to take out the bins.* He looks at me
and nods. *They don't go out until Thursday, but I won't forget.*
I watch him scoop up his oatmeal and jam the metal spoon in
his mouth. Scoop and jam, scoop and jam, scoop and jam, until
I feel sick.

My mother collects me from my apartment, squeezing my
hand when I get in the passenger seat. My brother leans forward
from the back. *Drowning, hey?* I say to him. *Should we play
'Bridge Over Troubled Water' at the funeral?* We laugh much
more than the joke elicits. When I walk into my parents' house
an hour later, I expect to feel some surge of emptiness, but it
feels exactly like every other time I've walked through the door.

My brother identifies his body the next day. I want to go, but
I am overruled. He returns home with Dad's watch and wallet.
Two things he removed from his body before he killed himself.

He slaps them on to the kitchen counter. *He looked...* he trails off, staring down at Dad's watch. *I didn't know water could fuck up someone's face like that.* These are the only words he'll ever use to describe what he saw. Eventually, I stop asking.

We have an open-casket wake, and everyone compliments the great job they did with his make-up. Irish people love to compliment the make-up of a dead person, as they sip on a cup of tea and rub rosary beads. To an Irish person, no one looks as good as three days after they've died. *He looks at peace*, my aunts say, and I have to double-check that we're looking at the same thing. He looks dead, so very dead. I wander around the house, going in and out of the living room, peering at this body that belongs to a man I once loved, but isn't him. *Tell your dad you love him*, my mum tells me, pushing me forward. The lifetime I had to say those words. I could have repeated them over and over, screaming them into his face. If I had said them enough, we surely wouldn't be here. *Dad is dead*, I remind her. *It's a bit late for that.* Still, I walk forward and place my lips on his slick, glistening forehead. My lips meet his frigid skin, and I am shocked by the nothingness I feel. Energy cannot be created or destroyed. I learned that in physics class when I was fifteen. But still, somehow, it has left him. I wipe away the invisible film of death left on my lips, and look around the room, wondering where it has gone.

Later that night, my cousin orders pizza. I knew him when he had a high-pitched voice, urging me to run faster down the field at our granny's house. He's a grown man now. I didn't recognize him when he showed up at the door. It has been so many years. I'm not close with any of my cousins on my dad's side; I don't know anything about their lives, of who they are, their passions and gripes, but in this room, I can feel the bond that ties us all together. We are all made from the same people. And now we are one less.

It's 1am, and I am tired, but my cousin tells me the body can't be left alone. It's tradition. We eat the pizza in the living room, shoving greasy pepperoni slices into our mouths while my dad lies there, untouched. My cousin tells me stories of my dad, when he was at his best. My fun father, full of vibrancy, making everyone laugh. My dad was always the centre of attention in every room he entered. He still is tonight, but when I look over at his body, I feel the gap from then and now, and it pierces through me. I close my eyes to forget it, and listen to the memory of my father. I let myself miss that version of him. When I open my eyes, it evaporates.

14

The wake carries on into the next day. Everyone reminds me to eat, because that's another thing people love to say during death. When someone dies, you better remember to stuff your face. I put out my hand to accept their plates. Lasagne and pasta and chicken curry. *Don't forget to eat*, they tell me, as I munch on ham sandwiches and quiche and cheese boards. I ask my aunt to make her raspberry and almond cake, which she only does on special occasions. I take slice after slice until my mum intervenes. *Show some respect, Marise*, she whispers. *People in grief aren't supposed to be pigs.*

In the late afternoon, when the sun is starting to set and pink shoots through the sky, I walk out to the garden and call my boss, to let him know I'll be out for a while. *My dad has died*, I tell him. I hear his English voice dance through my phone.

Oh wow, my God, I am so, so sorry, Marise. He pauses. *Was he sick?* I contemplate this. Was he? For me, a sickness is something you can see, or can measure. Like a bloody gash or broken bones, or test results the doctor presents to you. My dad didn't have diabetes, or cancer, or epilepsy. He might have said it, but it wasn't true. But what about sickness of the mind? That type of sickness can happen so gradually that you can't separate it from its host. It's in their head, so you think they've made it up. It's so subtle it can trick you into thinking it's not really there. You can only see after the fact, and after the fact is always too late.

Was he sick? *Yes, he was, but we didn't realize how bad it was.* My boss doesn't say anything, waiting for me to continue. I am not sure how to. I want to withhold the truth, but why? Who am I protecting? Not my father. The dead don't need protection. And I don't deserve it. I let his sickness kill him. I looked the other way while it ravaged his mind, ignoring his screams for help.

He killed himself, I eventually say. I'm met with silence. No one knows how to respond to suicide. Death is tragic, but suicide is more than that. It's preventable sadness. Or inevitable. Maybe they're opposite sides to the same coin. An optical illusion, changing whichever way you look at it. *Take as much time off as you need,* he tells me. I thank him and hang up. I walk into the kitchen and take a plate of shepherd's pie from the fridge. I am eight mouthfuls in before I remember I hate mashed potatoes.

15

The funeral is the following Tuesday, after the Easter weekend. Jesus died the day my dad died, but he was resurrected before Dad's funeral. *Lucky for some,* I say out loud.

In the spare bedroom of my mother's house I am wearing knee-high boots and a black dress that cuts above them, showing a slice of thigh. *A respectful amount*, I decide. I curl my hair and rub blush across my cheeks with my fingers. I look in the mirror and think *Holy fuck, I look good; grief must suit me*. I practise crying with poise and wistfulness. I wonder if my brother's friends have gotten cute. None of this feels real; I'm just playing pretend.

In the church, the priest talks about Jesus being resurrected, which I think is in bad taste. My dad isn't coming back. I guess he's playing pretend, too. He starts talking about how much my dad loved the GAA, but he's Canadian and pronounces it gay. *Tommy was very involved with the gay his whole life; it was such a massive part of who he was*. I look at my mum, and we start to laugh. So do the rows around us. The laughter ripples through the pews. The priest stares at us, confused, which makes everyone laugh even more. *And he passed on that love to his son Robert, who is part of the Dublin minor gay team*. The church explodes. I look around and see people wiping tears from their faces, bent over in hysterics. It makes me laugh even more. I squeeze my mother's hand as we try to straighten our expressions. *You know he'd get some kick out of this*, she whispers in my ear. I look at the coffin by the altar. My laughter quickly fades away. What's the point in laughing if he's not here to hear the joke?

When he was alive, Dad loved to plan his death. *Cremate me*, he said. *I don't want to come back to life. Once I'm dead, let me be dead*. He always side-eyed me when he said that, as if suspicious that I had plans to the contrary. *And get Daniel O'Donnell to sing at the funeral...actually, scratch that, I want Johnny Cash! But only if he's up to it. If not, Daniel is fine. But try to get Johnny.*

We play his favourite song during the cremation ceremony.

The words blare through the tiny room: *I hurt myself today, to see if I still feel.*

Bit on the nose, I whisper to my brother. He just stares back, and I know he has no idea what that expression means. *You really are thick as shit*, I say, and my mum shushes me. *Respect, Marise*, she reminds me. I roll my eyes. We're respecting my dad so much more in death than we ever did in life. *Everyone I know goes away in the end.* He would listen to that song on repeat, hours going by as he smoked cigars in the conservatory by himself. The signs: they were always there.

16

We're not sure what to do with the ashes. They stare at me from the mantelpiece every time I visit my mother, a reminder of how our family has failed. My dynamic father, trapped inside a cheap plastic box. *He chose it*, I remind myself as I pick up the remote and turn on the telly. *He chose to reduce his life to this.*

We'll bury him with your grandfather, my mum eventually decides. The whole family drives down to the most western point in Ireland, alongside the Atlantic Ocean. Where Dad grew up, before his mind destroyed him. We stop in to visit my granny. On good days, she remembers who we are. But at ninety-three, there aren't many good days. I kiss her cheek, feeling the multitude of her face creases. Every deep fold soothes me: a sign of a life lived. We've decided not to tell her that her son is dead. The youngest of seven. Her baby. We let him keep being her baby. *A kindness*, we say, keeping him alive through her gaze.

I was there when my grandad died. My first taste of death. The paramedics, the stretcher, the priest. Him leaving the house and never coming back. I trace my finger around his name on the tombstone. The year he was born and the year he died – eighty-seven years between the two. A life measured in years lived – thirty-two more than my dad.

My uncle has a shovel with him. This is the same uncle who refuses to admit Dad killed himself. *A terrible accident*, he tells other people. *He tripped and fell into that damn water*. He starts to dig into my grandad's grave, but the sides are surrounded by cement. It's impossible to break into it, so we move to the spot of grass just outside the grave. One slightly too-eager dig later, the shovel has struck solid concrete and the resulting stress has snapped it clean in half.

My uncle shrugs. *Hands and knees, folks*, he says, taking off his suit jacket. We all fall to the ground and dig with our hands, laughing as we do it. The soil has stained our formal clothes, there is sweat dripping from our faces. We keep digging. Once there's a shallow de facto grave, not in my grandad's plot but in a spot of grass beside it, we pop the urn inside and cover it back up with soil. My uncle wants to commemorate the moment with a song, but the only one he knows is 'Fairytale of New York'. He nods, and asks my cousin to count him in. He sing-shouts the song, every so often changing the lyrics to include my dad, but not in a way that makes much sense. *You scumbag, you maggot. Tommy, you cheap lousy faggot*, my uncle bellows, with tears in his eyes. *Happy Christmas, you arse*. It is July. We clap when he finishes. *Dad's looking down and getting some kick out of this*, my mother whispers to me. I smile and look up at the clear skies. Hoping what she is saying could be true.

During the five-hour drive home, I lean my head against the window watching the rain drip down. I guess which droplets will win the race to the bottom, like I used to do when I was a kid. Except this time, I have no real stake in the winner. There's no dad waiting for me when I get home, whichever one I pick.

The emptiness of that reality punches me right in the gut. But I force myself to think elsewhere, to think of the day that has just happened. Everyone on their hands and knees like idiots, and my uncle singing a Christmas song in the summer. Despite myself, it makes me smile. I feel glad that the day went the way it did, because I know it would have made my dad laugh, and I'm not sure life was ever better than when he was laughing.

17

He didn't leave a note, so I don't know what he was feeling. He did leave a Google search history of suicide methods, so I know it wasn't an accident. He did leave witnesses, who saw him try to drive his car into the water, and then stop at a boulder and sit by the canal for an hour. So I know it wasn't a rush, in-the-moment decision. He did leave empty vodka and cough bottles in his car, so I am sure he was inebriated.

But as I lie on my bed in my apartment in Dublin, my stomach turns thinking about the pieces that are missing. Everything I know reminds me of all that I don't. The how and where can't describe the why. All the knowing makes me feel sick. It leaves so many holes in the full story. *Why did you do it, Dad?* I ask my ceiling. As soon as I think that, I make myself unthink it. When there are no answers, asking questions is futile. What is, just is. Even if it's something I never wanted it to be. Even though I wished for it so many times, I never actually wanted to end up here.

I think if I try hard enough, I can forget my dad. I buy a t-shirt with a smiling sun on it, thinking the happiness will seep into my skin. I join yoga. I start to fuck girls. I plan a move to Amsterdam to go to graduate school. I tell everyone he is dead, but mostly use it as a punchline, so they know I'm cool with it. I say things like *It's sad he couldn't appreciate how beautiful life is, but I'm not going to make that mistake,* or *Even if I'd answered his call, I might have saved him that day, but he would have done this eventually; he was always going to kill himself.* People commend me on my strength.

Some days, I do such a good job at forgetting him, I will see a man across the street that looks exactly like him, and for a brief moment I forget my dad is dead and go to shout out to him. Then I remember, and the remembering crashes a pain into me that takes my breath away. On those days, the remembering is so much worse than the day it happened. I give myself a few minutes' window to think the unbearable. *I miss you, Dad.* I try to brush away the thought as soon as it comes, convinced if I let myself truly feel it I will fall down in the street and never be able to get back up. *He chose to die*, I remind myself whenever this sadness creeps in. *He chose to leave you behind.*

I get a coffee with my friend Ruairi before I leave for Amsterdam. *Sometimes I forget your dad died a few months ago, because of how you act*, he tells me. *Sometimes I forget too,* I say back, smiling. Forgetting doesn't help the missing parts of me that are him, but it does take away the sting. I wonder how long I can continue forgetting for; how long before a tiny crack will appear in that box, and the parts of him I've locked away start to slowly spill out. *That's tomorrow's problem*, I think, while downward dogging, *and I only live in the today.* Namaste.

THREE

MONEY

1

Harvey Norman is my favourite comedian, because he was my first boyfriend's favourite comedian. You love someone, and you end up loving what they love, just to get closer to them. That's often how it goes. Harvey records a radio show every morning in New York, with another guy who isn't as funny as him.

The first time I heard them on the radio, I was lying on my boyfriend's bed in Chicago. *Turn this shite off*, I yelled, but he ignored me. *These guys are geniuses, shut up.* Their voices were forced down my eardrums every morning for ten months straight, and I went from annoyance, to apathy to genuine enjoyment. That's often how it goes.

Three days after my dad died, I tuned in to Harvey's radio show. Away from my boyfriend I wasn't a devoted listener, but sometimes I liked to have it as background noise. The other host talked about the death of his father for two hours. Harvey made jokes as he did, and I laughed. For a few minutes, as I bent over in hysterics, I forgot my dad was dead.

When they closed out the show, they played Johnny Cash's 'Hurt'. I was lying on my bed as the words filled the room.

I hurt myself today, just to see if I could feel. It felt like more than a coincidence, that they talked about dead dads and played my dead dad's favourite song. It was surely fate. I sat up on my bed and typed out a long-winded email to Harvey Norman, about what a genius he was and how important his words were and that I hoped to someday meet him, because I was pretty sure I was in love with him. I knew I was coming on too strong, but I also needed him to know how important he was to me. He never responded.

I am almost twenty-four now, living in a studio apartment in Amsterdam, beginning the spring semester of a Master's degree I don't really care about. *Game theory,* I tell people, *like the guy from* 'A Beautiful Mind'. And then I sit back and bask in their awe. *That's a lot of maths?* they ask me, and I say, *Sure, sure, I'm smart and shit.* I leave out that I only accepted it to get away. I wanted to leave Ireland, so I could leave my dad's death behind, so I could get on a plane and shed every part of him from me, and Amsterdam taught in English, so I picked it solely on that. I leave out that I've failed most of my first semester exams, because everyone else got things much quicker than me, sailing on to the next chapter while I was left in the dust. That the professors speak with thick accents, so it's hard to follow, and I don't know how to put into words that I'm falling behind. My Chinese classmates have to translate Dutch-accented English into Chinese, in their heads, then work out the maths equations, before translating back to English and writing down their answers, and they still get it and I still don't.

I download Tinder, as a distraction, and adjust my settings to just women. I swipe, swipe, swipe, and don't have to swipe much further than that. Every girl in Holland is a ten. Each one is a hotter version of me. Blonder and thinner, with bigger tits and a prettier face. I go on dates with five, meeting in low-key bars that serve half pints, and I fuck them all. I smell their pussies on my fingers when I cycle home. I text them all, *That was fun!* But none of them stick. They all feel like placeholders, like commas in a long, run-on sentence. As much as I want them to, none of them feel like full stops. After the fifth date, I delete the app, knowing that no woman I meet will complete me. Maybe no person completes anyone, but I at least felt the want of that when I was with men. I'm not sure if I'm a bad lesbian, or just a bad person. Sometimes, I think I am just nothing at all.

During the last week of February, when the ice on the canals begins to melt away, and I convince myself I am also shedding a season along with them, I send Harvey Norman a message on Instagram, making a joke of something he had mentioned on his radio show that morning. I know he won't reply. After three unanswered emails, I've accepted that our correspondence is one-sided.

When I log into Instagram two hours later, and see his message waiting for me, I drop my phone in shock, before quickly picking it back up, ignoring the fresh crack on the screen. *Thanks, this is funny.* I dance around my room. I've never felt so validated.

He writes another message. I watch him typing it, the three dots looking like a Van Gogh painting. *So, what's your deal?* I quickly tap my screen. *I am a fan of you.* Two minutes later I get a response. *No, silly, I mean who are you?* I don't know what he's getting at. *I am a fan of your show*, I reply, confused that I have to spell it out to him. *Ha ha, you're cute*, he shoots back, even though I wasn't trying to be funny or cute.

He asks me questions about myself.

How long have you been listening to my show?
What age are you?
Are you single?

I smile and dance around my studio every time I see a message come in. I am pretty sure he is flirting with me, but I'm not fully sure, because real flirting is something I've only seen on TV shows like 'Tom and Jerry' – the dancing around each other, giving a little and then pulling back, allowing for a chase. That shit is like a fairy tale. Any time I've liked someone, I've just said the words right to their face as soon as I felt it. I've decided it, and pursued them, trying to drag them into my world of want. It's different with Harvey, because I didn't even consider I could fancy him. He is too old. So, I don't try to pull him into me. Instead, I just react to everything he says.

I try, very hard, to be funny and interesting back to him. I want him to keep messaging me. I am trying too hard, everything I say stinks of too-hard trying, but he doesn't seem to care. We message all through the night and into the next day. I have a date arranged for that next night, but I cancel. This is all too exciting to miss. I text my friends. *A celebrity is talking to me! And he's actually pretty cool.* They have to google his name. *He looks like a bald rat*, one says. *And he's not a celebrity, I've never even heard of him.*

He is! I insist. *Just a niche one. Like a Broadway star.*

He is so gross and old, another says, and I have to agree.

But he's very, very funny.

He asks for my number two days after my first DM, and I type it back within three seconds. He calls me, and I silently scream once I hear his voice. It all happens so quickly I can barely register it, but the excitement pulses through my body. *This is crazy*, I tell him. *I can't believe I'm speaking to you.* He laughs at me. *It's good to hear your voice too.*

We Skype each other a couple of weeks later, and I'm giddy, getting to see someone I idolize. His sound doesn't work. But then, suddenly, it does. We talk for ninety minutes straight, and when I click 'end call', I already miss him. He later tells me that he always pretends his sound doesn't work, and I'm the first girl he's talked to normally over video. Letting me know I'm one of many, but also that I'm special. Whatever trick that is, it works. I feel myself falling for him. I am shocked at how quickly I can go from seeing someone as old and gross, to them being someone I could love. All he had to do was pay me a little attention, and suddenly I am planning our wedding.

We continue messaging. Pretty soon, it turns sexual. I send him photos of myself in my underwear, my ass turned to the camera. *You're beautiful*, he responds. So, I take more. It hurts my back to take these photos, all the twisting and turning and holding, trying to stretch myself in a way I shouldn't be stretched. But all the aches are worth it, for that reply. In his eyes, I am beautiful. And that spreads into the rest of my life. *I'm a beautiful person now*, I think as I scoop grey-green beans onto my plate in the cafeteria then go sit at a table by myself. *Who cares? I'm beautiful*, I think as I get another F back on my midterm. When I cycle down the street, wind blowing, not in my hair but instead against it, so it wraps around my face and I have to peel it off to see where I am going, I scream into the wind, *I'M FUCKING BEAUTIFUL*.

Every morning, I wake up to a message from him. *Good morning, gorgeous*. I have to pinch myself to believe this is really happening. It doesn't matter that he's twenty-two years older than me, not really. *Age is just a number*, I repeat to myself. It doesn't really mean anything, because we could all die at any moment. We're only as young as when we take our last breath. When you write down twenty-three and forty-five, it makes it worse than it really is. We actually have a lot in common. We both love comedy, for example. And he tells me he's immature for his age and not ready to settle down. That's why he's interested in women much younger than him. They just get him more. When he puts it like that, it doesn't seem so bad. Twenty-two years seems like a lot of years on paper, but when a man who is twenty-two years older than you tells you it's nothing, you believe it's true.

He flies me out to New York to spend a weekend with him. When he asks me to come, I hesitate for a few days, wondering whether that's who I want to be. He eases all my concerns without me having to voice them. *I just want to spend some time with you*, he texts. *You're a very special person and I would like to know you face to face. We don't even have to do anything sexual.* I smile when he sends that. *I really want to kiss you, though,* I reply. And he sends back a smiley face. *That's the only thing I want.* I feel like I'm living inside a dream. He books the flights and gets me economy plus, with extra leg room. When I board the flight, I feel like a king. I shove my ticket into the air hostess's face. *Yes, that's 5A, thank you.* Before we take off, a different air hostess brings me a free glass of warm sparkling wine. I swallow it in three gulps.

What the fuck am I doing? I think at least nine times during the six-hour flight. *Why am I travelling thousands of miles to meet someone I don't even know?* But I push away that thought as soon as it comes into my head and stretch out my legs. *All this extra leg room I don't really need*, I think. *He must really like me, otherwise I'd just be in regular economy.*

When I get to the airport, he's not there to meet me, like I assumed he would be. Instead, there's a driver holding a place card with my name. *How often do you do this?* I ask him on the car ride to the city, but he just laughs. When we get to his building, a Trump tower, the driver opens my door. I step outside into the windy air and freeze. He takes the bag from my hand and walks me in. How often do you do this? A lot.

On the long elevator ride up, I breathe into my hand, checking my breath. My stomach feels like it's in my hands. *This is so fucking stupid*, I say over and over again, before checking my breath one more time. I exit the elevator and walk down the narrow corridor, glancing at the number on each door. I stop in front of 905, and check my breath one last time. I knock, and there he is. He leans in and kisses me, straight away, a smack right on my lips. I laugh and pull away, and he leans in again. We kiss, and I feel his tongue probe my lips. It feels so fucking awkward. When I pull away and look into his eyes, I know he doesn't share that feeling, so I suck up my nerves and lean in again, swallowing all the uncomfortableness I feel. I stick my tongue into his mouth and grab his head with my hand, as if he wasn't already as close as another person could be. I don't want him to be disappointed in me. *We're not going to have sex, because I don't want you to think I brought you here just for that.* So instead, he eats me out for forty minutes. I come so hard it gives me a headache. He hands me a wet face cloth as I moan in pain.

We go out for nice dinners, steaks in French restaurants and guacamole they make table-side. We eat breakfast in Upper West Side diners, diners with $20 meals. *How expensive can eggs be?* I think, already knowing the answer. $20 plus tax and tip expensive! He asks for something off menu. *Bacon cooked in olive oil, with fruit on the side.* They nod, obliging. I never knew you could even order something that wasn't on the menu. I had always thought the menu was all you got. I feel very special, being with someone who the menu is just a suggestion for. It makes me feel very…cosmopolitan. He pays each bill and leaves a fat tip. I knew he was doing well, but I didn't know he was rich.

We walk around New York in our scarves and hats, holding hands. He keeps making jokes and I have to stop walking, bending over in the middle of the street in laughter.

We go window-shopping in the West Village, because he wants to buy some furniture. We walk by Aesop. *That's my favourite skincare store*, I tell him. I've only been in this store once before. My friend Conell dragged me in, when we were in Berlin. *Smell how good this deodorant is*, he insisted. It was $30. *$30 for deodorant is crazy*, I told him. But damn, it did smell good. In New York, Harvey guides me into the store. I squirt lotion into his hands. *Smell how good this is.* He tells the assistant he'll take three bottles. *One in every scent.* He instructs me to pick out whatever I want. I pick out a cleanser, then hesitate. *No, really, anything you want.* I add moisturizer and exfoliator and body lotion. He swipes his credit card. $600, just like that. No one's ever spent money like that on me, and he does it without blinking. Like it's nothing. I try to ignore how good it makes me feel.

We stop for frozen yogurt after dinner. When I was nineteen, I spent a summer in New York, and me and my friend Maeve got Pinkberry every Tuesday, when it was half off. They swirled the frozen yogurt right into your paper cup, and it tasted exactly like ice cream. *But healthy ice cream*, we said to each other, like we were cheating the system. The real fun was in the toppings. Chocolate chips and jelly babies, fresh mango and strawberry and kiwi. Even with half off, it still cost more than a Big Mac meal.

With Harvey, I know not to worry about the price. I heap my yogurt with chocolate chips and brownie pieces and three spoonfuls of strawberries. He swipes his card and we sit by the window. *So good*, I tell him, in between mouthfuls. He doesn't respond. He looks around, agitated. I don't know what has got him so hot and bothered, but I stick my plastic spoon into my fake ice cream and put it to my lips. He stands up suddenly and says, *We have to leave.* He rushes us to the door, pulling my arm behind him, and I toss my half-eaten yogurt in the bin. Once in a taxi, he tells me some guy was acting weird inside the shop. *He was going to shoot up the place, I could just tell. I thought it was safest if we got the fuck out of there.* I want to tell him he's crazy. Tease him for being paranoid. But he scares me. Not just now, but especially now. Not in a 'he's going to hit me' way. It's a more subtle type of fear. He holds in his hands every feeling I have for him, and every feeling he's made me feel. I'm only beautiful if he says it, and he could stop saying it at any moment. Then, God forbid, I'd go back to being ugly. I grab his hand and thank him for saving me. He pulls his hand away and wipes it on his jeans. *Wash your hands when you get home, please.* I look out the window and nod.

The next night we hang out with his friends: other comedians I love. He does two sets at the Comedy Cellar, and I sit at the table made famous on 'Louie' and listen to them all make fun of each other. I pinch myself so I know this is really happening. *I am here*, I think. *I am really here.* Everyone besides the waitress ignores me, annoyed that I am here. I am sure I am just one of a hundred girls, and they are rolling their eyes when I look down at the table. *Another one*, I imagine them mouthing over my head. I don't care, though. I might be the 120th girl he's brought here, but for me, it's a first.

I think I'm really starting to like you, I tell him while sitting on his couch, straddling his legs. *Please just tell me if that's a dumb thing to do.*

Why would that be dumb? he asks, kissing my neck. I don't have the words to answer him. Except I do, but they get stuck in my stomach, miles away from reaching my mouth and being spat out. What I mean is, *I know I'm a thing for you to fuck, even though we're not actually fucking yet. Being a thing for you to get to fuck is probably more tantalizing. But I think you could be a thing for me to love, and how far is the bridge between those two for you?* I don't say those words because I'm embarrassed by them. I'm embarrassed over how quickly I've fallen for a man almost twice my age, a man my friends call the rat, a man who I know has done this exact thing countless other times. He looks at me and tells me words I've never heard before, and when I hear them my stomach does somersaults. But he is old, and I don't know how many times he has said them before.

I don't know why words mean less if they've been said more than once. It doesn't make sense. When someone tells me a secret, the first thing I ask is, *Am I the first person you've told this to?* And if they say yes, it makes it feel more worthwhile. Why is something more important if the words have been locked inside them up until then? Why is something more special if it's the first time? A closed book is our favourite type of person. If something is closed, if it's under lock and key, it must make it more valuable. And if you are the one to prise open a page, that makes you more valuable too, being the one to discover the mystery. And the people who scream their chapters, shouting from the rooftop what they feel, well, they're just crazy people. They're not worth anything.

I want, very badly, to tell him how I feel. I want him to placate my worries, to promise me I'm different, *Of course, ya dummy, of course you're special.* I want him to make me feel stupid for ever imagining I'm anything other than divine. That's not even a word he would use, because he wasn't raised in religion. But it's still a word I put in his mouth. I have a tidal wave I want him to hear, but I keep my mouth closed. I know what I could lose. Instead, I laugh when he makes a joke, and nod in agreement when he says something serious. I try very fucking hard to be the woman of his dreams. Which, of course, is just a woman without a voice. Forget Pornhub, the real porn is in the Disney film 'The Little Mermaid'. And I do my best to play that part.

When I leave, we kiss goodbye in his hallway, and tears form in my eyes. When I look at him, looking at me, he looks so pleased I let them free-fall, dripping down my face. *I'll see you again*, he promises me, smiling at my crying face. *I'd like that a lot*, I manage to push out, wiping my eyes with my sweater sleeve. On the way to the airport, the driver looks in the mirror. *Did you have a good time?* I smile at his reflection and shrug. *It was all right.*

He flies me out again a month later, but he's more distant this time. I don't know it then, but my ex-boyfriend wrote him a letter. Begging him to stop. Telling him he's getting in the way of true love, and to please leave me alone. That my dad has just died and he's taking advantage. He doesn't bring it up with me, and instead I just feel him growing distant. We don't have sex that trip either. We kiss when I leave, but he doesn't linger. And then things just fade away. His texts grow shorter and less frequent. It happens so gradually I can't put my finger on it until after the fact. And by then, it's already gone.

It ends exactly as I imagined it would. Him slicing down the guillotine, and me blind, only noticing what has happened when I hear the thump thump thump of my head rolling across the floor.

2

When things end, or when I accept they have ended, because he doesn't say it to me, I am itching to find another guy like Harvey. The celebrity bit might be hard to replicate, but the rich older part is surely easy. I take out my laptop, sitting cross-legged on my yoga mat, as the May sun hits my face. Last week

I found out I had failed my MicroEconomics repeats, which gives me seven months of freedom, before I have to repeat the class next December. The day I saw D, D, D, F flash on my computer screen, I applied for a visa and bought a plane ticket. My best friend, Conell, had moved to LA a few months before. I sent him a screenshot of my email from British Airways. *There's a room going in my apartment, so you can live with me*, he texted back. *!!!!* I responded. *We're going to have the summer of our lives.*

I first met Conell when I was twenty-two, sunbathing in a park in Dublin, on the one hot day of the year. *Are you in your fucking underwear?* were the first words he said to me. I laughed. *Yea, what's the difference between underwear and a bikini, though, really?* He shrugged. *I guess you're right. You could have picked ones without a raggedy hole in them, though.* He sat down beside me and we introduced ourselves. He was tall, with thick black hair and pale skin. He had a heavy beard and the type of blue eyes that pierced into you. *Jesus Christ, look at that babe.* I followed his eyes. Some hot dude was doing yoga poses on the other end of the green, topless, and our mouths watered as we both objectified him. *Imagine those arms around you? Imagine how big his dick is.* When he stood up to leave, I grabbed his wrist. *What are you doing tonight? Want to get drunk?*

That summer, we went out together five nights a week. We drank whisky in my apartment and stumbled to the only gay pub in the city. We danced together, then abandoned each other to hit on people we wanted to fuck. Usually, around 6am, I got a call from him, and would walk down my stairs, furious. *You know this isn't a hostel*, I'd spit out. And he'd be standing at my door with his sunglasses on. *Oh, you know meeee.* I'd laugh, and let him in.

*

MONEY

Sitting cross-legged in my Amsterdam studio, I google how to meet rich old men in Los Angeles. I hold my nose as I gulp down a celery juice, scrolling through the results. A website piques my interest. A different dating experience. I click into it. Pairing up young women to wealthy older men, for a 'mutually beneficial relationship'. I set up a profile. I post a bikini photo, taken in good lighting so I have abs. I add a face photo, a selfie of me smiling, mouth closed. Three filters applied on the photo so I look like a much better version of myself. I don't realize then how naïve it is to put a photo of your face on a website like this. How it could destroy your life if it got into the wrong hands. That there is a sea of potential consequence to everything we do. It's hard to see that at the beginning.

When I log in again there are fifty-six messages in my inbox. I respond to them all. One guy is from Australia. He is forty-seven and owns an investment company. He has salt-and-pepper hair, just like my dad. We talk over Skype. It's easy conversation. I tell him I've never done this before. *Me neither,* he says back. Within a week he has booked me first-class tickets from LA to Hawaii, to spend ten days with him at the Four Seasons in June. He sends me $1,500 to pay my rent. I didn't ask him to, and when the money lands in my account, I let out a scream. I message him immediately. *You didn't have to do that.* A text from him flashes up a minute later. *Yea, but I wanted to.* He wanted to. I repeat those words over and over in my head. *He wanted to.*

I didn't go to Hawaii; I chickened out of it, afraid of what ten days with a stranger who has already paid a deposit on me would mean, and he deleted his profile soon after. I never heard from him again. $1,500 and I never even had to meet him. He did it because he *wanted* to.

The day I landed in LA I had four dates lined up. All with older men who I found attractive from their limited photos. All men I enjoyed talking to through my computer screen. The first happened the night I landed. I laughed with Conell as I got ready, in my new bedroom in a converted loft that used to be a bakery. There were no doors or walls, and our rooms were separated with flowy curtains. That lack of privacy would have annoyed me with anyone else, but he was my favourite person to be around, so it never felt intrusive, only fun. *What if he's catfishing? What if he's ugly?* he asked. I shrugged. *All men are ugly.* I thought of Harvey. *He's gross*, my friends had told me. *He looks like a rat.* But I liked him. He had treated me well. What was so wrong with ugly?

The first date was a bust. He was arrogant and pushy. He bragged about how much money he made. *You're so tacky*, I told him, laughing. He didn't laugh back. I made up an excuse to leave as soon as we finished our food. *My roommate is locked out, I have to go.* The next date wasn't any better. He talked too much, and dripped grease down his chin as he ate a burger. My stomach turned when I looked at him. *Maybe this shit isn't for me*, I told Conell when I got back to our apartment. He laughed. *Just go on Tinder like a normal thirsty bitch.* I kicked him in the shin. *Tinder is full of broke loser guys who say condoms are too small for their dicks. These guys are refined.* Conell laughed some more. *You're right, it's very refined to need a walking stick.*

I meet up with Brian at a wine bar in West Hollywood. He shows up twenty minutes late, so late I am beginning to think he won't come. He's shorter than I was expecting, only a few inches taller than me. He's wearing a t-shirt and jeans. He looks younger than forty-eight. I look at him and feel relieved. Finally, someone I'm attracted to. *Sorry I'm so late*, he says, reaching out to hug me. *I was having a nap and overslept.* He runs his hand through his curly hair and laughs self-deprecatingly. *Wow, I may as well have just said, Hi, I'm Brian and I'm an old man.* I grin and cock my head to one side. *Well, sit down, old man. Don't want you to strain your back from standing.*

We drink wine and order cheese. I talk about my thesis and he talks about being a lawyer. We tease each other, settling into easy banter. We just click. We don't mention how we met. Two hours later, the bar is growing empty. We stay for another drink. He signals for the check while telling me he'd like to see me again. *If you have time in your schedule for some old fart who takes afternoon naps.* I laugh. *Sure. An evening I'm not volunteering at a nursing home, I'm all yours.*

We go on a second date, to Nobu in Malibu. A place I've only read about in celebrity gossip blogs. He orders me an Uber, and I do my make-up on the forty-five-minute drive. When I walk into the restaurant, he is already there, sitting at a corner booth. My stomach flips when I see him. We order cocktails, and I lean towards him as we talk. He asks me about myself. He tells me how interesting I am. *You're not like the usual LA girl.* And I laugh. Delighted to have beaten women I didn't know I was in competition with.

He orders for us. Yellowtail sashimi, seafood ceviche, king crab tempura, lobster tacos, octopus nigiri, squid pasta. $300 said in twenty seconds. *And oysters*, I add to the waiter once he's done. *I love oysters*, I tell him, smiling. *Oysters it is.*

Once the waiter has walked away, Brian smirks at me. *You know oysters are an aphrodisiac?* I roll my eyes. *Oh yea, I used to eat them with my dad when I was a kid and would just get so horny.* He laughs. *And now you're eating them with your daddy.* A bolt shoots through me as I look up at him in shock. He looks away and coughs. The air feels thick. Electric. Suddenly we're on a tightrope, and the next move decides whether we stay on course or fall into the ether. I love that moment in a date, when one person says something off script and you are jolted awake and have a split second to make a decision on how to respond – whether to ruin the night or keep it going. I decide to laugh too. *Don't be such a creep*, I say, throwing a piece of bread at him. I watch him relax. I smile.

Are your family back in Ireland? he asks. *Yea, my mum is. My dad…* I hesitate. *My dad moved to Florida last year. He has a new girlfriend and she's really pretty with massive tits. He got this crazy cool job, but I can't talk about it, because of NDAs.* Brian nods along intently. There's nothing a rich older man loves more than an NDA. The sound of those three letters together practically makes their mouths water. *We're really close, though; I talk to him every day and he gives me advice on things because he's really got his shit together, and I'm going to spend Christmas with him and we're going to go to Disneyland and…*

Disney World, he interjects. I look at him, confused. *Disneyland is in California, it's Disney World in Florida*, he clarifies.

Oh right, whatever. Disney World. But we're going to ride all the roller coasters and then get nice seafood for dinner and it will be positively sublime.

I sit back, my cheeks warm and fuzzy with the reality I've just created. *I'm glad you have a good relationship with your dad, it makes me feel less like a creep being here with you*, he says, smiling. *I have two daughters and a son. The oldest has just turned thirteen, and it's so interesting to watch him become a real person. It really makes me excited: to see what choices he makes and how he decides to do life. I think this is the best part of fatherhood, when you get to watch your kids become real people.* I lean forward, drinking in his words. The way he talks about his son makes me want to rip off his clothes. *But anyway, less about family. What do you do for fun?*

We talk all through the dinner. *I'm really into you*, I say after my third cocktail. He smiles, and picks up a piece of sashimi with his chopsticks. He slowly chews it, and I want to reach over and taste his lips. *I'm married*, he says. I feel my stomach drop. *That's why I'm on the site. I'm not looking for a relationship. I'm looking for some fun, no drama. Mutually beneficial. I'll make sure you are well looked after.* I smile, trying to hide my disappointment. I am embarrassed I ever thought it was something else. Of course, it is only this.

We skip dessert, and instead have another drink. He's not wearing a ring, but he's married. I wonder what his wife smells like. How often they fuck. If she knows he goes on dates with young women like me. I wonder if everyone else in the restaurant can see who we really are. Maybe they all saw it before I did. He gets the bill and pays with an American Express black card. He asks me if I want to go home, or spend more time with him. I look at him blankly, so he spells it out for me. *Do you want to get a drink somewhere more private?* I agree quickly, before I can think about what I am agreeing to. Because I already know.

We go back to his place, which is a hotel room in Santa Monica. *I got it, just in case*, he says as we stand in the elevator. I look down at the floor. In his room, I crack open the minibar, knocking back a mini Chardonnay when he's in the bathroom. I finger the miniature wine bottle, pulling back the label by the edges. *Am I really going to do this?* I gulp back the last of the bottle, and take a few deep breaths in. *Yes, yes I am.*

He comes out of the bathroom with a towel wrapped around his waist. His tan looks more leathered in this light. He has hair all down his back. For the first time, I see his receding hairline, how his black curls start further back on his head than I had initially noticed. It makes his forehead look huge. He sits on the bed, expectantly. I slowly undress and climb on top of him, pulling away the towel. I surprise myself at how easily I can play this role. We kiss, and I feel his wet tongue probe my mouth. It feels good. We have sex. That doesn't feel so good. He sticks his cock into me before I am ready for it, so it hurts. It's over before I can get too uncomfortable. He rolls over onto his back once he comes. *That was amazing.* I agree, putting my hand on his chest. *Incredible.*

He gets up. *I have to shower and get home.* I smile, relieved. He hands me an envelope and orders me an Uber. He kisses me on the lips as I leave. *Let's do this again.* I nod. In the car, I count out the money. $800. I leaf through the notes. It feels both filthy and divine. I send a photo of the bills spread out on my lap to Conell. *Shut up, you slut!* he texts back. I smile in the darkness.

Back at the loft, climbing the shaky stairs to my bedroom, I open the app and respond to every unread message in my inbox.

The next day, I am in the passenger seat as Conell drives along the I-10. We have the windows down, blaring Sinéad O'Connor, smoking cigarettes out into the wind. *I can eat my dinner in a fancy ressssstauraaaaaant,* we scream-sing to each other. We get Bloody Marys and breakfast tacos in a café near Venice Beach, then walk along Abbot Kinney, wandering in and out of the expensive stores. I buy Gucci sunglasses and a black dress with the stomach cut out. The $800 is gone, just like that. *Money is made to be spent,* I tell him. We check the app on our drive back to our apartment. We laugh at the men, and type out my responses. *You know you don't really need to do this,* he tells me, gently. *But I want to,* I say back. *This shit makes me feel alive.*

You're only a victim if you're not in control.

3

There was no real difference between a first date with those men, and normal men. Except there was now potential money. That potential money switched on some light inside of me. I became the best version of myself. I tried so much harder, knowing there was something tangible at stake.

By the end of June, I was going on a first date nearly every day. First dates are addictive. My favourite thing about them is that you get to talk about yourself. To someone you don't know, and they receive what you say based on their own life experiences. You get to view yourself in a new way for each person. So I guess my favourite thing about first dates is myself. My second is the food. My third is how easy it is to trick yourself into liking someone. I can have a good time with anyone, as long as I'm there. *God, I'm fucking fun*, I think as I order the crème brûlée. I don't even like crème brûlée.

I went on one first date with a rich Beverly Hills guy. I asked him what he did for a living, and he proudly told me, *Nothing*. That's when I learned truly rich people don't work. They just get money every month. From stocks or their grandmother. We went to a darkly lit bar where cocktails cost $30 and he watched me eat a plate of pasta. I slurped it with my mouth open. He name-dropped C-list celebrities and I pretended not to know who they were. It was driving him crazy. *You don't know who Michelle Rodriguez is?* I dribbled a bit of pasta on to my dress and grabbed it up with my hand back into my mouth. It left a stain. He drove me home in his Tesla and put his hand up my dress. *I like it rough*, I told him. I didn't really mean it. It was just something to say. Stopped in traffic, he leaned over and kissed me softly, then slapped me across the face. Not with full force, but the sting made me cry. *I thought you liked it rough?*

I nodded, wiping away my tears. We drove the rest of the way home in awkward silence.

One man, recently divorced, told me he was a 'finance guy', which apparently translated to fresh out of prison. He showed up to CATCH on a motorbike in a leather jacket. He told me his ex-wife was a biiiiiitch, and the way he enunciated 'bitch' made me think he hated women. We split a bowl of mussels. They tasted stale compared to the ones I picked from my granny's garden, but the white wine and garlic sauce made up for the extra chewing I had to do. I drank the broth straight, then drank eight cocktails until he was funny. *Ha ha ha! Women are evil cunts! Ha. Ha. Ha.* I made him order me an Uber downtown, to the bar my friends were at. I got out of the car at 6th and Grand, and told the Uber driver to keep the app open. *Drive around for another hour, make some money*, I told him, and he laughed. *I'm serious*, I said, shutting the door. *Consider me the Robin Hood of hoes!*

The only first date I felt unsafe on was with a doctor. We met in the rooftop restaurant at the Ritz Carlton and he promised me $1,000, just for the date. I was wearing a dress that when I sat down, rode up to my hips. I was worried that was too slutty for a doctor, so I desperately tried to pull it down. He spoke about percentiles and IQs and I nodded along, ordering another margarita. He leaned in to me, so close I could smell the egg on his breath. *Do you understand how smart I am?* Even though they were just words, they sent a shiver down my spine. I flagged down the waiter and ordered another drink. Getting drunk was the easiest way to enjoy these dates. When I am drunk, I can like anyone.

I was one drink away from liking him when he grabbed my

wrists underneath the table and said he wanted to see how much pain I could handle. It's hard to describe exactly the look on his face, but I did think, *This man is going to murder me.* So I got up and left. He walked me to the elevator, like the doctor gentleman he was, and then grabbed my wrists again and said, *This is your last chance, otherwise it's goodbye forever.* He stared at me so intensely as he spoke, I think I could have filed a police report on that alone. *No, thank you,* I said, looking down at my feet. *I'm sure your parents are real proud of what you do, you dumb whore.* I looked up at him, at the sneer on his face. I heard the ding of the elevator doors opening, and walked backward, not breaking eye contact. *Actually, my dad knows exactly what I do, and doesn't care. He thinks it's progressive. He's European like that. So, actually, fuck you.* I watched his angry face get narrower as the doors closed.

Karim was Egyptian and owned restaurants in Manhattan Beach. He never said how many, and I never asked, but the way he stressed the plural made me think it was probably only two. I met him on Tinder and he ordered me an Uber out to Manhattan Beach for our first date. It took two and a half hours with the LA traffic. I wore a white shirt that my friends called my tit top. It wasn't slutty, though, because I have no tits. He took one look at it and handed me a jumper belonging to his fifteen-year-old daughter to cover up. *Everyone in this town knows me.* Oh daddy! *Back in Ireland my dad owns a restaurant,* I told him. *They do fresh seafood and really expensive whisky.* He clapped his hands in delight. *A kindred spirit!*

We had lobster and tequila, and went back to his waterfront house where I wanked him off on the couch. He took off his glasses as he started to moan. I stared into his eyes and noticed something amiss. I couldn't quite place it. He noticed my noticing. *It's a glass eye. Don't look at it. Look at my good eye.* Then he came. He had lost it as a child when an American soldier accidentally shot him. We didn't see each other again. Not because of the glass eye. I loved the glass eye. It was so... resilient.

Conell was sick in bed when I was getting ready for one first date. I was wearing matching lingerie and no deodorant. He was sweating and puking and shaking. His boyfriend Timothy texted me as I was changing outfits. *What's the plan for later?* The three of us had been out together for the past three weekends, enough time to make it a trend. *There's an illness; night is cancelled*, I responded back. Conell had met Timothy a month previously, during a Pride party at the Ace Hotel. *I think I'm really into him*, Conell whispered in the Uber back to our hovel, *so don't say anything weird*. Once back in our loft, Timothy laughed as I cooked up a full packet of bacon in my underwear, drunk. *Watch out for oil spills*, he yelled, grabbing my body away from the pan when it was obvious I wasn't going to watch out for the oil spills.

I got Conell a wet towel and used it to correct my lipstick before placing it on his head. *I'm Florence fucking Nightingale,* I said, and we giggled. I weakly offered to cancel the date. *Oh no no, a reservation at Bestia is impossible to get. You have to go*, he reassured me.

I had oysters and braised lamb, and Tyler, fifty-two, a venture capitalist, whatever the fuck that means, told me I was obnoxious when I admitted I didn't recycle. During a shared brownie dessert, he told me he appreciated meeting me because it made him realize this wasn't what he wanted. I wanted to ask what 'this' was, but he said it with such significance that I nodded along like he was giving a powerful TED Talk.

I have a daughter your age, he said gently, when we were standing outside the restaurant waiting for my Uber and I was leaning up against him, to see if maybe he wanted to change his mind. *And I wouldn't want her doing what you're doing. Well, I have a dad your age,* I shot back, moving my body away from him, *and he sure wouldn't like you doing what you're doing either.* He smiled, sadly. *So we're in agreement, then?* I opened the door to the Uber, and turned to him. *Your daughter will still hate you even if you don't fuck girls her age. So good luck with that.*

On the short car ride home, I typed out a message. *I'm sorry for saying that. It was rude. It's not who I am. Maybe we could try again?* I read the message out loud, letting the words hang in the air, but never pressed send.

4

A first date is one thing. The cheese boards and mojitos and tuna tartare. The awkward hugs, the sometimes kisses, the Ubers called. But a second date is something else. It's a lot of bottles of wine from the minibar. A lot of forced laughter. A lot of clothes removed, then put on again. A lot of doggy style, to avoid eye contact. A lot of stacks of cash changing hands. A lot of boiling hot showers, to wash away their touch. Rinse, and then repeat. After the first date, I had a lot of second dates.

At this point in the story, when I am twenty-four, it is very easy for me to fuck someone I am not attracted to. My mind detaches from my body. It surprises me how easily I can do it. I can watch myself, lying on my back, with an old man heaving on top of me. Sweat dripping off them on to me. I don't wipe it away. When they start to moan, I grab my legs around their waist, hurrying up the process. The only thing that gets me off is the dangling carrot, the envelope of cash once it's all over. I think about counting the notes in the Uber home, and throw my head back in ecstasy. *Oh yes, fuck yes, yes, yes, yes.*

A young Asian guy who drives a Maserati and never asks a single question about me gives me $1,200 each time we have sex. He showers both before and after. He fucks me very formally. *Madam, I am pleased to inform you I have entered your vagina,* I imagine him saying. It's sex to the letter, and not one letter more. Pump, pump, pump, pumppumppump, and then it's over. I try to make him laugh as we lie in his bed afterwards, sure I can break through his wall, but he looks at his phone, bored. He always drives me home in his Maserati, turning up the radio so our silence is drowned out by Ariana Grande's latest single. When I kiss him goodbye on his cheek, he doesn't look at me.

A shy thirty-five-year-old Canadian gives me $3,000 a month. He doesn't live in LA, so I only have to see him a couple times during the month. We go to dinner, I get drunk, we go back to his house in the Hollywood Hills and fuck for five minutes. He apologizes every time for his quickness. *Oh, I like it,* I say back, *it's so passionate.* I never spend the night. That's the only rule I have. I can fuck anyone, but I can't sleep next to someone. He loves to ask prying questions like *Did you grow up poor?* or *Are you close with your father?* I know what he's looking for, but I never give it to him. *We had a holiday home in France growing up, and I talk to my dad every day.* He buys me leather jackets and designer boots when I ask for them. I can almost touch his loneliness every time he messages me. The pity I feel makes me hate him.

Josh is a married nerdy man who paid for my apartment on Airbnb before I had even met him in person. Even though I already had my dump in Downtown LA with Conell, I still accepted his Venice Beach offering. I figured I could use it as a weekend stay, like rich people do. It's right on the beach, and every morning I sleep over there I walk up to the rooftop, watch the waves crash onto the beach and forget all about him. When I get a cold, he drops off a three-day juice cleanse and texts me, *Come outside.* By the time I've crossed over the city in an Uber, he's already gone. Inside the bag of juice is $400. *Thank you, baby,* I text him.

We never sleep together. He's too nervous to make the move. *It will happen naturally, if it happens,* he tells me. And I smile and nod, taking the money from his hand, kissing his cheek. I don't say how unnatural it already is. *Why do you want to fuck a young girl?* I ask him one day, when he's bought me pizza from Gjusta and we're eating it on my weekend rooftop. That same question I ask to every older man I date. They never correct me, never interrupt to say, *Sorry, don't you mean a young woman?* Instead, they pour out the reasons. Men fuck us because the pussy feels better, because the ass is firmer and the tits don't sag yet. Because, of course, younger is more attractive, and anyone that cries otherwise is a fucking liar. Because that's how God built us; he programmed young girls to want to be nurtured, and old men to do the nurturing, and yes, women are better parents, but only because men nurture elsewhere; they focus on girls who then become good mothers, and there's something beautiful to that. This is their wisdom, their unifying theory.

If they're not religious it's because of biology. Somewhere written in our DNA is the desire for men to fuck much younger than them. Because that's how it's always been, since the dawn of time. Because women are in their sexual prime when teenagers, from the moment they have their first blood, and no, they're not attracted to thirteen-year-olds – that would be disgusting – but eighteen is okay, because we're all really just primitive beings, trying to reproduce, so it actually all makes biological sense.

Because women their age expect too much, because they're young at heart, because they don't want commitment, because they just fucking want to, all right?

Because they fucking can.

Josh chews his pizza as I ask him this question, and takes so long to swallow it I become convinced he's eating his tongue. The silence is so loud I want to interrupt it, but I pinch my thighs and say nothing. I read before that, when negotiating, the first person to speak loses. He swallows, finally, and grabs a napkin, wiping the film of grease from his lips. *Because I couldn't get hot girls when I was younger. I was awkward and had no money to impress them. And then I met my wife, and we had kids, and we poured our love into them instead of each other. And now I feel stuck. I want to have sex with you because I know I shouldn't, because you're young enough to be my daughter, and wanting you despite, or, honestly, because of that, is the only excitement I've felt in years.* He looks down at his lap. *I know that makes me a bad person.* I reach over and hold his hand. He has no idea how bad people can really be.

So, why do young girls have sex with old men? He's the first person to ask the question back, and I'm not prepared for it. *Some of us just find older men really attractive*, I tell him, licking my lips. *You don't need to perform,* he says. *You can just say the truth. I've already paid your rent for the next three months; you don't need to try with me.* I pick up a slice of pizza, letting the grease fall onto my t-shirt. I take a bite, and look over at the ocean. The sun is starting to set and the sky is shooting shades of pink against the dark palm trees. *This view, it's so beautiful, it's hard to get sick of it.* He nods. *I'm glad you like living here. I'm glad I could be a part of it happening.* I look away when he says that, afraid his desperation could be contagious. I stare at my pizza, pulling off the leaves of basil and throwing them on the ground. *I don't know why I do this. I guess I like pretending to be what someone else wants me to be. It makes me forget about myself, for a little while, and I like that feeling. Does that even make sense? Sometimes it's easier to just exist through someone else's gaze than try and figure shit out yourself.* I look over at him, and he smiles. *Thank you for being honest with me.* The way he says it makes me immediately regret being honest. When I look over at his dumb, eager face, I feel my stomach turn.

I don't bring him downstairs, into the apartment he has paid for, and fuck him. Like he said, he's already paid up front. But I feel obliged to give him something. I lean over and kiss him. I feel his body shake as my lips meet his. Then he pushes his tongue into my mouth, and sticks it further in than it needs to go. He thrashes his tongue inside me, so out of rhythm I think he could be having an epileptic fit. I open my eyes and see his are closed shut. He kisses like boys kissed when I was fifteen years old. When they were just learning what to do, when they thought more, more, more was the crux of sexuality. I disassociate while he kisses me, and plan my grocery list for the week. When he finally comes up for air, I move myself away before he can go back in for seconds. *That was the worst kiss of my life*, I think. *That was amazing*, he says. I smile and nod. *So good, but I have to go meet my friend soon, so you should go.* I walk him out of the building. He grabs my hand at the door. He is still trembling. *I knew, when I saw your profile, that I had come across someone special.* My insides turn as he talks. *Me too!* I say, and close the door.

They aren't all so desperate. Or, at least, they're desperate in different ways. There is a sixty-three-year-old movie director who gets #MeTooed a few years after this. I will see his name on the laptop screen and think, *Well, that figures.* He picks me up in his Lamborghini and I am 90 per cent sure he's wearing a toupee. I tell him my dad has the same car. *Impossible,* he bellows, *there's only a few of these made! Well, it's true,* I say, defiantly. *My dad is very rich and makes movies, too. Intellectual European ones, with subtitles and shit.* He waves a hand to dismiss me. *That stuff doesn't make any money, there's no way he's as wealthy as me.* Then he laughs, a deep, cackly laugh that has him in a coughing fit a few seconds later. I look out the window as he hacks into a tissue.

When he drops me home that evening, he parks in the alley behind my apartment building and leans over to kiss me. It feels like I am being strangled by an octopus. He grabs my hand and places it over his crotch. *Take it out and stroke it,* he gruffly demands. When he comes, his ancient sperm covers the handbrake of his $200,000 car. I watch him wipe down the handbrake with a used tissue. *Girls like you can be such trouble for men like me,* he says, smiling as he shakes his head. He throws a wad of bills in my lap. *Don't spend it all in one place, darling,* he winks, and I am positive I feel my soul actually leaving my body. Still, when he texts me a week later, all in capitals, 2PM TOMORROW LETS GET CRAB LEGS DARLING AND HAVE SOME FUN, I respond with a yes.

There's a married forty-five-year-old who asks me to never wear perfume or scented lotion, in case his wife suspects anything. *I love her,* he tells me as we're both lying naked in a hotel bed. *It's just complicated.* He deposits $800 into my bank account each time I see him, and that never feels complicated to me.

The German man, who is so hot I want to pay him, gives me $500 after I come. I want to see him all the time, but he's only available once a month. I don't ask why.

A fifty-year-old Chinese man, who writes me cheques in calligraphy that the bank won't cash until he comes into the branch in person, to verify. *She did some work in my garden,* he says to the bank manager, an explanation for the $1,500. That's a lot of flowers planted.

A fifty-eight-year-old blond-haired man, whose photos looked like Leonardo DiCaprio but, when I show up at Shutters on the Beach in Santa Monica, looks like Philip Seymour Hoffman. He orders my food for me, and tells me he has a semi. He tells me I look like his daughter. I laugh and say he looks like my dad. He hands me a cheque for $4,000 before we have sex on his sofa. There's a view of the ocean from it. I look out at it in the darkness as he pounds me. He doesn't want to use a condom, but I make him put it on. He cancels the cheque the next day. *You don't have the appetite for me, so let's make it $700 a go.*

And I go, and go. After a while, they all morph into one.

I feel myself beginning to change under the weight of these men. Hardening. I like the power I feel fucking an ugly, ageing man. The power they transfer to me. The power that I know of always belongs to a man. All I can do is take a little piece of it. I inhale the morsels they give me. I turn them into nothing.

Men have become dispensable, a thing I can use to get what I want. I enjoy them using my body to make themselves come. I like the transaction of it. There are no feelings involved. But we all love to play pretend.

I act reckless with them. I go to the homes of strangers, men whose last names I don't know, to fuck them. I feel the underlying threat that exists during every meeting. They could kill me. I don't care. I don't care if something bad happens to me. The murky waters between me and a brown envelope are my favourite part – the thrill of the unknown, each step as uncertain as the last.

These men are using you, Conell tells me over beers. *Yea, and I'm using them right back. A victimless crime.* Some of the men know exactly what we've signed up for. Others are just searching for connection in an empty void. None of them are bad. Even if I don't know it at the time, none of the men are bad men. Still, I don't know if any of us are good. Just hollow people, using sex and money so we can feel.

5

I am sunbathing on the roof of my building. My bikini top is tossed on the concrete beside me. The rays beat down on my body, as I lie on an old picnic table, careful to avoid the splinters. I watch a rat scutter by as I cover myself in factor 50. Every twenty minutes, I rinse myself off with a hose that spurts out lukewarm water. I lie back on the table, closing my eyes, feeling the sun sink into me. *This is the life I am meant for*, I think to myself.

I feel something hit my thigh. *Hey, bitch.* When I open my eyes, Conell is standing over me, smoking a cigarette. I sit up. *How can you wear a turtleneck in this heat?* I ask, taking a cigarette from his pack. *I don't like the sun on my skin*, he shrugs. *Look how big your nipples are!* I look down, and laugh. *You know they're massive when they're soft.* He holds out his lighter to me and sits down on the picnic table. *So what loser is it tonight?*

His name is Brad, can you believe? How fucking American. He's fifty-six. That's a year older than my dad will ever be. Isn't that crazy?

Do you really think that's crazy, or does it make you sad?

I ignore his question. I hate when he asks me questions like this.

I look to my left, at the buildings that make up Downtown LA. I blow out smoke. *I pretend to these men my dad is still alive.*

Conell looks up from his phone. *Why?*

I don't know. I laugh once I say that, realizing how stupid it is. *I actually honestly don't know. I did it once, and I liked how it felt, to make up a life that can never actually be. Like I was playing God with myself. And then I did it again. Not on purpose; it just slipped out. And now it's almost a habit. I don't plan it, but I like imagining these lives for my dad that he can never have.*

Conell taps out his ash on the ground beside me, and I hear it sizzle. *You know you don't need to do this.*

Oh, come on. What else would I be doing?

Literally anything else. What about the girls?

He's referring to the dates I go on in between the men. Beautiful lesbians who are out of my league, with tiny waists and soft lips and long hair. Girls whose conversation I drink up, whose eyes I can stare into and not want to look away. Girls who I can lean over to and make the first move. With those girls, I get to be the man. That power excites me initially, but then it scares me. Once I am aware of it, nestled in the palms of my hands, it becomes scalding hot, and I need to throw it away from me before it sears right into my bones.

The girls stay over in my bed, and then I bring them to brunch the next day with my friends. We hold hands as we wait for our table to be called. We all laugh together, eating eggs and drinking Bloody Marys. I kiss them on the sidewalk while my friends try on jeans in Silver Lake boutique stores. I smell their hair, out there in the hot LA sun, and promise them the world. *I want to take surfing lessons with you, I want to bring you to Catalina Island, I want to meet your parents.* And they say, *Yes please, I'd fucking love all that*, and my hands start to burn. All that power is too much for me to own. So, I throw each one away and open up my phone and swipe, swipe, swipe, until I find another. It's a new girl every few weeks, but my friends greet them like they're the one. Like there's never been a girl before them. Like there won't be another after them. When the girls are gone, they make fun of me.

What new girl are we meeting this week, who we have to pretend is going to be in our lives past this one brunch? And I laugh back. *This week, her name is Kelly.*

It wasn't that I didn't like them. In fact, I liked them all, but I didn't like them liking me back. They suffocated me with their liking, and the only solution was to try again with a new one, replaying those first few weeks of a pseudo relationship over and over again, until there was nothing left but muscle memory.

The girls don't count, I tell Conell dismissively. Girls never count; that's the whole point of them. *Besides,* I say, rolling over on my side, *money is more permanent than feelings. Even if you spend it, you still know it exists, because you feel it in your hands.* Conell stands up and stamps out his cigarette butt, ignoring my gaze. *I don't think you actually believe that, but fine. Enjoy Brad.*

He walks away. *I won't enjoy Brad,* I scream at his back, *that's the whole fucking point.*

Conell looks back at me when he gets to the building door. *It's okay to miss him, you know,* he shouts over. *Your world won't fall apart if you admit that.*

I squint, barely able to make him out because the sun is shining directly into my face. *How could I miss Brad?* I yell. *I don't even know him yet.* I hear the door slam shut before I can see he's gone.

6

You've spent three months taking advantage of men. You think you know what it looks like. Wielding power is so all-enforcing you can't miss it. Until you do.

Your first date with Mark is in a seafood restaurant in Santa Monica. He has already cancelled on you once, so you're not sure if he will show. You arrive after spending the day on the beach, your hair knotty from the salt water. You are wearing jean shorts and Birkenstocks, your bikini straps slipping down your shoulders. You look out of place among the business suits and high heels. He orders you a drink, something you've never heard of, but when you taste it, it becomes your favourite drink. He asks you questions about yourself. He asks them in a way that makes you feel like he's the first person to ever ask them. He said he was forty-two on his profile. He now tells you he's fifty. He says it in a way that makes you like him even more. *I don't fuck on the first date*, you tell him. You have grown confident from your months of first dates; you know how to communicate what you want. *That's perfect*, he says, smiling back at you. Like what you said was his idea. Within thirty minutes, you are drunk on him. Before an hour is up, he checks his watch. *I've got to go now, but this has been great. I'll call you.* All you can manage is a smile in return. You're afraid to open your mouth; afraid of what desire will come spilling out. So, you just nod.

He calls you up later that evening, when you are home in your apartment in Downtown LA. *I'm over in your neck of the woods for a business dinner. Let's meet for a late-night drink.* It's not a question. You quickly shower and do your make-up, drawing your lips in red. Lipstick is something you can never get your head around; your hands apply it too shakily so it's all over your mouth. You use a cotton bud to clean it off, but take off too much. You scrub your lips in frustration and try again, watching a YouTube tutorial to guide you. It still doesn't look right. *The bar will be dim*, you think to yourself, and grab your bag and leave.

When you see him, you immediately want to fuck him. Your whole body is on fire. The bar is closing when you both arrive.

He convinces them to stay open for just one more drink. You'll find out very soon how good he is at convincing people to do things.

You talk, but mainly listen. He tells you he has a girlfriend. *I hope that isn't a problem? You seem cool, so I assume it isn't.* You swallow the problem. *I guess it's fine, yea.* You both keep talking. You drink up every word he says. He speaks with an authority and awareness you find tantalizing. You lean forward every time he says a word, desperate to feel it all.

The bartender comes over to the table. *We really got to shut.* All the chairs are up on the wooden tables, and most of the lights are out. You ask him if he wants to come back to your place. *Because technically, this is the second date.* He says yes.

He controls the tempo, the movement, the actions. He steers you to a shape he wants. You give in so easily to his control, it makes you wonder if you've been waiting for this your whole life. You have the best sex you've ever had. Every other fuck feels like stabilizer sex, and he has taken off the training wheels. When you come, you look straight into his eyes. A bolt shoots through your body. You think you are in love with him.

When it's over, he strokes your hair as he sits up on the bed. *Let's go on a drive to an ATM. I want to give you some money.*

You don't need to do that, you tell him.

I do, I want to be good to you. Every time I've done this before, I give $600 each time. It's not about the money, but the money is important. I know you're smart enough to get it. You smile, not getting it.

You drive around with him to a few ATMs. His card doesn't work in any of them. *It must be because it's a new card*, he tells you. *I'll get you back next time.* He never does, and you never bring it up. Really, you like that he didn't give you money. It makes you feel different to the other girls. If he doesn't give you money, it means it isn't about the money.

You see Mark a couple of times a week. You talk to him every day. You are desperate for every interaction with him. No matter what you get, you want more. You are infatuated with every part of him. Especially the part of him that makes you feel seen.

When he fucks you, you feel connected in a way you've never felt before. *I don't think anyone has even seen me how you do. You pierce right into my gut. When I am with you, I feel completely exposed.* The words just spill out of you. *I love that,* he always says back. *I love your power.* He always speaks about your power. Even back then, you know he is the one with the true power. Any power you have is only a result of him giving you it. How grateful you feel for getting even a drop.

Mark's name isn't really Mark, but you never ask what it actually is. You don't need to know. You know what you both have transcends any of that bullshit. *Mark, Mark, oh yes Mark,* you scream from your bed.

He texts you all the time. He knows you fuck other men when he's not around, but he likes to check in, to make sure you're still thinking about him:

What guy is it tonight? Tell me everything about him.

I'll be over in an hour. Go for a run and don't shower after :)

Tell me your darkest fantasy. You know I'll never judge you.

I have to cancel on tonight. I haven't seen my daughter in two weeks :)

I can tell I don't have your full attention, so let's chat some other time :)

You are working when he sends that, as a hostess in a whisky bar. You immediately run to the bathroom, leaving a queue of people standing at the entrance, waiting to be seated. *No, I am here. I am here. I am here.*

Mark isn't a good person. And you know that, deep down. It's a part of the attraction. You love how easily he controls you, how easily you let yourself be controlled. *There's no such thing as bad or good*, he tells you, *just people trying to get what they want.*

What do you want? he asks you. *You*, you reply. He laughs. *Well, then you're one of the lucky ones, getting exactly what you want.*

He comes to your bar one night with his friend. It's a high-end place; they serve just whisky straight, with hand-chipped ice. People have to ring a hidden bell to get in. Mark kisses you roughly when he walks in. *It took us a fucking hour to get here*, he says with annoyance, like LA's traffic is your fault, and you say, *Oh, sorry?* They sit on the patio and drink whiskies that are $60 a pour. You bring them hot towels, leaning on the arm of Mark's chair to talk. You are delighted to meet his friend; surely that means there is something real here, if he wants to introduce you to him. Surely this means what you want it to mean. When you want something very badly, it's so easy to imagine it to be true.

When you bring the bill, he passes it to his friend, who pays. *Give her a nice tip*, he instructs. And he does. They drive back to your apartment, with you in the back seat. *You have to see where she lives*, he says to his friend when he pulls up at your building. His friend hesitates, at the same time you do. But still, you all get out of his Jeep. You wonder if you are going to have to fuck his friend. You decide you will do it, if he wants you to. You decide it's not really your choice at all.

Isn't it so bohemian? Mark says, his words bellowing in the open apartment. *They don't even have doors in here!* You hope Conell isn't home, rolling his eyes from his bed. Mark's friend awkwardly looks around, not moving from his spot at the entrance. *Yea, very cool. We should head, though.* Mark pulls you closer to him and sticks his tongue down your throat. The only sound you hear is his friend coughing. You hear him, and pull in closer. You feel embarrassed for his friend, but glad he is a witness and not a player. Glad Mark is choosing you, just you. You catch eyes with the friend, and he shrugs. He gets it.

Sometimes, Mark comes straight to your apartment, and you fuck. He complains about your soap brand when he takes a shower, and you tell him you'll replace it. Other times, he brings you out on dates. He's never nervous about being caught. *I don't know anyone who lives in East LA, so we're fine*, he tells you. You nod, like it's the only thing you're worried about too. Mark has been cheating his whole life, he tells you. *I know you're too smart to judge that.* He is so sure about parts of yourself that you're hazy on. It feels very welcoming to have someone tell you who you are when you're so uncertain.

One night, he pulls up at your apartment in his sports car, with the roof down. He drives erratically, sometimes stopping in the middle of the street to say something to you. The cars around him beep aggressively, but it doesn't seem to concern him. He pulls up to an Italian restaurant in Silver Lake, and hands his keys to the valet. *I know everyone's staring at us, old guy with money, hot young girl.* You can tell he gets off on it. You do too.

He asks for a table outside. He orders for you, but picks exactly right. *Oysters and steak, medium-rare, and a bottle of pink Champagne*, he tells the waiter. You've had this food a hundred times with other men, but you really taste it with him. Afterwards, you take out a cigarette, shaking your lighter when it won't produce a flame. *I don't mind if you smoke, but I don't find it that interesting.* You quickly stub out the cigarette. You desperately want to be interesting.

You talk with him about politics and desire and insecurities. You say how unsure you are of your future. He assures you that everything you need to figure it out is inside of you. You smile when he says that. He fills up your empty glass. *I've never met someone like you*, you say. He laughs. *People tell me that a lot.*

I've just figured out who I am, and what I want. People are drawn to that. You look away, embarrassed. You don't want to be people. You want to be something he's never had. You want to be special.

You look at him across the candlelit table, your cheeks hot from the warm Southern California night. *I'm not crazy, am I?* you ask him. *We really do have something unique, don't we?* He ignores your questions, but hones in on your want. *I wish I could bring you into the bathroom, bend you over and suck on your pussy.* You instantly contort your brain to be what he suggests. You slide your legs apart under the table; you open your mouth and stick your thumb inside, slowly sucking it. He smiles. *Good girl.* You look into his eyes. You know you are smart, but you also know he is smarter than you. A part of you can see how he is playing you. Another part of you likes being played.

He fills up your glass again. *My cock is rock hard, baby.* He stands up to beckon for the bill. You stare at the bulge in his pants. *See? Now everyone else can see how much I want you.* You laugh. You never want the night to end.

Mark gives you money when he feels like it. He likes to pay your rent the day before it's due, right when you're down to the wire and feel sweat running down your back. *My hero*, you text, because you know that's what he wants to hear. His assistant drives to your apartment on the last Saturday of the month, and passes an envelope from the window of his Beetle. You laugh as you take it, but he just smiles, embarrassed. *Have fun*, he yells, speeding off. You wonder how often these drop-offs happen. Maybe it's written into his job description.

As the months go by, Mark slices off deeper parts of you, parts you didn't even know you could give. You feel special, every time he asks for a little bit more of you. *He really wants me*, you think, carving off new chunks to give to him. When he tells you his fantasy, three months in, you want to say yes before he can even finish his sentence.

You know how you tell me about the other men you fuck? And you nod, because you do. *It turns me on when you talk about it. What if I got to watch you with another man? Watch him fuck you until you come. Watch him use you to pleasure himself.*

Your body betrays you; when he says it, you make a face without realizing, because really, you don't want to do it. You don't want another man; you only really want him. He can sense this. *And then, of course, afterwards, I would take you in my arms and hold you and kiss you, and then you'd truly be mine.* You like this idea. *Yea, maybe that could work.* He smiles, and repeats himself. *Then you'd truly be mine.* You decide you love this idea. It becomes your idea.

He tells you to set up a Craigslist profile. Craigslist, that website you've used in the past to find apartments. The Craigslist Killer. Women have been murdered in these classifieds. *Specify a black man*, he tells you. *That would be so much hotter.* You don't ask him why. You get eighty messages from the profile. You read them out loud to your friends while you're all drinking beers in your living room. The room fills with laughter as dick pics flood your inbox. One guy tells you he coaches high-school football. *I've never done this before.* He sounds believable, but who ends up by accident on a Craigslist threesome ad? Then again, not everyone ends up there by choice. *My idea*, you repeat to yourself, every time you feel unsure.

You present a shortlist of guys to Mark. You don't really want to do this, but it's your idea, and you want to please him. Pleasing him pleases you. Still, he can feel your apprehension. He's very good at reading people. *You don't seem that excited about this, which is disappointing.* You don't want to disappoint him. You make an argument about how much you want it, how hot it is, how much your body desires it. *It would be the hottest thing to me if he fucked you raw, and came inside you*, he says. *Oh well, yea, I guess, except that's really risky. I don't want*

to have sex with a stranger from Craigslist without a condom.
Mark always uses a condom with you, so you're sure he gets it.
Within a week, he has you agreeing to no condom.

You never do it. When it becomes obvious it's not going to
happen, you realize he never really wanted to do it. He just
wanted to know you would. That power, you get it, it's addictive.
To control someone is something. To be controlled is something
else. They are two sides of the same coin. There can be opposites
that are the exact same. *Do you like it?* he asks, while leaving
red marks on your ass. *Yes, yes, please, yes,* you moan.

He didn't take control away from me. I gave it to him, willingly.
I wanted him to make every decision for me, from what I smelled
like, to what I wore, to who I wanted to fuck. I wanted him to
decide what I liked, and who I was, because having to choose
it for myself was overwhelming. I could begin the thought,
I want to… and then my brain would cut out. It just went blank.
I couldn't decide the ending to that sentence, so I was grateful
for him taking over. *You want to please me.* And I smiled,
relieved at my fate being decided by someone else; at becoming
a you instead of a me. *Okay, yes, great. Thank you. I want to
please you.*

Once back in Amsterdam, I take out my phone and delete
his information, taking away my choice. I know if I ever said
one more word to him, my whole heart would spill out. I know
how much he'd enjoy that game. Because that's all it was to him:
a game. And me, the willing player, twisting to his every move.

Matthew. His real name was Matthew. I heard it from his
phone when it was connected to the Bluetooth of the car. I acted
like I didn't notice it, and he let me get away with not noticing.
Matthew and Mark. One half of the evangelists. *Oh God, oh
God, oh God.*

7

When I was fourteen, I had teeth pulled out so my braces could fit on. Four back molars: big teeth with roots entwined deep inside my mouth. I was afraid the injection would wear off before the dentist got them out, because I had watched a YouTube video about how that can happen. It was like something from a horror film. Patients screaming out in pain. What if it happens to me? I was scared, and I had just learned about the Cold War earlier that day in history class. I remembered the opening paragraph from my textbook. *The Cold War was the cooling down of relations between the USA and former USSR. It was not a war per se as no actual fighting occurred, but was more a war of nerves.*

I sat in the dentist's chair and repeated this sentence over and over again so I could concentrate on something else. My dentist was a middle-aged man with bad breath. It made me wonder if dentists go to the dentist themselves, because this guy was surely due a check-up. He stuck the long needle in my mouth without any warning. His assistant steadied my shaking jaw. *The Cold War was the cooling down of relations.* He probed and drilled and pulled. *It was not a war per se, because no actual fighting occurred.* I squirmed each time his tools bore down on me. *It's just pressure*, he told me. *Why won't you relax?* He tossed each tooth on to a metal tray beside him. I gripped the chair as he went in for more. *The USA and former USSR was a war of nerves.*

It was over fifty minutes later. *See, that wasn't so bad*, my grumpy dentist told me. I nodded in agreement, holding in tears. Three months later, that same dentist would clip the inside of my mouth with his pliers and not bother to apologize. I hated that man, but not yet. *Very brave girl*, the assistant told me, and I knew it was a warning. *Good, brave girls don't make a fuss*, is what she was really telling me. I wanted to hysterically wail and cry until I made myself sick, just spill out every emotion I was feeling on to their floor that this stupid old bitch would have to clean up, but instead I just continued to nod, swallowing my anger.

My mum was waiting in the car. She asked me how it went when I got in. She wasn't allowed inside with me anymore, because when I was nine she saw blood in my mouth while I was on the chair, and fainted, and they had to get me off the chair and her on to it, and it was a whole big scene that no one wanted repeating, so she stayed in the car. I knew she didn't drive off and come back fifty minutes later. She just sat there in the car park, listening to the radio. My mother loves in such a silent language, you'd be forgiven for missing it. I used to think if you couldn't see something immediately, if it wasn't screaming in your face, that meant it didn't exist. *I'm a brave fucking girl*, I spat out, and then started to cry. The big ugly tears I was desperate to release now came out, in the safety of the car and my mother. *Language, Marise*, my mum told me as she reversed. *When are you allowed to eat? Let's pick you up something for later. Do you need some painki —*

I interrupted her. *Why are you not listening to me? You don't even care*. My mother said nothing, quietly changing gear.

When I am twenty-five, back in Amsterdam, I get myself into a bad situation. It's not surprising I have ended up here. I have been making choice after choice for a while now that I hope will be the end of me.

I am having sex with a man right now. Two hours earlier, he held a key of coke across the bar where I worked. I leaned down and sniffed. He told me women were the devil's children.

I laughed, even though I didn't find it funny. Then I sold him a bottle of Champagne. He asked for two glasses. I filled them to the brim. We made 25 per cent commission off the Champagne sold. More off the coke. He paid in cash and left a €500 tip. I folded the notes into my skirt pocket and walked around the bar. I held his hand and followed him up to his hotel room on the third floor. I sat on the bed as he locked the door. My gut told me to leave the room. I ignored it. I inhaled two miniature bottles of Chardonnay to quell the uneasy feeling in my stomach. As usual, my body knew before my mind did. I slammed down an empty wine bottle on the bedside table, making the conscious decision to ignore my body's alarm bells.

He stops fucking me. He stares down from atop me. I know something is wrong. I look at the lines around his eyes. I knew this man wanted to hurt me from the moment I stepped in the room. I still chose to close the door behind me. I look back into his dark, empty eyes, and take a deep breath in. I choose this.

The Cold War was the cooling down…

He puts his hand around my neck.

Of relations between…

You're a stupid little bitch, he whispers in my ear.

The USA and the former USSR…

His grasp is getting tighter.

It was not a war per se…

My breath becomes shallow.

You think you're smarter than me? Look at you now.

As no actual fighting occurred…

He hits me in the face.

You worthless stupid whore. I could kill you.

Something snaps inside me. Usually, when you agree to have sex with someone, you can't back out halfway when shit gets weird. Well, you technically can, but it's considered impolite. You just have to lie there and wait for it to be over. And I am normally very good at doing that. But his apparent death threat wakes me out of my passivity.

Get off me now. I don't want this anymore.

He ignores me. I try to push him off me but the weight of his body is on top of me and he is so much stronger than I am. I have been doing chaturangas every day for the past two years, building cute yoga-arm muscles, and yet, when I need it, my strength is nowhere to be found.

The Cold War was a cooling down of relations between the USA...

I can't move. He's pressed himself on top of me and my breath is becoming desperate.

And the former USSR...

I try to kick but my legs are pinned down.

It was not a war per se...

He leans his mouth down to mine.

Per se per se per se...

I shake my head from side to side to avoid his lips.

Please just don't kiss me.

I can ignore his dick ripping the inside of me but I do not want him to kiss me.

The former USSR...

He smashes his mouth against mine and forces his tongue inside.

The Cold War...

I could kill you, his distorted mouth snarls at me.

I nod in agreement.

The Cold War was the cooling down of relations...

I wonder if I'll die. If he'll kill me. I wonder if he's thinking the same.

No actual fighting occurred...

He moves his body from atop me to change my position. It's two seconds of a window. I kick him in the balls with my knee.

It was not a war per se as no…
I kick and kick.
YOU STUPID FUCKING BITCH!
No actual fighting occurred…
He slaps my face and lets go of his grip. He releases me.
I grab my dress and run out of the room, naked. *You worthless cunt*, I hear as I stumble down the stairs. I want to cry, but I hold it in.

Security are upstairs within two minutes. They kick him out. One of the bartenders throws him on the wet cement outside, and slams his boot into his face. I hear about it as I sit in the changing room. Sprays and eyelashes and bras are littered around the floor. Hair curlers still plugged in. I stare at my face in the mirror. I wipe away the specks of red lipstick on my chin. All the mean Russian girls I work with, who I hate almost all the time, make sure I am okay. They don't know how to do that in words, so they hand me cigarettes and brush my hair. *How so knotty? So dry, too*, they murmur softly as they do it. Within ten minutes, I am laughing, swatting away the brush. *Get off me, and bring me a fucking drink!*

As I cycle home at 3am, swerving around the drunk men vomiting on the streets, I think about what happened tonight, as the cold air hits my face. I know that I got out of the room not because I fought back. I got out because he released me. I am alive because he let me go. And that's always the fucking way. The power that I know of always belongs to a man. From the dentist's chair to the bedroom, and much in between. It's always been a thing that has happened to me, never something I have really owned.

It's only when I'm locking up my bike that I think of the Russian girls, teasing out the knots in my hair as they blew smoke in my face. I think of my mother, parked in the dentist's driveway, listening to the radio. There is a kindness in women that could be considered a power, I suppose, but it's often so silent it gets eclipsed by anything a man is destroying. It's so fucking silent I usually miss it completely. If my dad had been waiting for me, he would have beeped the horn. And I would have rushed out, holding the bloody gauze to my mouth, and apologized for keeping him waiting.

I put the keys in my door and double-lock it once inside. I change into my pyjamas and get under the duvet. I stare at the ceiling, thinking of the lines around that man's eyes, how they deepened as he threatened to kill me. That man. I don't even know his fucking name.

I spend two hours thinking about him, before I ask myself, *why?* Why am I so transfixed on the power of men? Why are the men who have hurt me more important than the women who brush my hair afterwards? Why have I never let women matter at all? *Girls don't count*, I hear myself say. What a lazy way to think. I have let myself become engulfed in the loud destruction of men, and in doing so have missed the quiet strength of women. I think of my mother's perfect square scar on her left cheek. I think of me kicking that guy in the balls. Women are so much stronger than I've ever allowed them to be.

As I fall asleep that night, I realize there's so much that I have missed.

8

My last relationship with an old man begins much like the first one: an established comedian who I looked up to, who was openly damaged, who paid me attention and made me feel special. There's twenty-five years between us.

MONEY

I meet Oscar Mayer after a show of his in Amsterdam. I hang around afterwards, waiting to take a photo. He flirts with me and gives me his number. We meet up the next afternoon by the canal beside his house, drinking cans of Coke, and talk about comedy and him.

He was an alcoholic, but now he's not. Except you're never not an alcoholic. It's a badge you wear for the rest of your life. And he wears it, with pride. He talks about his drinking days with a reverence that tells me he'll drink again. My aunt quit smoking, after fifteen years, when I was seven. She spent the next five years telling anyone who would listen that, if she won the lotto, the first thing she'd do would be to buy a pack of cigarettes. She started smoking again when I was twelve, and has been sucking down forty a day ever since. We like to think of ourselves as befores and afters, like we can draw a clean line between who we used to be and who we want to be. But no after is permanent, and every after is definitely only temporary if you miss the before so much it keeps you up at night.

Here's how I know he'll drink again: his drinking stories never involved hurting others, they only centred around the pleasure and pain drinking afforded him. But as the child of an alcoholic, I know how impossible it is to localize the effects of your actions. They cover the ones who love you, like a blanket, until they quietly stop breathing. If you can't see that, you will drink again. And even if you see it, even if it slaps you awake every morning, you might still pick up the bottle. Mr Cummins taught me that when I was fourteen, and I cried, because I knew, deep down, what he was saying was true. When I tell Oscar Mayer this, he laughs at me. *Stop projecting*, he says, waving me away with his hand.

Three weeks later, we fuck in his ex-wife's bed. She's away, and he's Airbnbed his house to make some extra cash. I pretend to come. The next morning, he brings me a croissant from the local deli, and sits on the edge of his ex-wife's bed, telling me how beautiful I am. I smile and eat the croissant in three bites, spilling flakes all over her sheets. When I get out of bed to get dressed, I leave them there.

We continue to see each other. I cycle over to his house before work, because he doesn't like leaving his surroundings. He likes to stand out on the tiny street in front of his house, commenting at people who walk by. Sometimes, he sweeps the pavement. His teeth are stained a burned yellow. His hair recedes so far back his head it's a wonder it doesn't just give up completely. He puffs up the remaining hair, pulls it forward, and I watch him look at himself in the mirror, wondering if he sees what I do. His ass is so flat it looks like he has a really long back. Which wouldn't be so bad if he didn't criticize every woman that walks by his house, pulling her apart as if she exists for him to masturbate to, and she's ruining his porn. *All these average women just waddle along like they're good looking,* he moans, *with their flat asses and thin lips.* I look at his mouth, at the barely there slivers of pink surrounding his rotting teeth, and I kiss him. *You're so much above any of these people.* And he agrees.

He loves plants, and expensive cheese, but most of all he loves himself. What we have in common is him. We both think he is a misunderstood genius. We speak, for hours, about how unappreciated he is.

He has two sons. Only one of them is fucked up. One in two doesn't seem like bad odds to me because I know that alcoholism destroys the children of the drinker much more than the drinker themself. But he views that son as a thing that happened to him, not something he caused. He complains about him when he's in the house. *Would he ever just fuck off and do something?* But when he's not there, when he's just an idea instead of a person, he frets and loves. *What can I do to save him? I'd die for him.* I roll my eyes when he spouts that bullshit. We can all die for someone; it's living for them that's hard to do.

I don't like his son, because there's something too familiar about him – it makes my skin itch just to think about. When I speak to him, I focus on the floor, because it's like looking directly at the sky. It hurts too much to keep looking straight on. Living is something that has been thrown at him, and he has let it splat on to his face. And he's content just to watch it drip down, from his body to the floor, and the thought to wipe it up doesn't ever cross his mind. His agency is absent; he just lets it all happen to him.

His son, the fucked-up one, is my age. He somehow separates the two of us. Son, girlfriend, child, woman. Oscar Mayer asks for my advice on what to do with him. He asks me to speak to him, but I refuse, reminding him he is not my son, not my problem. What I don't say is that his son makes my body shudder when I even think of him, because he reminds me so vividly of what I hate about myself. Instead I say, *Not my problem.* And he calls me a bitch.

When I am sitting on his couch, straddling him, I take off his glasses and look into his eyes. I see death. Not in his eyes exactly, but in the delicate skin around them. The folds upon folds. How they crinkle without him moving. It disgusts me, and I can't look away. Sometimes, when I look at him, it feels like I am looking at a ghost, but one who is still alive. They're the worst type of ghosts. They can haunt you for the rest of your life.

He infantilizes me. He babies me. He laughs at things I say, because he's the only one who truly understands anything. He complains about how I eat, how I don't brush my hair, how I throw my stuff on the floor when I walk in his house. *When you have a place of your own, you'll understand. You're too young to get it*, he says, smiling, patting my hair. If he had a pacifier near him, he'd stick it in my mouth. I swat away his hand. *You're giving me knots! And anyway, it's not even your house,* I argue, *you're just renting. And you're two months behind.*

He hits on every young, pretty woman he sees, even if I'm there beside him. He can't help it. He's a mosquito, drawn to the light of youth. It's only really embarrassing when she's grossed out by him. Answering his invasive questions while tapping her foot, checking her phone. Entertaining him like I would my grandad. It's embarrassing, because then I go home and fuck him. Doing the thing these women shudder to think about.

He won't kiss me when we have sex, and he leaves the moment it's over, jumping up off his bed like it's covered in fire ants. I roll my eyes, but accept it all.

One night in January, when it's cold and dark outside, and there's no sign of any release in the clouds, and everyone has accepted the drudged fate of a life in purgatory, he calls me when I'm at work, demands I come down to the street, makes me buy him cigarettes because he's all out. I do, walking dutifully across the street to the supermarket. Except no one makes us do anything. He asked without a question mark, but I still said yes.

And still, he is the genius. I am lucky to be around him, be a part of him. I am always lucky, so lucky, to be an extension of these men. I am a parasite, sinking my teeth into someone more interesting than me, gaining life from their blood. I live as if I'd stop existing if they looked away. Like I'd turn to dust if they weren't around. Or worse, I'd exist, but only half so, just the outline of me but no colour in between the lines.

Thank God your father killed himself, otherwise you wouldn't be damaged enough to go out with me, he says to me, not once, but over and over again, like it's a prayer. And I laugh every time, so it becomes a joke we're both in on. As if everything that has happened to me is just a prequel, so he can fuck me.

*

I go to London during the spring, nine months into our relationship, to visit him. He is house-sitting for a friend. His son, the non-fucked-up one, comes to visit the last three days I am there. The first day we watch bad reality TV and eat pasta that my boyfriend, his father, makes for us. He hands us our plates as we sit on the couch, watching '90 Day Fiancé'. He acts like we are both his children, fussing over us with some sort of resentment. *Be careful of the couch, and close your mouths as you eat.* My blood goes from normal to boiling in sixty seconds flat. *I'm your fucking girlfriend, not your kid*, I snarl at him, in front of his son, who has the decency to look down at his phone.

We have an argument later that night, in strained whispers, while his son is asleep. *Don't even think about going crazy right now, not while my son is here*, he shout-whispers at me. He emphasizes the *crazy*. A dirty word. The crazy I can be is an inconvenience to him. He wants to sweep it under the dirty couch he takes naps on. He wants to fuck me, sticking his old cock inside of me until he comes. He wants to laugh about my dad killing himself, so he can fuck me. But he doesn't want to have to deal with the crazy all that is rooted to, the true reason why someone like me would have sex with someone like him.

I stay with him for six months after that. One night, we get dinner in the Asian restaurant at the end of his street. We order sashimi and tempura, his favourites, then he leaves the table for a cigarette. As the waitress places the napkins on our table, she smiles at me. *Your father, he always comes in here*, she says. I laugh, but don't correct her. I tell him what she's said when he comes back inside, and he's delighted. *Wouldn't you love me to be your dad?* I smile at him. *Do you promise to be a better one?* He takes my hand and kisses it. *Yes, little girl, I'll be the fake father of your dreams.*

Except the men who fuck girls half their age, who fuck crazy girls and then get annoyed at the weight of their craziness, who fuck girls with dead dads and say a quick prayer of thanks for the dying, those men are never the men you want to be your fake father. They are the men your dad warned you about, if you had a father who was around to give you the warning.

He's not just the last old man I go out with. He's every older man I've fucked. All of them tied together make up the same one person. Handprints over handprints, until there is just a black smudge left on my body. At least the ones who paid me gave something. The others just took, took, took. Or maybe I handed it over to them, without them having to ask. Complicit in the theft. Because at least when someone was taking from me, it made me feel I had something worthwhile to give.

And still, I can't reduce my part to that of a victim. Life isn't just things that happen to me; it's choices I make. None of these men happened to me. They made decisions, and I did too, even if the decision was to close my eyes and accept. Passivity is a choice too, just one I'm too afraid to own. It's easier to pass it off to someone else, to make villains of other people, rather than look in the mirror at the monster staring back at me. Everything that has happened to me happened because I let it. Happened because I chose it. Happened, in some way or another, because I wanted it to happen.

In the end, not the actual end, but the end up until now, after I have wiped my hands of all their creaky joints and fat wallets, and thrown out the thickening shampoos and 'Reader's Digest's, I am left with myself, just myself, and the numbing realization that I am as bad as any of them. Somewhere, some father is giving his daughter a warning, and the warning is about me.

FOUR

TROUBLE

1

I have always been a crier. I love to cry. I've never seen it as a sign of weakness. Crying has always been a sign to myself that I am alive. I cry watching those returning-from-war videos, when a man in combat fatigues surprises his daughter at school. I cry when I argue with some asshole who tries to skip past me in line at the post office, my words spitting out of me and my voice rising and then the tears fall out. I cry when the chain goes on my bike and it's fucking raining and cold and I just want to be home already. I cry to get out of trouble. I cry when a boyfriend describes why he loves me. *And what else?* I'll ask in between sobs.

Sometimes I like to watch myself in the mirror as I cry, especially when I am in the big heaving type of crying, snot dripping out of my nose, ugly splotched red face. No one expects you to be pretty when you cry. You're off the hook. You can be as ugly as you please. You're not something for other people to ingest; you don't have to watch yourself from someone else's gaze. When you cry, you belong just to yourself. I watch the salty water drop out of me, on to me. I touch my fingers to my face, feeling my emotions trickle down it. Wet cheeks remind me that I exist, that I am a conscious being who takes up space in this world, that I am here. I have always been a crier, but from ages fourteen to seventeen no tears came out.

When I look back at that time in my life and sift through the memories, I do so lazily, with a wide-tooth comb in hand. It catches the big, messy knots, and if I pull hard enough, they come right off. But anything lesser runs right through the comb. It's easier to remember the things that happened to me than it is the things that happened inside of me. But omitting part of the story is just erasing it. It doesn't exist, without it all. Admitting is different to remembering, though. The truth is, I have many lost memories from this time, when the slow fog of depression quietly crept up on me. I can only pull out strands of it; I can only make sense of disjointed jagged pieces. The full picture will always be missing.

I remember starting secondary school, and the tiredness that crept into my bones. How heavy it felt in my body. How much of an effort it was to keep my head upright. I felt exhausted, all the time, but I reminded myself that my father slept until noon every day. Tiredness was surely written in my DNA. It wasn't something to worry about.

At fourteen, something else started to seep into me. There didn't seem to be rhyme or reason to it. I woke up one day, and everything felt just a little off kilter. There was a heaviness pressing on top of my spine, causing me to think crookedly. I had sudden bursts of intense anger, I was so overwhelmed by myself.

That's her hormones, my mother tells my brother, as I throw another tantrum, smashing a plate on the floor and screaming hatred to everyone. *Marise's horbones*, my brother repeats, making my mum laugh. *Shut the fuck up!* I scream at them. I keep screaming – at my family, and my friends, and my teachers. I have so much anger pulsing through me, but I don't know the root of it, an explanation for why I am this way.

My mother brings me to the doctor the morning after I attack her. That is her word: attack. I can't remember what she is talking about. The word rolls around my head. Attack. Like an animal.

The doctor puts me on 60mg of Prozac. No one uses the word depressed, so I don't know that is what I am. To get my prescription, I have to attend a children's clinic every second week, and meet with a man in a suit who asks me how I feel. No one uses the word therapy, so I don't know that is what it is. My dad picks me up from school every second Tuesday at 3pm, and drives me over. We never speak about where he is driving me to. I sit in the waiting room, with little kids playing on the floor. I feel pathetic, sharing a waiting room with a bunch of five-year-olds. What childish problems I have that a toddler can share them. *Grow up*, I urge myself. *Snap out of this.*

Every second Tuesday afternoon, I sit opposite Dr Edama for our therapy session. I spend the hour glaring at him. He asks me questions, about how I feel or what is on my mind, and I stare back in silence. I treat his questions with suspicion. *Very nosy*, I think as he probes. I come from a family who pride ourselves on our silence; who bury our feelings as deep as they can go and slam shut the door. *I can't understand you, you're not making sense*, I spit out, when he pronounces a word wrong. *Yes, my accent is quite thick*, he replies, smiling at me. *Well, speak properly*, I say back. When you're fourteen years old, you are well versed at being a bitch. You know how to hurt other people with ease.

Dr Edama resorts to reading out statements during our sessions. He asks me how much I agree with them, from one to ten. I always choose an eight. *Everything can't be an eight*, he warns, after two sessions of *eight, eight, eight. Well, it is*. I hate sitting in this room, and I hate him, because if he wasn't there, I wouldn't have to be either. I spend a year going to see Dr Edama every second week, and I never say more than eight.

I knew there was something wrong with me, but I believed the wrongness was flowing through my veins, right alongside my blood. It was as much a part of me as my kidneys and lungs and left knee. If I was cracked open and the badness was scooped out, I really believed there would be nothing left behind. So I protected it, thinking I was protecting myself. I never gave him the chance to help me. You can't help someone who refuses to admit they need help. They have to crack themselves open, even just a tiny chink, before anyone else can come in. Back then, I couldn't grasp that I needed cracking open. I didn't see the cause and effect between my dad and myself. It would take me another ten years before I was able to look at the wounds inside of me, show them to others and ask for help. So I told Dr Edama, *eight, eight, yes, another eight*, and smirked at his frustration. Thinking I had somehow won.

The Prozac didn't make me better, either. Prozac took away everything that was left of me, so I was a walking zombie. It voided me of feeling. It took away the bad, but also all the good. Life went from a shitty array of colour to a constant sludge of grey, and rendered me such a vegetable I couldn't even articulate that.

I knew the Prozac was supposed to fix the depression, because I had googled 'Why do you take Prozac?', but I didn't see myself as depressed. Depression was for tragic figures, like Sylvia Plath and Eeyore. It wasn't for normal people like me. Even my dad, who had tried to kill himself, wasn't really depressed. He was just mad, and an alcoholic, and a drama queen. If he had been depressed, he would have said it to me, and he never said it.

I keep gulping down the Prozac, even though I'm not depressed, because I know there's *something* wrong with me, and if anything can save me, it has to be the thing I got on a prescription. Doctors don't lie, not like normal people do. They're similar to priests in that they're removed from ordinary people; they're one step closer to divine. A doctor prescribed this to me, so either the Prozac will save me, or else I am just a rotten apple, someone who should be tossed out in the trash. I need the Prozac to save me, because it's the only thing that can. Day after day, week after week, month after month, I shove those pills into me, waiting for my absolution.

Out of all the badness I have felt in my life, being on Prozac was the worst. I felt like I was living underwater, each step I took laborious and dragging. Any time I would speak or think, a water bubble would pop up in front of me, containing nothing. I was in slow motion, and no matter how much effort I put in, I couldn't move faster than a sloth. I couldn't even remember what it felt like to feel anything. Not anger or sadness or joy. I lost all my tears. Prozac took away everything and left a vacuum in its place, a flimsy replica of real life. I might have looked like me, but I wasn't me. *If this is getting better,* I thought, *please let me die.*

Please, just let me die, I beg, lying in my bed. *This isn't working, and I know that's my fault, so please just take me. Give someone else my place, someone who knows how to exist in this world. I don't know how to be happy, so just fucking let me die.*

There are so many lost memories from that time of my life. I don't remember much, except the hazy feeling of nothing, of watching myself instead of living as myself, and being convinced I wouldn't be alive by my eighteenth birthday. I couldn't fathom a reality in which this went away. I never thought any of it was Prozac's fault at the time. I didn't know medication could be wrong. I didn't think you could question a doctor's expertise.

They have spent years studying this stuff, and you're just a stupid teenager, I thought to myself. If a doctor gave it to me, it must be right. I took medication when I was sick, and it made me better. I thought this had to be the same. I just wasn't trying hard enough. I just wasn't good enough.

2

I have wanted to die so many times, but I've never really wanted to be dead. Wanting to die is my solution when I don't know how to get out of a bad situation, when my mind is too unhinged to think logically. The simple thought that would get me out of it is *This feeling will pass.* But I'm unable to think that when I'm in it. It swallows me whole.

It's not depression. It happens when I am depressed, but depression and wanting to kill myself are separate things for me. Depression is that hazy fog, where I sleep fourteen hours a day and am still so tired. It slowly creeps up on me. I wake up one morning and I haven't showered for five days. *How is it Friday already? At least it's only June. Oh, fuck, it's October?* That's what depression is. Always fucking October.

Wanting to kill myself is different. It almost gives me energy. It's exciting, but it also makes me feel at peace. It's the missing piece to the 5,000-piece puzzle. It's a sudden quick rush that engulfs me, consumes me, and I can't think of anything else because it's so fucking tantalizing. It's usually over something trivial, something that is not a thing at all. But the stupid hazy fog of depression doesn't let me see that.

The first time I want to die, I am sixteen. I have a half boyfriend. His name is Euan. He is six foot two, with thick black hair and broad shoulders. His big hands hold my cheeks as he kisses me, and I know he could crush my whole face, if he wanted to. He speaks slowly, in that careful way people whose native tongue isn't English talk. There's a military precision to the words he speaks. Nothing is said that he couldn't back up in a court of law. No thought of his slips out by mistake. When we are together, I don't have that same filter. I spill out parts of myself quickly, saying words I'm not even sure are the truth, and I keep going when he doesn't interrupt. It's only after four months that I realize I know very little about him, but he might know even less about me. *You don't say much*, I say to him one night, when we are in my bedroom and I am wearing my school uniform, my knee-high socks falling down my calves. He shrugs. *You talk for both of us.* And I laugh. *Brooding,* I think dreamily, when I look at his closed mouth, *exactly how a man should be.*

He grew up in Africa, and carries a knife around with him, just because. I find that exciting. *He's different*, I tell my friends. *I know he's white, but he's actually African.* A few weeks earlier he had brought me to a shitty hotel, and I sucked his dick for the first time, then freaked out and locked myself in the bathroom, missing our dinner reservation. We ate Burger King at midnight, and then slept in separate beds. For Valentine's Day, he bought me a necklace. I thanked him, and threw the box into my wardrobe. I didn't want to hurt his feelings, but it was hideous. He doesn't seem to notice that I never wear it.

I say he is my half boyfriend, because there is another guy called Pascal, who collects me in his car every Friday night. Pascal has curly blond hair and an Adam's apple that bulges through his neck. He has scrawny hands, and when I watch him change gears in his car, I think about how different they are to Euan's. If Pascal tried to kill me, I'm not sure who would win. I go on these car dates with Pascal because Euan doesn't give me enough attention. He goes days without texting me, and when he does show up, he never gives me enough to feel full. I need someone to supplement what he gives me, so I respond to every text Pascal sends. *Tonight?* I read from my phone screen. *I'm waiting*, I reply.

Pascal pulls into McDonald's every Friday night, and we get Cokes, and then drive up to the mountains and sixty-nine on his back seat. I always pretend to come. It seems like the polite thing to do. I don't feel bad about what I do, that I am letting another boy come in my throat when I already have someone who gives me a Valentine's card. When I think about both of them, I decide they make up one full boy. Someone I could maybe love. Except I definitely don't love Euan, and I'm not sure I even like him. We have nothing in common, and I hardly ever think of him when I'm not around him. And yet.

I am sixteen, and depressed, and still don't understand what that means. Tonight, I am supposed to meet Euan. I text him to ask when he's picking me up, and he doesn't respond. He doesn't respond to the next ten messages I send. And then, it happens. I become a toxic mixture of frantic and despondent. It almost feels good, this terrible feeling of rejection. It doesn't matter who is at the hand of it, what matters is that it floods my whole body and I feel alive. I am not tired, for the first time in a long time. I am full of a terrible energy that is burning through my body.

It feels so good, until it doesn't. It's too much now, and I want to get away from it. I throw my phone across the room, so I can't see it. I lie in my bed, lights off, hoping to go to sleep. I'll wake up tomorrow, or maybe the day after that, or maybe I'll sleep for a month, but when I wake up, this will be over. My heart is racing and I can feel the thump thump thump against my chest, and I'm shaking. I'm never going to get to sleep with this pumping through me. I get up out of my bed and walk over to my dresser. I'm not sure what I'm looking for, but I know, once I find it, I'll be right again. I open up my bag of medication and thumb my birth control. I get really bad periods that wake me up in the middle of the night and have me grabbing my stomach, crying out in agony. My doctor prescribed this to make the pain go away. And it did. I throw the tabs of pills back in the bag. I take out my Prozac. 60mg. There's a three-month supply here. I pop out one pill, and swallow it. This feels like the right thing to do.

I run downstairs, and there's a skip in my step. I grab a big glass of water from the sink. *I'm just thirsty*, I tell myself. I go back to my room and sit on my bed. The light is still off, and I feel around for the pack of pills. I quickly pop another out and swallow. And again and again and again. There's an urgency now; I need to finish them all, otherwise they'll burn a hole in my duvet. I take thirty, forty, fifty pills. I'm gagging now when I swallow, so I pinch my nose and keep going. I stop at sixty.

I don't know at sixteen that it's almost impossible to overdose on antidepressants, so, as I sit on my bed, in darkness, and breathe out, I think I will die. Everything feels calm. *This is the right thing to do.* I think I'm meditating.

I sit there for what feels like two hours, but is really ten minutes. The thoughts rush back in as quickly as they left. *Oh God what have I done fuck I am an idiot why did I do this my parents my brother why would I do this?*

I am running to the bathroom. Before I know what is happening, I am sticking my fingers down my throat. I gag, and nothing comes out. I do it again. And again. Tears are streaming down my face, and piss is slowly streaming down my leg, making my pyjamas wet. I go deeper and deeper until I hit the right spot. The vomit burns on the way up. It's thick and slimy. It doesn't hurl out of me; it slides along the bathroom bowl, slowly. I keep pushing and there's a pool of piss on the floor now, because I'm trying so hard. The acoustics from the tiles make my retches echo.

I'm sixteen, and I don't know that if I had taken something toxic, it would already be swirling inside my bloodstream, so vomiting it out might not save me. I don't know that yet, so I think I am saved.

I crawl back to my bedroom, on my hands and knees, weeping. I feel both sorry and angry at myself. *Poor Marise, you victim, you don't deserve this*, I think on one hand. *Bad Marise, you perpetrator, you deserve this*, I think on another. The two thoughts fight it out in my head, lovers in an argument, throwing plates at each other, screaming at the top of their lungs. I cover my ears with my hands, but the screaming doesn't lessen. It only intensifies. Bang! Bang! Bang! *Poor girl! Stupid girl! Worthless girl.*

I see a dandelion in front of me, and I reach out to blow. *Live, die, live, die, live.* Before I can finish it, and get my answer, it is flattened by a steel-toed boot. Bang! Bang! The boot is kicking my head now, stomping over me. The noise of my thoughts is being drowned out by a piercing ringing. It's all inside my head. I slap the side of my face, hoping the bad thoughts fall out. But nothing happens. Maybe I need to hit harder. I slam my head against the wall, and again. *Get the fuck out of me*, I scream out to an empty room. *Leave me alone.*

My parents come home close to midnight. I am crying in my bed, feeling slightly out of it, my jaw chewing on itself. My dad comes into my room and sits by my bed. I tell him what I've done. I don't know why. The words just come out, and then there they are. *You fucking idiot*, he says to me. I bury my head in my pillow. How rich. Him, of all people, calling me an idiot. Maybe things look different when you're peering in from the outside. Maybe he forgets. *All over a boy*, he adds. He's got a tone to his voice like he's relishing this role of wise man, preaching from his throne. I'm too weak to fight him, so I just whisper, *I'm sorry*, over and over again, until he grabs my head into his chest, holding me. He rocks me slightly, until I fall asleep. I am embarrassed at what I tried to do. Embarrassed at how easily I took it back. Embarrassed that my dad looked into the mirror and thought, *Pathetic*. At least I know this won't be mentioned again. I'm lucky to be part of a family that buries our defects deep within us. The only embarrassment is in remembering.

3

It went away the same way it arrived: slowly, without me noticing at first. I looked around one day, and I was eighteen, and felt normal, and couldn't remember not feeling normal for a long time. *I was just being dramatic*, I thought to myself. *None of that was real. It was all inside my head.* Depression is always that illusive. All-consuming when inside it, but so easy to dismiss when you step one foot outside its grasp.

I had a momentary slip in my final year of university – four months of bed rest, sleeping fourteen hours a day, not showering or eating. Nothing bad had happened – there wasn't anything to pinpoint the change. Nothing I could grab hold of and say, *This is it*. Instead, a heaviness just attacked my body, so I couldn't move. When I made it into class, people complimented me on my weight loss. *You look incredible!* they told me. *Whatever you're doing, keep it up!* My doctor was less enthusiastic. She put me back on medication: Lexapro this time. I cried in her office when she wrote the prescription. It felt like she was signing off my fate for the rest of my life – it wasn't childish bullshit; this is who you are.

I couldn't accept it, so I didn't take the pills. I let them collect in my drawer instead. I decided they would be insurance; if I ever got to a place where I wanted to kill myself, I would have the tools to do it painlessly. I definitely didn't want to kill myself, but I also didn't trust myself not to ever want to. So, I kept them, just in case. As I hoarded those pills, I did other things, things that I believed would stop me ever getting there. I taped a Kurt Vonnegut quote to my wall. *I urge you to please notice when you are happy, and exclaim or murmur or think at some point, 'If this isn't nice, I don't know what is.'* I memorized the words. I repeated them in my head each night when I was going to sleep. Forcing them into my brain. I wrote a list of things that made me happy on the back of a McDonald's receipt. The smell of garlic on my fingers, roller coasters, fresh sheets, comedy shows. I rewrote the same list every time I found a new receipt in my bag. I thought that if I did it enough, it would become muscle memory. I would remember how to feel happy, and it would be so burned into my psyche I wouldn't ever forget again. And it worked. I started to feel better. *A false alarm*, I thought, relieved. And if that isn't nice, I don't know what is.

4

Three months after my dad dies, I move to Amsterdam to start my Master's programme. I collect the keys to a tiny studio apartment, with the heating included in the rent. I stock up my fridge with vegetables and cold-pressed juice, smiling at the cashier. I Instagram a photo of one bottle. *#greenjuicehealthymind*. I force myself to be happy, because he obviously hadn't been, and I am damned if I'm going to follow in his footsteps. I show up to the first day of classes in my favourite navy jumper, with a crisp white shirt underneath. *How fucking studious*, I decide, catching my reflection in the classroom window.

I cycle through the Amsterdam streets, making sure to appreciate all the trees dusting off autumn. *Gorgeous colours*, I think, and snap a photo of the fallen leaves. *#lifeisgood*. I sit in the front row of the auditorium, my notebook open and two different-coloured pens lined up beside it. I am ready. *Hello, class,* my lecturer begins, *welcome to the next chapter of your lives*. I smile back at him. I decide it's going to be a good one.

As is always in life, the initial excitement fades away into a routine. I get home from class every day and crank the thermostat up full blast, hanging in my underwear. I guzzle down awful green juices, plugging my nose as I swallow. When I look out my fifth-storey window, I see grey concrete and murky canals. If I squint, I can't tell which is which. At the weekends, I can go a full three days without saying a word to another person, just sitting in my studio in my underwear, sweating. I feel myself beginning to slip. College is hard. I don't know the basic maths they are teaching. Everything accelerates at a rate I can't keep up with, and I don't have any friends. I am not eating my lunch in a toilet cubicle, but I don't connect with the people I am sitting across from. Sometimes it's lonelier to be around a group of ten people you can't relate to than it is to be by yourself. When I shove a spoon of potatoes into my mouth, pretending to laugh at a joke I don't get, I feel hollow.

I am slipping, but so slowly it's barely noticeable. Maybe it's just in my head. Or maybe it's real. My dad's recent death is a stark warning of what could be, and I decide to take the warning seriously. *I am not my father's daughter*, I tell myself. *I can get through this*. I sign up for yoga classes, and cycle over every morning, my mat tucked under my arm. I push open the door and the hot air mixed with too much sage overwhelms me. *Very intense*, I say to the receptionist, coughing. She beams. *Amazing, isn't it?* I stretch and twist and hold for ninety minutes and, at the end of the class, will myself into a meditative state.

It doesn't work, but at least from the outside, lying on my mat, sweat dripping down my exposed stomach, I must look at peace. *A healthy body is a healthy mind*, I remind myself, as I shove some free tea bags into my backpack on the way out. I don't even like tea! But it's something healthy people drink, so I force it into me.

At home, I practise every evening on my mat, doing handstands over and over again until I am dizzy. I set up my self-timer to capture my scorpion pose. *#bendybodybendysoul*. I eat pancakes made with coconut sugar for breakfast, and quinoa salads for lunch. In the evening, I brush my hair and apply mascara, then pinch my cheeks to make them look healthy. I change into a fresh pair of €100 leggings, and cycle over to a café in my neighbourhood. I order a vegan salad while trying to do my homework. I take a picture of spinach entering my mouth. *#cleaneating*. If I can look the part, that very curated image of healthy, it is only a matter of time before it seeps into my bones too.

Despite doing all the right things, despite forcing myself to be happy, and all the hashtags that go along with that, my mind continues to slip. When I lie in bed at night, after a day of yoga and salads and smiling at strangers, my head still wanders into a bad place. *You'd be better off dead.* That thought attacks me, over and over. I don't know where it's even come from, because I'm drinking enough spinach juice to make Popeye jealous. I've come in all guns blazing, and still it overpowers me. I know I can't fight this kind of thought with just chia seeds, so I go looking for outside help. The doctor is free in Amsterdam, and she refers me to a therapist, who is also free. My therapist is a beautiful woman named Yvonne, who has long blonde hair and a tiny nose and massive tits, which are not important per se, but they are noticeable. She welcomes me into her office and sets out a plan of action. We start with CBT – Cognitive

Behavioural Therapy. *This will help you understand your thoughts and the patterns around them. It's a very successful method.* It doesn't work. *You're not giving me enough*, she tells me during one session. I think back to Dr Edama and the questionnaires. *But I'm giving so much more than I did.* Somehow, that isn't good enough.

Seven weeks later, she repeats that same sentiment. *You aren't giving enough. This isn't working out.* I am floored. I didn't know therapists could break up with a patient. I assumed that was against the law. *I don't think I can see you any longer.* Is this a Dutch thing? I'm here. I show up to her office almost every week. How is that not enough? How can't she see I'm trying so fucking hard, just by being here? *I want to get better, that's why I'm here*, I think to myself. I see the words dance in front of me, and they're strangers. So I don't say them. I'm not sure if they're true. Do I really want to get better, or do I just want to fail at getting better? So I can say to myself, *At least I tried*?

I say nothing. Not because I'm feeling nothing, but because I don't know how to transfer those feelings into words. I've spent so long pushing them down they're barely recognizable to me. I am trying to make sense of them, but I'm not doing it quickly enough. It's like the maths in class. I am trying, but that doesn't matter if I'm still failing. *We don't give marks for trying*, my professor tells me. We are looking through the mid-term test that I have failed. I had almost all the concepts right, but I made stupid arithmetic mistakes. I forgot to carry the 1. So, my final answers are wrong. But they were right, right up until I made that tiny mistake. *My dad's dead*, I offer up feebly. He ignores it. The Dutch don't care about trying, or that my dad is dead. They care about the final result. And so, I fail.

I cycle home and get into my single bed. I don't get out of it for five days, except to piss and eat a loaf of bread. I miss all my classes and one assignment. I'm not worried; that professor is American. I'll tell him my dad just died and he'll surely let me off. *Your dad's death is the gift that keeps giving*, Conell says, laughing, when I tell him how often I play that card.

I don't feel sad, I just feel heavy. My bones are so heavy, they're pulling me down every step I take, and my head is a fuzzy haze, like when you turn on the TV and there's no signal. That black and white buzzing. I have to stay in bed, because I don't have any energy to move. When I finally get up, it's to go to the grocery shop and I have to drag myself there. I buy ingredients to make sandwiches for the next week. Tomato, cheese, bread, chorizo. When I get home, I have to lie down. It's all so exhausting. I close my curtains and lie on my bed, staring at the ceiling. It feels like an hour, then suddenly it's a week. I get up, take a shower and go buy those same groceries again.

This continues for a month, until one rainy Tuesday I force myself back into class. And a new routine grows. I wash my face, then make breakfast. I cycle to school, sit through lectures, cycle to the grocery shop and cycle back home. I assemble a sandwich and eat. I lie back in my bed and sleep. I buy one beer a week that I drink on a Friday, only so I don't lose track of time. I am drinking a beer, so it must be Friday evening. Another week down. That is all I do, for three months. There are no thoughts in my head. I don't think about how I feel, or what is happening. Anything else but what I'm doing seems impossible; this is already too much.

After my therapist fires me, I meet with the general doctor every week instead. It's not so I can get better, though; it's so I don't get worse. *I read a story in the paper about somebody dying, because their bike got caught in the tram tracks during the rain*, she tells me one day. *I was worried it was you.* I dig my fingers into my palm, because it's an easy thing to do to distract me from this room, and her. *Well, it wasn't,* I say, smiling,

I'm still here. I'm glad you are, she tells me softly. I pinch my palm, hard. The quick jolt of pain reminds me that I am here. Here. I stare at the concrete wall behind her. The framed photo on her desk, facing away from me. The wrinkles around her eyes. Here, here, here. *I'm lucky*, I say. *Lucky to be here.*

My doctor prescribes me sleeping pills. *To help you sleep*, she says. My problem isn't sleeping, though; it's getting up. I don't tell her that. I know these can be insurance. I collect them from the pharmacy every week, and add them to my collection. One week, then two, then a month. Now I have three months. *That's enough to die*, I think. And I breathe out.

One Thursday night, at the grocery store, I am wandering through the aisles, picking up things and placing them back down mindlessly. I go to pick up my usual beer. But then I find myself placing it back down, instead picking up two bottles of wine. *I want to have fun*, I think to myself. I am suddenly very tired of feeling nothing. I circle back through the store and add expensive cheese and pizza and homemade energy balls to my basket. Kombucha and lemonade and herbal tea. Quinoa and lemons and doughnuts. Two different types of hot sauce.

I keep adding until my basket is overflowing, and the organic natural crisps fall out. This is my life, God damn it, and I'm going to feel it. I cycle home with excitement, passing other cyclists on the way, a race between myself and everyone else. I make small talk with a guy in my elevator, and tell him to have a good night when I reach the fifth floor, and mean it. We all should be having so many good nights. I try to fry the pizza on the stove, because when I bought it I forgot I didn't have an oven. It's burned in some places, and soft dough in others. I still eat it. I drink my wine, and dance around my studio in my underwear, listening to Chance the Rapper. *Rap just make me anxious, and acid made me crazy, Na na nanana na*. I text old friends, telling them I love them. I feel happy. I feel alive.

I dance over to my insurance box, and take out my sleeping pills. *Na na nana*. I pop one, and another, and another. I'm still dancing, and happy. *I want to die*, I scream over the music, laughing. And I pop, pop, pop. I take more than thirty. I wash them down with more wine. *Na na nana*.

I am twirling around in my kitchen, smoking a joint, turning and turning and oh shit – I realize what I have done. In one quick swoop, everything stops being fun. I put out the joint on my stomach, feeling the hot burn surge through me. Localizing my pain. *Fuck fuck fuck*. I am frantically pacing my studio, trying to think what I can do to get myself out of this, but my mind can't keep up with what is happening; it's gone blank. I email my boyfriend in Chicago. I plan to tell him I love him, but the words my fingers type and the words that end up on the screen are not the same. *I'm so sorry I'm sorry I did something dumb I am so sorry*. Chance is still playing in the background as I type. I read what I've sent to him and shut down the laptop in horror. I take two more sleeping pills and hold my pillow over my head. Just fucking be over already. Going, going, just be gone.

5

I wake up the next day with a pounding headache, my tongue stuck to the roof of my mouth. When I peel it away, I wince. Did I eat a pack of fucking chalk last night? I cover my head with my pillow and feel around the bed for my phone. I peek one eye out from the delicious cold pillow, and the bright screen shoots into my brain. *Jesus Christ*, I shout out, and then grimace at the sharpness of my voice. Everything is too fucking bright and loud. 14:32 flashes on the screen. I sit up. Shit, shit, fucking shit. I see multiple emails from my boyfriend, an ocean away. Oh fuckidy fuck. I slowly piece together what happened last night, assembling the jigsaw of what I did. I get close to the finished picture and then slap my phone against my head, trying to unscramble it. I roll over and stuff my face into the pillow, cringing. *AHHHHH! How! Fucking! Embarrassing!* I delete the emails before I can read them, before I have to really acknowledge they exist. I scroll down further and see two missed calls from my doctor. I call her back immediately, knowing she'll be worried something bad has happened, and I don't want her to overreact. She answers after two rings. *I am so, so sorry*, I rush out. *I slept through our appointment, I forgot to set an alarm*. The air hangs heavy between us. *You don't sound right*, she eventually says. *You are slurring your words*. I blink. Am I? *Are you...are you okay?* It's not the words she says, but the gentleness of her voice, piping hot with concern, that makes me spill out the truth. *I am so sorry, I, I took loads of pills last night I don't know why I didn't mean it God I am sorry this is so fucking mortifying.*

Twenty-five minutes later there are paramedics pounding on my door. I stand up, unsteady, and walk over, letting them both in. They instruct me to sit back down. I only have two chairs, so one of them stands awkwardly by the bathroom door. I see dirty underwear on the floor beside him, and hurry over to kick it under the bed. I smile, embarrassed. *I wasn't expecting company...* Neither of them smile back. I'm not sure of the protocol, should I offer them something to drink? I look over at my sink, at the two empty wine bottles beside it, and decide against it. It's not my problem if they're thirsty. I didn't invite them over.

They unload their equipment and check my heartbeat and my pupils, and ask me twenty questions. I answer them all while looking at the floor. Their little machine beeps back at them. *Your vitals are normal*, I hear. *That's good, right?*

I ask weakly. *Everything's good?* They ignore me, and confer in Dutch, making a decision about me that I am not privy to. I am suddenly furious at myself for never bothering to Duolingo the language. They could be saying anything right now; calling me stupid or crazy, deciding to lock me up and throw away the key. Or they could be complaining that I am a dumb little bitch who is wasting their time, precious time that could be spent saving people in actual trouble. Or, for all I know, they are planning their lunch, trying to decide between McDonald's and a kebab. The not knowing is making my heart race. I chew at my thumb, pulling away skin with my teeth, watching the blood flood my nail bed. *Come on, guys!* I want to say. *You're not deciding the score of an Olympic gymnast's routine. Hurry it up.* I clear my throat. *Everything is good, right?* I ask them, firm but forceful, like I already know the answer. They look at each other. *Yes, you are okay, so we will leave.*

I sink back in my bed once I hear the door shut. I feel relieved. If something bad had happened, they wouldn't have left me here. If something bad had really happened, there would be alarm bells ringing in my ears. Instead, I stare at my ceiling in silence. Whatever I did wasn't serious. I was just being a dumb bitch, looking for attention. I feel a weight lift from me once I realize that. When enough time has gone by, when I have breathed out all the bad that wasn't really there, when I feel positively light, ready to levitate off my bed, I call my boyfriend. I am calm, ready to explain everything, to rationalize what happened. When he answers my call, he's already crying. *I thought you were dead*, he says, his voice high and somehow so small. He sounds like a child. *Please don't ever do that again, please.* He sounds more scared than I've ever heard a person be, so I throw out all the words I was ready to say, and make a promise to him that I'm not sure I can keep. *I am so sorry. I'll never do this to you again, I swear.*

I can't keep doing this to people, I think later that night. *I need to commit, or stop.* I count the empty pill pockets scattered on my floor. Thirty. So thirty is the magic number.

I continue stockpiling my antidepressants and sleeping pills. After a month, I've replenished my supplies. I cycle back from the pharmacy and delicately place the paper bag on my bedside drawer. It sort of looks like a shrine. I eyeball the pills, counting them up in my head. I pop one out, fingering it around the palm of my hand, like a bowling ball that keeps spinning, and I'm not sure if it will fall into the drain or give me a strike. That gamble is so fucking tantalizing. I lift the pill to my mouth. I kiss it, just to feel it against my skin.

I didn't actually promise that I wouldn't do it again. I just said I wouldn't do it to him. I turn off my phone, and stick the pill in my mouth. I let my saliva disintegrate it, the bitter taste making me gag. I wash it down with gone-off coconut water from my fridge. I pop another. And another. I keep going, until I reach thirty, and stop there. Now that I know I can't die with thirty, I let myself enjoy the effects. I splay out on my floor, the cool tiles tickling my body. I smile as I lie there. My mind starts to leave my body, slowly moving up into the room, dancing over me. A small enough gap that I can reach back down and come back to myself, but enough distance that I can still be removed from who I am.

I swallow thirty pills every time I feel empty, in the hope it will make me full. And it works, briefly. For a couple of hours, I am so high I can't remember anything that led up to it. For a few beautiful hours every month, I am allowed to forget.

6

One morning in spring, I wake up with stabbing pains in my stomach. They are piercing the insides of me. I cry in pain, but no one is here who can hear me. I sit in this agony for half an hour, then put on my coat and shoes. I am not wired to handle pain very well. I begin the mile and a half to my doctor's office. I am a mile in, and the pain becomes unbearable. I fall off my bike, lying down on the street, clutching my stomach. A group of tourists come over and help me up, flagging me down a taxi. *Lock up my bike*, I say to them. And they do. They pay for the taxi, which I don't realize at the time. Good people exist, and they're all around us, if only we are able to look.

At the doctor's office, when I have stumbled out of the car, and a strong arm has guided me inside, I am surprised to see it belongs to a man. *Where are the women?* He ignores me. *I need the woman*, I say, confused, unable to remember my doctor's name. He sits me down on a chair, without any of the delicateness a woman gives naturally. I start to cry. *Please give me the woman.* He shrugs. *I am all there is right now.*

I try to tell him what is happening, try to describe what I am feeling, but I am in so much pain most words don't come out. He loads up a syringe and injects me with morphine. He tells me it's morphine when he removes the needle from my thigh. *Wait, no, wait. The woman.* I blink, slowly, and then there is an ambulance, sirens silent but lights flashing, and two men are loading me onto a stretcher. *Will I die?* I ask, and one of the men smiles at me. *You'll be okay, let's just get you to the hospital.* I cry the whole twenty-minute journey. A blank male face stares back at me, looking over at some equipment when I reach out for his hand. *Please, I need you*, I beg, but he focuses on the wires coming out of the rectangular box in front of him. I am mortified at my want, at how much I am laying it bare in front of me. I know I should be stronger than this, but I'm not. I'm so fucking weak.

Once I'm wheeled into a room in the hospital, after I've been shifted to a bed, I stand up and projectile vomit across the room. The nurse come in, furious. *Why didn't you tell us you were going to be sick?*

I didn't know, I offer back feebly. I thought morphine was supposed to make you feel better. A doctor comes around and asks for my symptoms and my history. I don't tell him about the pills and my depression. That is mental, and this is physical. I don't tell him because I don't think to tell him – they are separate problems. They run all sorts of tests and keep me overnight. I fall asleep easily and wake up the next day at 3pm. *You sure slept a lot*, the nurse coos at me. *Must be the morphine*, she adds. *Mmmhmm, must be.*

The doctor comes around an hour later, when I am shovelling jelly into my mouth. *The tests all came back fine. You're very healthy. We're not sure what happened here.* I nod along. He discharges me, and I walk out of the hospital holding a plastic bag with my belongings. When the sun hits my face, I stumble backward. I sit down on the side of the street, trying to figure out where to go from here. I thought I was hours away from the city, but when I check my phone, I'm only a thirty-minute walk from my flat. I get up and put one foot in front of the other. I unlock my door, on automatic, and get into bed. Once under the safety of my duvet, I don't leave for a week. *There's nothing wrong with you*, I tell myself over and over again. *They tested for everything. It's all in your head.*

7

Because of the multiple old men I fucked in LA, I can afford a one-bed apartment on my return to Amsterdam. I marvel at the door separating my bedroom from my kitchen. *What luxury*, I murmur. One month turns to five. My classes are over. I passed by the skin of my teeth. I have just my thesis left to write, and then I'm done. And I can write that anywhere. I have no reason to stay in this city anymore, but I am still here. For a reason I'm unclear on, I feel anchored to Amsterdam.

I am living right on a canal. I have a view of the water from my balcony. When I lean over the metal rail, hearing the water softly splash against the canal's banks, I feel at home. I am drawn to a job in a members-only club. I knock on their door, my CV crumpled in my hand. A fat woman answers and beckons me inside. She looks me up and down, and ignores the paper I'm holding. *Do you have clothes that are more sexy? Short skirts and low-cut tops, that type of thing?* I nod. *Great! And do you know how to handle men?* I'm not sure if it's a trick question. I look at her face, and it gives me none of the answers. *I, uh, yea, sure, I know men. I know what they want. I, uh, I think I know how to make myself into what they want.* She nods. I loosen up. *I know how to use men, if that's what you mean?* She tells me I can start next week.

I put in hair extensions before each shift, clipping long blonde strands to the back of my head. I wear short skirts and thigh-high boots, circling layers of bright red lipstick on my mouth in the dressing room provided for the girls. I survey my reflection, convinced I look like a clown. But in this job, how I feel is irrelevant. I only exist in relation to the customer. And he likes red lipstick, so I apply another layer. I think about getting lip injections. I've looked at my lips long enough in the mirror to know they're lopsided. I used to be proud of my lips; they were just like my dad's, and he got them from his father. They were an heirloom passed down between us, but now I want to correct the generations before me; I want to make my lips perfect. One of the girls sends me her doctor's number. *He can fix that*, she tells me, waving her hand at my mouth. I make an appointment.

The degrees of separation between myself and pretty are getting smaller. It feels good. I visit a clinic that uses lasers to burn off cellulite. I part with €350 for ten treatments. I order whitening strips from the internet. They burn my teeth, but I keep them on for the recommended time. The separation decreases. If I'm lucky, soon I won't be able to recognize myself.

I set myself up in the bar, the dim lighting making it hard to decipher the different mixers. I use the flash on my phone to pour myself a rum and Coke. I knock it back in three quick gulps, and pour another. When a customer sits himself at the bar, I lean towards him, closer than I need to be. The music is blaring around us, and I use that as an excuse to brush my lips against his ear. He smiles, and I rub my lipstick from his cheek. *Sorry for that, babe*, I say, and his smile grows wider.

I cycle home in the early mornings, exhausted. But I like the tired feeling. How I can feel it in every part of my body. All the coke I am doing in my job starts to spill over, so I am bringing little baggies home, only because I don't like to waste. I finger the plastic in my pocket as I hear the water crashing against the ferry. The comfort pumps through my veins.

I stay up until seven o'clock every morning, probably because of the coke. I pace around my apartment, chain-smoking in the living room, taking lines every hour, writing my thesis about ISIS. When I first presented the idea to my advisor, he was excited. *Trying to find rationality in a terrorist group, how interesting*, he told me in his cramped office. *Maths isn't prejudiced, so you might be able to decipher some predictability from the group.* I nodded as he spoke. *So, you approve?* He slammed his hands down on the desk. *With gusto. Maths sometimes has the answers that emotion can't see. This could be something very special, if you work hard enough.*

He now replies to my progress with less enthusiasm. *None of this maths makes sense, try again,* and *There's no coherency here, try again.* I go to sleep each morning, and when I wake up, it's dark again. I don't see sunlight for a few months. You need to see light in order to remember it exists. It's unnerving how quickly you can forget.

One night, my laptop freezes. It's a new MacBook Pro that three different men I was sleeping with in LA paid for. They each thought they were the only one, so I made a profit on it. I walk out onto my balcony and throw the laptop down, into the water. It doesn't make much of a noise. I ignore how empty that makes me feel – how the water can just eat up something that is, and a second later, it's like it never existed at all. *Fuck you, Steve Jobs,* I yell, *I won't be confined by technology.* I walk back inside and snort another line. I start writing my thesis out on paper, which I then burn with a lighter. These words were there, and now they're not. I am God. I laugh, and take another bump.

As I pace my living room, I get into a habit of pulling my hair out. I tear strands out, collecting them in the palm of my hand, and don't know what to do with them once they're there. To counter this problem, one night I shave half of it off. Thick, long clumps of hair stare at me from the floor, and I leave them there. I touch my baldness as I watch beheading videos, for research, and feel a tingle down my spine.

At three o'clock every morning, when most of the world is asleep, I walk out of my building and lie on the concrete beside the canal. During daylight, these canals are a comfort to me. Their ebbing and flowing reminds me that I still ebb and flow; that I exist. Once the sun goes down, it becomes more sinister.

These bodies of water remind me how other bodies can just slip away inside of them. How they can quietly engulf the people who don't want to exist anymore.

I drum my fingers against the side of the bank, hearing the soft waves splash against me. I think of my dad, and what he might have been thinking when he threw himself in. Did I enter his mind? Did he hate me? Did he think I hated him? Does it even matter? I dip my foot in the water. The cold shocks me. I wonder what it would take to fall into its grasp. Just roll my body, from the cement to the water, and stay under. I wonder if I'd struggle; if my body would fight against my mind. I wonder who would win.

Seventeen minutes. That's how long it takes to drown yourself according to lostallhope.com, a website I have bookmarked that ranks suicide methods. It's a long time to commit to. I once watched a documentary on people who had jumped off the Golden Gate Bridge, the mecca of suicide. Every person who survived, when interviewed, said the same thing. As they were on the way down, they realized their problems weren't so bad, that they didn't want to die, they wanted to live. They got to, but so many didn't. Did the dead ones want to die the whole way down, right up until their bodies broke the water, or did they change their minds too?

I wonder what went through my dad's head during his seventeen minutes. If there was ever a point in those 1,020 seconds he wanted to take it back. Or if he wanted to die until his last breath. Did he fight against the water, or did he just sink, sink, sink?

I don't believe in God, but I talk to Him while I lie beside the canal. I know we're on bad terms because of all the masturbating I did as a child, and all the sex I've done as an adult. I know He's sent my dad to Hell, because suicide is a sin. *He looks in peace*, I remember my aunts saying at his open casket. But if God exists, He's thrown my dad to the devil. After drowning, he is in the pits of Hell. Lostallhope.com ranks death by fire as the number one worst way to kill yourself. My dad is suffering as much now as he did then. There's no absolution when your pain is of your own making.

I don't believe in God, because I know He doesn't exist; I've read 'The God Delusion'. I hate God, because He is punishing my father, and I'm the only one who should be allowed to do that. But I talk to Him, out loud, like we're old friends. I did go to mass every Sunday for twelve years. Sure, my mother made me, but I still showed up. That has to count for something.

I let Him know what ISIS are up to, just so He can be prepared. *I know you see everything, but have you seen their tweets?* I let Him know He has some competition, that there's another god out there, who people are dying for, right now, as we speak, so He might want to up His game.

I tell Him about my day. I describe the food I ate, and ask if He knows what a toasted cheese sandwich is. *I don't want to tell you how to live your life, but if you add hot sauce and jalapeños, it really elevates the meal.*

I ask Him for a sign. Not to live, but to die. Just a bird or a feather or something, anything, so I know He's signing off on this. He never responds, because He doesn't exist. *I know you aren't real!* I sometimes scream into the air, but I cross my fingers behind my back, just in case.

I haven't seen light in two months, but I know it exists, somewhere inside of me, because I don't do what my dad did. Each night after my chat with God, I get up from the canalside path and walk back to my apartment. I chug a bottle of water, my mouth dry from the talking and the coke. I get into my bed and pull my duvet over me, rubbing my cold toes against the warm blanket. That's the duality of water and heat. Too much will kill you, and just enough can keep you alive.

(What I am trying to say is that if I really wanted to kill myself, I would be dead.)

8

After three months of self-imposed exile, I grow paranoid. I am convinced someone will murder me if I leave my apartment. When I walk to the shop, I see groups of kids playing on the street, and I break out in a run, knowing they want to hunt me down. When people in my building smile at me as I walk up the stairs, I grab the knife in my pocket, ready for their attack. Someone is trying to kill me every time I leave my flat. So I stop leaving. I miss three weeks of shifts, and then am fired through email. *If you ever want to come back, you know where to find us*, I read. I count the stacks in my bedroom. Six grand. I can max out my credit card: another five grand. That's enough to retire on. I can stay here for the rest of my life.

I order food in, and don't unlatch the chain when the delivery guy arrives, forcing him to squeeze the plastic bag through the crack in the door. If I give him the chance, he'll try to kill me too. I think I want to die, but I want to do the killing. I don't want it outsourced to someone else.

I hold my pocketknife in my hand; a knife I ordered off the internet, for protection. It has a heavy wooden handle, and I grasp that heavy wooden handle as I imagine a perpetrator right in front of me. I slice through the air. I see a head tumble down in front of me. Like one of those ISIS videos. I stare at my left palm and see blood trickle down my arm. I glance around the room, wondering who has infiltrated my bunker. But the only person I can see is myself, staring back at me from a mirror. I kick down the mirror, smashing it in two. So then I am left with nothing. I delicately pour another line on to my dirty coffee table and lean down and sniff. I shake my head as it runs through me. *Don't let them kill you*, I tell myself, without knowing who 'them' actually are. *No one can ruin you but yourself*, I think, holding my hands

189

in a prayer. I doublelock my door and pace the living room, as the hours turn into weeks, always telling myself, *don't let them kill you*. Like I am absolved from the decision. Like it's not my choice at all.

But I can see it all so clearly now. The threat was never from another person. I walk out to my balcony and look down at the canal. This city is trying to kill me. I will die here, if I stay here. I flush the almost empty baggie down the toilet, praying it doesn't cause a clog. Then I go to the nearest internet café and book a one-way flight back to LA. Two weeks later, I pack my bags and leave.

9

I'm not allowed back into my Downtown loft. The landlord, who occupied the room beside the kitchen, when he hears about my return, texts Conell, *Over my dead body. I can't listen to that girl have loud sex every night again. Tell her to find somewhere else.* So I book a room in West Hollywood on Airbnb.

I walk along the weed-covered driveway, pulling my suitcase behind me, and when I reach the porch, the front door is slightly ajar. I walk in, and some curly-haired man is pounding down on a piano in the living room, like he's a modern-day Beethoven. He spots me, but keeps going, and I stand there awkwardly, surveying the room. Instruments litter the floor; two guitars and drums and a fucking flute, of all things, and there's a stack of records beside the fireplace, but I can't see any record player. On the walls are movie posters for films I've never even heard of. I sigh. I hate people that clutter a space with who they are. When he finishes banging on the piano, ending with a theatrical glide along the keys, I am not sure what to do, so start to clap. He stands up and takes a bow.

He brushes the hair out of his eyes as he walks over to greet me. *Gal, it's a pleasure.* I look at his face, trying to suss him out. *Your name is really Gal?* He picks up a guitar and drums the strings. *I'm from Israel. It's a common name there. More for women, but sometimes for men.* I nod. *Well, I have a boy's name, so guess we have something in common.* He laughs much harder than is appropriate, and grabs my shoulders. *You are so fucking funny! Let me show you your room.* He pushes me up the stairs. *I'm having a dinner party tonight, with all my favourite musician friends, and you should come. I'm going to make my famous chicken casserole.* I look around the room, the sunlight splitting in the windows, and turn to him. *I'm actually busy tonight, but have fun with that.*

June, July and August all fall into each other. I roll out of bed at noon each day, pull my shorts up my thighs and stumble down the stairs. I run my fingers through my knotty hair as I stand in the kitchen, drinking coffee. I smoke a pack of cigarettes before 3pm. I go down to the local Walgreens and buy a twenty pack of Rolling Rock, and another pack of Marlboros. I sit outside and bake in the sun, drinking and smoking. Other guests at the Airbnb sometimes join me, but mostly I am alone. I have fun either way, lying on a wooden chair outside, feeling the sun beat down on me as I sip my cold beer. Some days I go to a coffee shop and pretend to write my thesis, and some days I get an Uber to the beach and dance in the waves, but most of the time I just lie there, in the back yard, thinking. It starts with good thoughts. Then slowly, the bad creep back in. I drink more, to forget them.

I have a friend in LA, Josh, who is much older than me and a TV producer. He's best friends with Gal, who makes trailers for movies. One night the three of us are out to dinner, with another TV guy. They're all talking about their jobs. *I don't have talent like you guys*, I say proudly. *I have no creativity inside me, no desire to make anything.* They react like I've called myself ugly: *No, no, no, of course you do. You have something you are good at. Everyone does.* I counter-argue: *No, not everyone does. Some people make the thing, but others have to consume the thing. I consume, and that's okay. We don't all need talent in order to matter.* I smile smugly, delighted with the last sentence that comes out of my mouth. Very poignant.

When I boarded that flight to LA, I decided to give up all my older men. Just as I thought the coke was the problem, I also saw fault in all of the grey sagging bodies that had entered me. They had been destroying me, a white powder but in a human form, and I believed that if I didn't go cold turkey on them, I'd die. When I flushed the drugs down the toilet, I also gave up all of the old men. Without them, my evenings now stretch into infinity. Rather than using my extra free time to finish my thesis, I add more drinking to my schedule. I drink once I wake up, I drink in the afternoon, I drink while dancing to Britney at a club. Around other people, my drinking is positively magical. It's only when I am back in my bed at night that I am brought back to my emptiness. On good nights, I am too drunk to notice it. I get to sleep without any badness pumping through my body. I want more of those good nights, so I drink even more.

Sometimes I miscalculate, and drink too much. Everyone around me is vibrating, and the room is spinning. I can't make conversation. I stare a hole into the floor below me, counting to ten. I spend the rest of the night, and much of the next morning, vomiting into the toilet. It begins as a rare occurrence, and next thing I know, I am spending multiple mornings a week lying on the cold tiles, crying in misery. Holding the toilet seat with my hands to steady myself. Throwing up until my throat burns. One day I get sick so hard I piss myself. A hot stream runs down my legs; a dark spot in the sweatpants grows, as I retch and heave. I don't have a problem, though. They're just miscalculations.

I talk with Harvey on the phone. After he flew me out to New York a couple of times, and then closed the door on me, we kept in sporadic touch. He's been sober for more years than there are between us. Rehab is as American as hot dogs and guns. He checked himself into one at seventeen. *No one is an alcoholic at seventeen,* I think, *they just haven't learned how to drink properly yet.* I don't tell him that, because I still want him to see me as a person to love. Just so I can say, *I don't love you back, ha ha.* I want to claw back the humiliation I felt at his hands, and the clearest path to that I can see is him waking up one day and saying, *Why don't we give this another try?* So, I keep my mouth shut when he talks about his AA meetings, because there's no surer way to get an alcoholic to hate you than by saying they don't really have a problem. Instead, I nod to everything he says. He tells me I need to quit drinking. It will solve all my problems. If I start going to AA meetings, I will get better. He promises me that.

He sounds so convincing. But I'm still not convinced. I like drinking. I like the act of raising the glass to my lips and gulping the liquid down, while smoking a cigarette. I like how it makes other people seem. It makes everyone more interesting, so I can listen to some drone shite on about her kids and think, *How bloody fascinating,* and I'll mean it. Every beast becomes a beauty, when I'm drinking. I'm also a nicer person when I'm drunk. I'll send *I love you* texts to my mum, and buy my roommate doughnuts, just because. I am the best version of myself when ten bottles of beer deep.

But mostly, I drink because I like how it makes me feel. It somehow makes me lighter. All the bad thoughts just fade away. I like myself so much more when drunk. I am a fun girl, an interesting girl, a good girl. *Your life will be exponentially better once you quit,* Harvey tells me. Even though I nod at his sober pitch, I know I don't believe him. Sober, I hate everyone, especially myself. But when I'm drunk, my perception shifts, and everything bad is funnelled into something good. Drinking gives me the happiness I've been searching for. It is the missing jigsaw piece. Life makes sense when I am drunk, in a way it never could when I was sober. There is no way I can let that go. I agree with Harvey when he texts me, but I know, deep down, I'm not willing to give drinking up, not for anyone.

10

When I wake up one morning, hungover and depressed, much like every other morning, I turn my pillow over and try to fall back to sleep. Before I can sink back into nothing, Gal barges into my room and pulls open the curtains. *Get up, you bum,* he instructs, *you're not allowed to sleep till 2pm anymore. I'm forcing you up. We're going on an adventure.* He tosses me his keys. *I'll even let you drive.* He hasn't let me drive since I crashed his car into a tour bus parked on La Brea. I wasn't going fast, so the only damage was one dent in the passenger side of his convertible, but he swore he wouldn't let me near it again. I jump out of bed and grab the keys from his hands.

Once I've taken twenty-five minutes to parallel park, and only hit the kerb three times as I manoeuvred the car, we aimlessly walk around Silver Lake. *This is so dumb,* I moan after an hour of wandering. *It's just houses and cafés and bars, exactly like there is in West Hollywood. I want to go back to bed.* We pass by a Scientology building, and he grabs my arm. *Let's go in,* he says to me. *Could be funny.* I wiggle out from his grasp. *You're always trying to put yourself in funny situations, and that's because you're too boring to come up with anything interesting in your own mind.* I turn around to face him. *I feel sorry for you, because you're old and boring. But I'm not going in there, and you can't make me.* He reaches over and sticks his hands in my armpits, tickling me. *Your dire 'woe is me' attitude is so annoying,* he says, as I try to kick him away, *and if you want to go home right now, you can walk. Otherwise, we're going in.*

There's an old man in the waiting room. He makes conversation with us. His daughter works here. He says how proud he is of her. He reminds me of what a dad should be. The receptionist calls our names. She brings us into a back room. There's a woman sitting inside, a goddess of a woman, who looks around my age. *It's a pleasure to meet you,* she smiles, not leaving her seat, *my name is Casey.* I plop myself down on the chair closest to her. *That's a boy's name. Just like mine.* She laughs when I say this, shaking her head, her blonde hair bouncing off the sunlight coming in the window. *You're funny,* she says, and I blush. She crosses her legs. Her thighs are half the size of mine and twice as long. I stare at them. I can't see any hair. I wonder if she shaved them that morning. She makes small talk with us. She cracks a few jokes. She seems so normal. I wonder if it's her dad sitting out in reception.

You have really long eyelashes, I tell her, interrupting whatever she is saying. She smiles. *They're like spiders, the worst! I wish mine were like yours.* I put my hand to my stubby lashes. *Thanks, I guess.* I'm close enough to smell her. If I stick out my tongue, I bet I could taste lavender. I decide I like her.

Gal brings up the 'Going Clear' documentary. *Oh, I've never heard of that,* she says brightly. *The biggest documentary about your religion that is fucking everywhere right now, and you haven't heard of it?* I stare at him. What's his fucking problem? You can ask a question without being an asshole about it.

Casey ignores Gal, and keeps talking, looking directly at me. As she speaks, I imagine what it would feel like if I leaned forward and kissed her. How soft her lips might taste. The vibration of her manicured hands running through my hair. *What about Louis Theroux?* I ask, snapping myself out of my daydream. He made a documentary about Scientology too, and during it the Scientologists started making a documentary about him, a kind of tit for tat, because they're strategic like that. She has to know about that; the tape is probably nestled away in this building somewhere. *Hmm, not ringing any bells, no. I must check it out!* She smiles at me again. I forget whatever I was thinking.

She changes the subject. She changes the focus. She asks us about ourselves. *I'm feeling a bit depressed,* I admit. *I read somewhere you guys don't like depressed people, though.* She laughs. *Oh no, that's completely untrue. There's a lot of untrue things out there about us.* She smiles again. *We can actually cure depression! If you take six weeks of our tailored classes, you can cure your depression. We've had people in here wanting to die, who have tried every medication and every therapist in this city, and have seen no light. Six of our classes, and now they are the happiest people I know!*

I bite down on my fingernails as she talks. I know what she is saying is bullshit, but I also don't *know* that. I watched the beginning of 'Going Clear', but then I got bored and switched it off. I did see 'The Master', but also isn't Hollywood notorious for exaggerating? Also, okay, maybe they do all that crazy stuff, and it's really bad, but maybe also, at the same time as the bad stuff, they do cure sad people? They could be both bad, and cure sad people. It doesn't have to be one or the other. All I know for sure is that I have tried three different types of official medication, and been to two therapists, and tried to self-medicate with coke and alcohol, and I am still fucked. I know Scientologists are supposed to be batshit crazy, but what if they can fix me? Is there really so much harm in just giving it a try?

I give her my phone number and sign three different forms, making me an incoming patient. Gal elbows me when I give my signature, but I ignore him. *This is the beginning of the rest of your life*, Casey tells me, brightly. I smile back. *I thought you guys were nutjobs. I guess I was the nutjob for making assumptions. I really hope you can fix me.* She types into a computer. *Oh, don't worry; we can fix everyone.*

Two days later, I get a call from an unknown number. I answer, hoping it is them. *We're so excited to begin treatment*, the voice tells me. *First, we need your credit card. Classes are $100 each, and you need twenty to begin with, then we'll reassess.* I do the maths. *Um, I don't actually have any money*, I begin, silently cursing myself for giving up fucking old men with money. *That's okay*, the voice tells me, and I sigh, relieved. *We accept credit cards.* I pause. *I actually don't have a credit card because I'm not American.* The voice on the other end takes a beat to respond. *Do you not have any family members that can loan you?* I think of my dead father, and poor mother. *Eh, no, I don't come from rich people. But maybe we can figure something else out? You know, I could maybe clean the building – my yoga studio once offered this type of exchange and...* She interrupts me. *No, that won't work. You clearly don't want to help yourself. Contact us when you're serious about making changes and have the funds to do it. Goodbye.* She hangs up the phone before I have the chance to convince her how serious I am.

I walk into my kitchen, dejected, and pour myself a whisky, my hands shaking. *Fuck those cult cunts*, I scream out to no one. I down my drink in three gulps, and pour another. *Like you fucking dopes don't know who Louis Theroux is.* As soon as my glass hits the counter, I pour another. *I've seen The Master, I know what you devils do*, I text the number that called me. And I pour another when I don't get a response.

I drink until I forget who I am, then spend the early hours of the morning puking up my amnesia. *Something needs to fucking change*, I tell myself as I grip the toilet bowl. *Something needs to fucking save me.* As I lie on the bathroom floor, I notice the dried blood on my arm. I piece together what I did a few hours earlier, when I was forgetting who I was. I removed the blade from my roommate's razor with a knife. I held it over my arm, and closed my eyes. You go vertical, not horizontal, if you really want to hurt yourself. I drew the blade along my pale flesh. Then it all went blank.

I have woken up Gal with my puking. He sees my bloody arm when he walks into the bathroom, and bandages it up, telling me how stupid I am. *I know, I know,* I plead, *just please leave me the fuck alone.* He walks out of the bathroom as I continue to vomit. *Get help,* he says, before he closes the door, *you need help and I'm not the one to give it to you.*

Sitting on the bathroom floor, sweat dripping down my face, I try and devise a game plan. I might not be able to do a Tom Cruise, but there's surely another path to my absolution. I reread the texts Harvey has sent me. *I'm going to quit drinking*, I type out to him. My phone buzzes almost immediately. *This is the best decision of your life! I've looked up local meetings, and here's all the ones close to you.* I scroll through the list, and decide on the one that starts in two hours, so I don't have time to take it back. When 9am rolls around, I rinse out my puke breath with mouthwash, slip on my Birkenstocks and walk the five blocks there.

11

The only entry requirement of AA is that you have to have a desire to stop drinking. But they don't do a lie-detector test. They just believe you if you say it. Even though I've decided to stop drinking, I don't actually feel the desire to quit burning through me. Instead, I feel like I'm trying it on for size, wearing the dress of sobriety but keeping the tag on, tucked inside, just in case. When I walk into the stuffy warm room, on the third floor of a crumbling building on Sunset Boulevard, I take the seat nearest the exit, and make a plan to dip if it gets too weird.

Unlike Scientology, AA is free. They don't charge you to attend. Anyone can take a seat, and there's no membership due. Everyone who works there is a volunteer. There's no hierarchy, no CEO of AA. They designed it that way. They knew that people love power, so if they gave them the chance, someone would try and become the Jeff Bezos of drunks. So they made a rule that you can't.

At that first meeting, five minutes before it officially even begins, when my head is beating into my chest with a brewing hangover, I am approached by a man who is either my age or sixty-five. It's tough to decipher through his unwashed beard and army jacket. *I…haven't seen…you…here before….man*, he eventually pushes out of his mouth. *No, uh, this is my first time*, I say while looking at the wall behind him. A good way to get someone to shut up is by never addressing their face.

This shit, it… He wanders off for a few seconds, nodding to himself. *Oh right! This shit…saved…saved my life, dude.* I nod politely and continue looking at the wall. I'm sure I can make out the shape of a cat from the pieces of paint that have fallen away. *Take my phone number and call me anytime.* I snap back to attention. This motherfucker really has the audacity to hit on me in an AA meeting? Is nowhere sacred anymore? I now look directly into the eyes of this dirty hippie. *No, thank you,* I hiss. *Jesus Christ, do you have no decency?* He meanders off without taking offence, and after another two meetings, I learn that it's just a part of AA. Everyone gives each other their number, and everyone texts each other to check in. AA is big on support systems; no one person can beat their demons by themselves. Nobody is trying to fuck; they're just trying to save.

AA is also anonymous. I'm still not sure what that means. Every sober person I meet tells me they're in AA.

There is a Bible of AA. It's called the Big Blue Book. It gives the history of AA, and the Twelve Steps to recovery. You're supposed to study the Big Blue Book like you would the gospel. AA technically isn't Christian; your higher power can be anything. It can be your mother or a tree. But it works best if it is God. AA isn't religious, technically, but it is holy. And there's nothing more holy than God.

When you introduce yourself during a meeting, you have to follow your name with *and I am an alcoholic.* And then everyone says hi back. I don't know if that's a written rule, but everyone does it, so you have to too. I think it's so there are no accidental show-ups. Maybe once someone showed up who thought it was a cancer support group. It's like when you fly, and you are boarding the plane, you have to show your boarding pass to the flight attendant, even though you wouldn't have gotten through the gate without having it. It's just a double check.

Someone facilitates the meeting, like an MC, or a priest, and they change who that is every meeting, so no one person can hog the limelight for too long. They start the meeting with some ground rules. Then they ask if anyone wants to say anything. If you're attention-seeking, like I am, you throw up your hand and walk up to the pew. It's not an actual pew, but it reminds you of one. There is something divine about AA. Maybe because you know people have died for your sins.

You describe how alcohol is messing up your life. You don't have a great description, because honestly it hasn't messed up your life – you've done that yourself. You hold your arm up as a visual cue to your rock bottom. It's covered in a bandage from your wrist to your elbow. *I tried to slit my wrists last night, but it is harder to do it than it seems, and it really hurt, so I stopped before I could properly hurt myself. I barely made a dent. But I think I am at rock bottom, for just attempting it.* You hold your arm up again. People look impressed. Maybe that's just in your head. But you feel it all the same.

Then there is a keynote speaker. This is the best bit. Someone who has been sober a long time, either a year or thirty, comes up and speaks about their journey to getting to where they are today. It's the best bit, because of the stories before the sobriety. They talk about crossing the Iran border with coke up their ass, and two friends getting thrown in the slammer there, fingernails pulled off. Or fucking a prostitute, and her filming it, and then trying to blackmail them with it, sending copies to their wife and kids when they don't cough up the cash. Or pissing on their boss's computer at work, in front of the interns, and then losing their home because of it.

Everyone's story is different, but they mostly involve pissing themselves in front of someone important. That's one of the cornerstones of AA. The keynote speakers always get caught up in the before stories, the glory of the before days, before they knew they had a problem, and then suddenly they have two minutes left and rush through: *...and yea so I realized I needed help and joined the programme and now am the happiest I've ever been thank you.* Everyone claps. If you look around the room, there is usually someone crying.

The MC then asks if anyone has a burning desire to drink. A burning desire, as opposed to a regular, lukewarm one. Someone might raise their hand. Usually shaking. In an uneven voice, they admit they want to drink. They are scared they will do it. Most times, they are the person who has been crying during the keynote. Their eyes are still red from it. You shouldn't judge, but you can't help yourself. The thought *Pathetic* forces itself into your brain, and you let it stay there. It might make you a bad person, but it is a bit pathetic. No one says anything back, besides the moderator, who sing-songs, *Thank you for sharing.*

Chips are handed out. Plastic silver coins. To commemorate time. *Anyone here twenty-four hours sober?* That's the entry-level chip. You shoot up your hand, because you're near enough, and go up to collect your medal. Everyone claps as you return to your seat. The next level is thirty days. You will have to wait twenty-nine more days for another go at the podium.

At the end everyone holds hands, which is the least fun bit, having to touch some stranger's sweaty palm. The chant is recited. *God, grant me the serenity to accept the things I cannot change, the courage to change the things I can, and the wisdom to know the difference.* Even if you're not an alcoholic, they're pretty good words to live by. It all lies in the wisdom to know the difference.

12

I loved my first AA meeting. I found it magical. It was organized nonsense. Structured madness. I go back every day. *You want to do ninety meetings in ninety days*, someone tells me. *I can do that!* I reply excitedly. If I'm not drinking, I need to find replacements that erase time, because otherwise I will be alone with my thoughts, and if I am alone with my thoughts for long enough, they always turn to me wanting to die. I need the distraction.

After five meetings, I can't remember what it feels like not to belong to these people. I text them throughout the day, and meet at coffee shops to study the Big Blue Book. I show up thirty minutes early to each meeting, to chat with my fellow former drunks. We fist paper cups of coffee, knocking them back quickly like they're high-end tequila. The people who go to AA aren't normal people. They are ex-addicts, except there is no such thing. Once an addict, always an addict, or so it goes. These people have just transferred their fixations on to something else. The Twelve Steps. They treat the Big Blue Book with the same intensity they once had for downing a bottle of vodka on a Monday morning. We cannot create or destroy; we can only transfer.

They aren't normal people. That's why I like them. They are crazy, but they're now channelling their crazy into something non-destructive. They aren't destroying their families or losing their homes anymore, but they are still slightly off kilter. You can see it in their eyes, and the way they move. There's something unhinged inside of them.

I like the old men of AA especially – the ones who have families, children, daughters who they have destroyed almost to the point of no take-back. But then they took it back. I like these men because they are still here. Not all old, alcoholic men with daughters are still here. Some of them didn't even get to be that old. But this isn't about those dead men. It's about the ones still alive. I knock back lukewarm bitter coffee as I laugh at their terrible jokes, waiting for the meeting to start. It feels like I'm looking through the lens of what could have been.

When I was fourteen, Mr Cummins told me most alcoholics who stop drinking go back to drinking. As I look around at the group of people surrounding me, licking their lips as they turn the pages of the Big Blue Book, holding eye contact for too long when they speak to me, I know he was speaking the truth. These people don't drink anymore, but the thing inside of them that made them drink? That is still there, festering away. Ready to pop. A lot of these people will drink again. For every person with a twenty-year chip, there's someone else who got to nineteen years and 364 days, only to fall down at the same hurdle they've jumped over thousands of times.

Does anyone have a burning desire?

Most of us do, every day, and sometimes it wins.

And those that don't, they still hold the fire inside of them. They push it into other things; but it is always still there, ready to ignite. A desire ready to burn, burn, burn. Just waiting for the match.

13

After seven days of meetings, I am getting into my groove. I still don't feel I have a problem with drinking, but I like this new identity: someone who is part of AA.

After my seventh meeting a girl in the programme invites me to get some food. She drives me to Denny's, telling me her redemption story on the way. She's been sober for three years. *The best three years of my life.* The sober time is always the best time for AA people, and they have to tell you that. To remind them it's true. We go over passages in the Big Blue Book as we eat bacon and eggs. She tells me she is proud of me, which is wild because she doesn't know me, but that's another thing AA people do. Have pride in strangers. I push my plate away from me, full. She is still talking and eating. I look over at the clock behind her head. I stare at the second hand as it moves.

A bell dings every few minutes, and middle-aged waitresses rush past me with plates of greasy eggs. I hear the chatter of the tables beside me, and the buzz starts to leak into my brain. I look back at the clock and it ticks faster than time should pass. The bell keeps dinging, louder each time. My leg starts to shake. I need to get the fuck out of here. *I've got to feed the dogs*, I say abruptly, standing up to leave. My new friend smiles, not noticing anything amiss, and stands up to hug me. *I'll see you at tomorrow's meeting?* I nod, and lean over to rub a finger around the grease left on my plate. I stick it in my mouth and feel my stomach turn. *See you then.*

I walk fourteen blocks, the sun beating down my neck, the sweat collecting in my underwear. Every step I take, there's less of me. If I keep walking, I might stop existing altogether. I stop in at the café beside my house. I order an iced coffee and sit down at a table outside. I hear an American man give English lessons to a young Asian girl at the table beside me. He's describing the continuous tense. The cuts on my arm are itchy, so I stick my plastic straw underneath the bandages and scratch. I keep scratching, until I see a circle of red appear through the white gauze. Fresh. I hear the *tick, tick, tick* of a second hand, moving time. When I look around, I don't see any clock.

I leave my empty glass on the table, leave the *I am starting, they are learning*, and walk across the street to Walgreens. I ignore the fridges at the back of the shop, where I used to grab a twenty pack of Rolling Rock every morning before I joined AA. There's a comfort in walking away from the fridge of who you used to be, but there's a fear with it too. I stand in the medicine aisle, suddenly terrified, scanning the rows of pills. Wondering what will fix me. When I reach out to grab a bottle of pills, I don't feel like it's really me moving. I am watching this girl bring a family-size jar of Tylenol to the register and pay. *In case I get a headache,* I tell myself, bringing myself back into my body. Thoughts are hissing around in my head and I can't make out what they are, but the buzzing is driving me insane.

I walk into my house, kicking off my sandals, feeling the cold tiles of the kitchen on my feet. I eye up the bottle of Jack Daniel's in the pantry. *I want a drink*, I say out loud. No divine entity leans in to stop me, so I pour myself a glass, adding a couple of cubes of ice from the freezer. I pace the kitchen with the drink in my hand. I smell it, intaking the delicious fumes. I hold it to my temples. I want to drink. But I don't drink anymore. I am in AA. I pour out the glass in the kitchen sink and run up the wooden stairs to my room.

I lie in my bed, and the buzzing turns into hammering. I open my eyes, and everything is fuzzy. I close my eyes again. And the whole world drops dead. From one second to another: the world is alive and then it dies. Tick, tick, tick.

I breathe out. I am back here again. I always end up back here. Life may be a maze, but there's only one exit for me. It always comes back to this.

You'd be better off dead.

That is not my thought, but it's in my head all the same.

Better off dead.

Dead

Dead
Dead
Dead
Dad.

I am so tired, I say out loud. It's too exhausting to be alive.

Sometimes, that is all it takes. Wanting to die and not wanting to live are not the same thought. But they can cause the same result. And maybe that's all that really matters.

It will always be like this. You will never get away from this.

I pick up the bottle of Tylenol and pour out a handful of pills. I swallow. I pour out another handful. I swallow again. Each time I swallow, the buzzing lessens. So I keep swallowing.

I know what amount can kill me.

I take double that amount.

I am not trying to die. I just want the noise to stop.

God grant me the serenity to accept the things I cannot change.

I lie back on my bed. My thoughts are swirling, and I still can't make out what they are, but the pace of them has slowed. Maybe this is the serenity.

Get the fuck up, get the fuck up, get the fuck up.

Who is that speaking now?

Don't move. Just wait it out.

I am willing myself to either die, or live, and I'm not sure which voice is right. Which one I should listen to.

Without making a decision in my head, my body takes over. I get up and head towards the bathroom, to vomit up what I've done. *Thank God, I can take this back.* I reach out to open my bedroom door. Instead, my hand locks it. My mind screams at my hand to unlock. My hand does not comply. My body walks back to the bed, and my mind pleads it to go the other way. I lie down and pull the covers over my head.

Breathe in, breathe out.

Breathe in, breathe out.

Breathe in, breathe out.

Again, again, again. Until you can't. It's that simple. Breathe until you stop. And then, stay stopped.

I float away from my body again and watch what is happening beneath me. A girl with long blonde hair and dark roots, lying on a double bed, her little belly pouch poking out as her grey t-shirt rides up her stomach. Her tanned legs thrash around the bed, and the way the sun shines through the tall windows makes her cellulite glisten. She reaches her arm over and pushes a pillow into her face. A muffled noise escapes into the room, but no one is around to hear it. *This girl isn't important*, I decide, looking down. *It will be okay if she dies.*

And I breathe out.

Gal comes home. I am not sure how long it has been. He knocks at my bedroom door. The light banging brings me back into my body. I don't answer. He keeps knocking, louder each time. I laugh. The knocking inside my head is now matching this knocking outside my door. I can't tell the difference.

The knocking stops. I hear his footsteps walk down the stairs, growing more faint with each step. Maybe he's given up. Maybe he's left me here to die. Maybe he's decided I'd be better off dead. I want to call out his name, now that I know he's not behind the door to hear me. Now he's left, I want him to save me. I push the words out of my chest, but they get stuck in my throat. My head is spinning, growing heavier with each breath. I am falling. The light decreases, getting smaller and smaller as I fall. A dream within a dream, except it's all real. I hear his footsteps again, growing louder. He's back. He starts drilling. Maybe I'm imagining this sound. It's puncturing my brain instead of the door.

He breaks the door down, piercing through my dream. He

looks at me, and the Tylenol jar on the floor. *What the fuck have you done?*

What I was always going to do.

My head is heavy. It's too hard to keep it held up, so I let it drop back.

Now I am in the hospital. This is the same place Britney went when she had her breakdown. And Kanye. It's the crème de la crème of emergency rooms. The same place Gal brought me when I had a panic attack two months ago, after watching 'Inception'. That film fucked me up. A dream within a dream. I couldn't figure out what was real. I was lying on the couch afterwards and breathing so heavily, and then suddenly I couldn't move my arms or legs. My whole body seized up and I couldn't move. I thought I was having a stroke. So did he. When we arrived at the ER, the gay receptionist said, *It's a panic attack. Here's a paper bag. Just breathe, girl.* And I did.

I knew once I had arrived that I would be fine. I wouldn't die. I didn't even want to die, so I guess it was good that I wouldn't.

I am processed through intake, still conscious. My head keeps falling backward. It's like it's made of lead. My eyelids get heavier. The nurse keeps shaking me awake. *It's imperative you stay with us*, she says.

I am lying on a trolley in the hallway. No one is panicked, so neither am I. I think I'll go to sleep. I don't care what the nurse says. I want to fall in.

I hear my roommate yelling at nurses, asking where the doctor is. The nurses reply calmly, *She'll get here when she does.*

The doctor comes by. She asks what I took. Gal hands her the half-full jar. She counts. *Did you take all of the missing ones?* I nod, smiling up at her pretty face. *If she took all of the missing ones, that's a toxic amount. We don't have time to wait for her bloods, she needs the antidote now.* She sounds alarmed. I open my eyes. Suddenly, there is movement. Everything is rushed. I am confused. Why is there panic? I start to cry.

I grab the wrist of whoever is wheeling me down the hall. *Please, please, don't let me die. I am sorry I did this, and I know I don't deserve it, but please just save me anyway.*

I wake up the next day, in a hospital room, with an old woman sitting on a chair beside me. I pinch the skin at my elbow, to see if I am dreaming. No, I am still here. A dream within a dream. But somehow, still alive.

14

That afternoon, when I am allowed visitors, Gal steamrolls in. He throws a pile of clothes on my bed, and curses the doctors, and me, and the parking attendant who redirected him to a lot three streets away. *It's too hot to have to walk around this fucking city*, he moans, pacing my room. I laugh. *Calm down, you drama queen.*

I'm not a drama queen, he snaps, *I'm Jewish – we have stress sewn into our DNA. And you scared me with the shit you pulled, so forgive me for being afflicted.* I hold up my arm, with the tube sticking out of it. *But I'm still kicking. I'm like Jesus, risen from the dead.* He throws my denim shorts at my face. *You're such a cunt. This is serious.* I give him the finger. *Relax*, I say, *you're going to give yourself an aneurysm.* He slaps my finger away. *I probably already have one festering, so thank you for that.*

He forces me to call my mother. He thinks if I tell her what has happened, it will make it real and I'll have to take it seriously. I don't want to worry her. I know she can't do anything to help me, not just because she's an ocean away. *What's the point?* I say, but then give in. I call her up on loudspeaker. *I don't want you to worry, but basically, I stopped drinking nine days ago, and then two days ago I took an overdose, and now I'm in the hospital.* There is silence. A very long silence. I hear her clearing her throat. *Why do you think you have a drinking problem? That's probably just Americans getting in your head, you know what they are like...* I lean back onto the bed, smiling. I see the horrified look on the nurse's face, and I laugh. I am the only one who can make sense of the conversation. I don't want to talk about this, and she doesn't want to hear it. We are opposite sides, but the same. I am mostly my father's daughter, but every so often, I am my mother's child.

15

A psychiatrist came by when I was waiting for my life to be saved, lying on the trolley in the hallway of the ER room. She asked me a bunch of questions. I don't remember what I answered. Now, another psychiatrist comes by. This guy asks me what I did. Why I did it. I know he is asking this to decide whether to commit me to a psych ward after this. I am earnest. *I don't know why I did it. It wasn't me who decided it. But I regret it, and I won't do it again.* I tell him I don't want to be committed. That I choose not to. He nods, and scribbles down in his notebook.

He made it seem like it was a choice. It wasn't. I am informed I will be going to a psychiatric facility when the hospital discharges me. It's a law in the state of California. If you're considered a risk to yourself, you can be locked away for seventy-two hours. It's called a 5150 hold. Kanye got the same thing. No one is above the law, and especially not when they're considered crazy.

I argue and scream and cry, but it's no use. None of the doctors will listen to me. When Gal comes back to visit, I tell him of my plan. *The nurses change shift at 4pm, and right around then you're going to sneak me out of here when no one is looking.* He shakes his head at me. *You need help, Marise, please, just accept it.* I call him a cunt, and he leaves my room apologetically, promising I will thank him some day.

After a week in the hospital, when the doctors are confident my liver levels are normal and there's no more poison in my bloodstream, two paramedics enter the room, a man and a woman, to take me to the psych ward. They have a trolley waiting in the hallway, with buckles around the sides. They ask me to get onto it.

Hahaha, that's okay, I'll just walk out with you.

Sorry, ma'am, it's procedure. We need to strap you down.

Strap tightened over my left wrist; buckles clasped. A slight tug to make sure it's secure. Repeat to each limb so I can't move. It's just procedure.

Just procedure, I spit back at them, *that's exactly what the Nazis said.* The woman paramedic laughs. *I'm Jewish, you can't say that to me.* I look down at my legs. *I didn't mean it like that, it was just a metaphor.* I am too embarrassed to put up any more of a fight, so I just close my eyes and accept my fate.

I am wheeled through three floors of the hospital, tied down to this trolley, a blanket over me to hide the thick restraints. Patients stare at me from their beds as I pass by their doors. Real patients, in hospital with a broken leg, or cancer. With balloons and flowers on their bedside lockers. Real sick people, who didn't choose to be sick. Looking at me. Feeling sorry for me. I am someone who chose this. The cancer inside of me is myself.

I am loaded into an ambulance that will bring me to the psych ward. My nose starts to tingle once we drive away from the hospital. I want to itch it. I know I can't. The pain gets worse, because I can't. It burns on top of my face. I move my hands against the restraints. I feel desperate. I ask the woman paramedic to scratch it, and she does. She repeats the move each time I ask, laughing as she brings her fingernails to my face. *Usually, you'd have to buy me dinner to get this type of treatment*, she jokes, and I laugh too. For a moment, I forget where I am.

An hour later, we arrive at the ward. They wheel me through secure door after secure door, until I am in the reception area. I am still tied down. Other people walk by, barely looking at me. This is it. I am here.

16

I am taken through intake, again. I sign each form put in front of me, without reading them, because reading is for people with a choice. I might not be strapped down now, but I am stuck here. Whatever door I choose, the same fate is waiting for me. What's the point in pretending to decide?

When I have finished scribbling my signature on each page, I am brought into a tiny room behind the reception. A nurse takes my blood pressure and sticks a needle in my arm. Right in the same arm that's had needles in it all week. *Can't you just call the hospital? They just did this yesterday*, I plead, and she stabs into me anyway. *We need our own, for our records*. She sounds like a computer. I imagine how bored she is. How mundane, to take the blood of crazy people. It looks just like any other blood.

When she is finished with me, she sends me back into reception, where I sit opposite a woman named Jane. Jane is someone who would describe herself as 'no nonsense', I can just tell. Jane fucks missionary-style once a week, and slaps in her retainer before the guy has even come. Jane hosts a 'The Bachelor' viewing party every Monday in her apartment, but chastises her friends when they put down their glasses on her IKEA coffee table without a coaster. Jane thinks dogs are annoying, and has definitely uttered the expression *Boys will be boys* when her boyfriend has farted in front of her.

Jane roots through my belongings. She takes the laces out of my shoes. *A potential weapon*, she tells me flatly, as if I already know that and am trying to pull one over on her. She takes my phone, but lets me write down any numbers I might want to call while I am here. I write down Gal's number. Surely he will be feeling bad about demanding I come here. Maybe his guilt will make him let me off rent for the month. I take down Conell's cell. I wonder what he'll make of where I am. I think we'll laugh about it someday. I don't know if that day will be tomorrow, or in five years, but I know we'll laugh once it comes.

Jane hands me a toothbrush and a bar of soap. *You're not allowed to keep toothpaste in your room, that's another potential weapon, so you need to come get some from reception each morning and night.* I laugh. Who is killing themselves with toothpaste? She hands me the starter pack: a notebook, a dull pencil (pencils are okay, but pens are another potential weapon) and a schedule. I glance down at the page:

7AM BREAKFAST, 8AM FREE TIME, 9AM THERAPY, 10.30AM SNACK, 11AM ART CLASS, 12PM LUNCH, 1PM THERAPY, 3.30PM FREE TIME/DOCTOR, 5PM DINNER, 6PM RECREATION ROOM, 8PM MEDICATIONS, 9PM SLEEP.

It's the same every day, she says.

What if I need to take a shit? She ignores me. *You are on Tier 1. Everyone starts on Tier 1 when they arrive. You're not allowed to leave this section of the building. Food is brought to you, and you can't go to art class. After twelve hours, you move to Tier 2. Bad behaviour brings you back to Tier 1. Once demoted you stay on Tier 1 until we decide otherwise.* She doesn't look at me while she's talking, so I use the time to stare at her. She has a scar on her left cheek, and deep dents all over her face from acne. She's got a massive honker that takes up most of her face, and tiny thin lips that don't take up enough of it. She's ugly, but in a very matter-of-fact way. Like she decided being pretty was frivolous. I can't decide if I hate Jane, or if I want to be her.

She shows me to my room. It has three single beds. *You're lucky, only one other patient is in here*, she says. I glance over at a lump in one bed. I'll never see this girl move from her bed the entire time I am in here. So lucky.

You'll meet the doctor at 3.30pm, so show up at reception then. It's 12.30pm now. Therapy is in thirty minutes, in the room at the end of the hall. You can settle in until then. She leaves, and I sit on the bed staring at the clock, counting down each second. One Mississippi, two Mississippi. I close my eyes, and I can hear the clock ticking, getting louder with each second passing. *Tick, tick, tick.* I fucking hate that sound. I get an urge to burst my eardrums, to stick a knife inside my ears and twist, so I can stop hearing that fucking ticking. The urge leaves as quickly as it arrived, so it barely even counts. Three Mississippi, four Mississippi.

I walk down to the therapy room at 12.50pm. I meet the other patients. There's maybe fifteen altogether, give or take. They quickly surround me, welcoming me into their fold. *There are two doctors here. You want Dr Cabera. He doesn't give a shit. Dr Jones – if you get him, you're fucked. He doesn't let anyone out in three days.* This is news to me. I'm here on a 5150; it's a three-day hold. What the fuck are these crazy people talking about?

I thought the law was… I begin, but am interrupted. Crazy people have terrible social etiquette. You can forget ever finishing a sentence if you're among crazy people. *The law isn't on your side*, one guy offers up. *There's the 5150, sure, that's what brings us in here. But then there's the 5250, a two-week hold after those three days.* A fucking 5250? How many more of them are there? I look around at everyone, and half of them have eyes that suggest a 6050. They've been in here a long time; I can sense it. Three days was already a nightmare, something I didn't want to do. The idea there could be more makes me want to swallow the toothpaste.

A young Hispanic man enters the room. He introduces himself as Juan, the counsellor. *We have some new faces*, he says, smiling.

Welcome. To begin, let's do an ice-breaker question. What's everyone's favourite candy? Sharon, do you want to start? Sharon is a tiny woman who is overweight. You can be both. Take up both wide and negative space. She is visibly shaking. When she speaks, it is in the high pitch of a child. *Sharon, and I, really like M&Ms.* Before you have a chance to focus on her, the attention is diverted away, and I can feel her sigh with relief.

What about you, Mary? Juan asks, still smiling. He's looking at a woman in a wheelchair. She looks like she is 105 years old. She is the skinniest person I've ever seen. *Why you bother asking Mary?* some guy chimes in. *You know she don't say shit.*

Maybe Mary wants to speak today, Juan says, still fucking smiling. *Mary?* The guy sitting beside me nudges my ribs. *That's Mary the mute. She's been here forever. Last time I was here was a year ago, and she was there in her wheelchair, ignoring everyone. Time doesn't pass with Mary. Technically, she should be in the eating-disorder ward, but they decided she was suicidal, so she's with us freaks.* He nudges me again as he says freaks, like it's a joke I'm supposed to be in on. I ignore him and look at Mary. Everyone is staring at Mary. Silent cheerleaders, willing her on. She doesn't acknowledge the room, instead staring straight ahead. *Okay, maybe tomorrow,* Juan concedes.

Next up is an obese man with a badly shaved head, with tufts of hair growing out in sporadic spurts. Even though he's on the other side of the room, I can tell he smells. He rubs his eyebrows every time he talks. *Hi guys. I am a schizophrenic and I'm homeless, this is my eighth time in here. I love Hershey's, man, I would kill for some Hershey's right now.* He grins, showing a row of missing teeth.

An older man in a tweed waistcoat speaks after the schizophrenic. *My name is Robert, I am a jack of all trades, master of none. Ha ha ha! No, I am actually very skilled. I used to be a Hollywood producer, and now own multiple businesses.*

I shouldn't be in here; it was a Grade A fuck-up and someone will have to pay. I will be suing this place, and it's looking like I'll get a couple mil'. I am a lawyer so am very well versed on the law, and you guys have broken the law having me here.

Thanks, Robert, Juan says, of course still bloody smiling. His permanent grin is starting to get under my skin. *But if we can focus on the ice-breaker question right now.*

Robert copies Juan's demeanour. *Thank you, Juan. You really are doing a fantastic job. I do enjoy Skittles. What about you, Chan?*

Beside Robert is a young Asian man, with a scar across his left cheek. *Yo, man, Robert, you think I can get in on that money? I shouldn't be here either.* Robert inhales sharply. *No, no, NO. You clearly do not understand the LAW.* Chan nods thoughtfully, accepting Robert's annoyance. *Well, I like all candy, really. My dad tried to molest me.*

All hell breaks loose at this. Most people in the room gasp, but in big dramatic ways, making sure everyone else can hear them. *MOLESTED,* someone screams. I look around, but can't tell who. They are all suspects. Sharon starts to cry. Heavy, wailing sobs. Juan is pale. Someone down the back whispers, *Gay shit,* and I see at least one other person nod in agreement. An older woman comes over and grabs Chan's head, trying to rock him against her breasts. Juan tells her to sit back down. He clears his throat, silencing the buzz in the room. Everyone looks at him expectantly. *Thank you for sharing that, Chan. For trusting us with that massive part of you. You are welcome to discuss this further. Only if you want to.*

Well, he didn't actually touch me, because he knew the cameras were watching. But he wanted to. He would fuck my mom and think of me. I received his thoughts into my head because I can do that. That bastard was crazy for me.

The balloon in the room quickly deflates. Everyone settles

down. Some people look disappointed. Juan takes a breath and resumes the ice-breaker question. As if on cue, a girl in the back pipes up. This room is an orchestra, moving and speaking in some synchronized rhythm for the crazy.

Bitch, if you look at me one more time, I will break your neck. Everyone looks over to where the girl is staring, hoping it isn't at them. She isn't looking at anyone, focusing on a spot on the wall in front of her. *Yes, bitch,* she continues, *one more fucking look.*

Who are you talking to? Robert asks, in a forced gentle voice, turning his chair towards her, leaning forward, like he's fucking Robin Williams in 'Good Will Hunting'. *Oh, she knows. She fucking knows.* Sharon starts to cry again. *Yea, it's you, cunt.* We all stare at Sharon.

I'm going to give you a warning, which is your final warning, about threatening behaviour and offensive language, Juan says to her, resigned. Juan's smile has left his face, left the building, is twenty miles down the road. An older man gets up and walks to the door, pointing at the clock on his way out. The two and a half hours are suddenly over. We didn't even get to hear half of the room's favourite candy.

17

Cigarette breaks are every two hours, at ten to the hour. At 1.46pm, I join a small queue at reception. Sandra, the prettiest staff member, with her thick black hair and massive Bambi eyes, unzips my bag of belongings and takes out my cigarettes. I remove two. *Everyone's gonna ask you for one,* she warns me; *you don't have to say yes.* I slide one back in the pack.

Everyone huddles at the side door at twelve to the hour, waiting. Most conspicuously without any cigarettes. We are let into the yard at exactly ten to the hour. The five of us with cigarettes circle Sandra, who holds up a lighter attached to a piece of string. Once lit, I walk to the other end of the yard, away from everyone else. I stretch my legs, feeling the heat of the sun on my thighs. I close my eyes and blow out smoke and pretend I'm on Venice Beach. When I lived part time in my apartment right by the boardwalk for three months, that was paid for by one of my sex benefactors, I drank cold-brew coffee every morning, then walked down to the beach in the afternoon, wearing my bikini underneath my sweatpants. Throwing my bag on the sand, and undressing. Walking into the water. The hot sun beat down on me, as I jumped over each wave, screaming in delight. When the sun started to pierce through me, I remembered my Irish skin and ran out of the water. My wet hair stuck to my back. My feet thumped against the sand. My breath fought up my throat. My heart bounced against my chest. So many signs I was alive.

I can feel the droplets of salt water on my body, quickly evaporating. I have my sunscreen and a beer on my towel beside me. I can smell candy floss and hot dogs from the vendors on the boardwalk a couple of yards away. I hear the crazy Venice boardwalk people from a distance. The crazies are stuck on the boardwalk, screaming at each other, music booming from never-ending speakers. They never step on the sand, in case it turns them to dust. I like the invisible barrier between them and me, clearly indicating there is a them and a me. Never an us. My feet are in the sand, so I am not them. I am me.

I keep my eyes closed, and when I hear *Hey, can I have ends?* I cock my head in the opposite direction until I hear footsteps fade out, the waves of the ocean hitting against the shore as they retreat. When I open my eyes, no one is around me. It's just me, leaning against a table that is bolted to the floor. Railings around me. Granite underneath me. Less alive, but still here.

The girl who wanted to hit Sharon is stalking around the yard, with no cigarette in hand. Uh oh. I see her circle in on those smoking, standing as close as she can to them without touching, whispering sweet nothings into their ears. I watch each person step back and dutifully hand over the cigarette they are smoking. She sucks on them, eyes quickly darting around the yard, like she's plotting murder. I can't recreate what that look is, but it exists, because she has it. It exists, because I see it. Then she sees me. And she's breaking out in a run, directly toward me.

Yo, dumb bitch. Dumb bitch? I guess that's me. I stare at her as she grows bigger with each step she takes toward me. When she reaches me, she snatches the cigarette out of my hand. *You're wearing shorts. You're not allowed. Shorts ain't allowed, and I wasn't allowed, so fuck you, bitch, you're not allowed either. Sandra. SANDRA. She ain't fucking allowed.*

Sandra sighs. *Time's up*, she yells. Sandra grabs my arm as we all walk back inside, directing me into the nurses' station. *I'm sorry*, she says, shrugging, *but Mercy is right*.

I laugh. *Her name is fucking Mercy?*

Sandra nods, and winks. *Shorts are against the rules, though*, she continues.

But it's LA, I counter, *it's so hot*. She shrugs again. The shorts are taken off me, and I'm given paper trousers to wear instead. They're not made from actual paper, but they sound like it when I move. When I walk back out, Mercy is sitting at the bench in front of reception. She looks down at my legs, and smiles. *Bitch*, I mutter, but not loud enough for her to hear.

18

It's 3.30pm. In the same tiny room where my bloods were taken, a fat man is sitting where the nurse was before. He has a salt-and-pepper beard, so I trust him, because doctors with grey beards know what they are doing. It's science. He reads through my chart. He asks me my history. He brings up my overdose. I am careful with my reply. I'm not going to be caught out again. *It was a big mistake. I don't want to die. I really want to live.* I am not sure I believe what I am saying, but that isn't the point. I just need him to believe it. He prescribes me Lexapro, because I was on it before. It doesn't matter that it didn't work before. *You can get sleeping pills from the nurse at 11pm each night, if you can't sleep.* I decide I like him, because I sure do like sleeping pills. As I stand up to leave, I remember, and ask him his name. *Dr Cabera.* I let out a sigh of relief. I have just sixty-seven hours left, if I play my cards right.

I look down at my itinerary. Dinner time. I wait in the therapy room with the six other patients on Tier 1. We are brought trays with pork slices, mac and cheese, and green beans. Everything is a sludgy texture, like they boiled it all in the same pot and forgot about it for an hour. I pick at the mac and cheese, and leave the rest untouched.

Are you not gonna finish that? I look up, and some goggle-eyed boy is leaning forward, three inches from my face. He looks like if Timothée Chalamet quit acting and took up being bipolar. When I shake my head, he quickly snatches my tray from me, afraid I'll change my mind. *I love the food here*, he says. *This place is the fucking best. I feel like I'm on vacation when I come in here.* Food spits out of his mouth as he talks.

I fucking hate this guy, taking joy in what is clearly a decrepit situation. How he can act like he's on holiday, when I'm in a fucking nightmare. I imagine holding a gun to his head and popping, watching his brains splatter against the wall, bits of skull mixing into the green beans. I smile. He smiles back. *You're cool, I like you. Hey, maybe we can hang out outside of here? I'll get your number before I leave.*

After dinner, it's a free-for-all. You can play board games, or write in your journal, or lie in your bed. I don't like Monopoly, so choose my bed. My room is beside the phone, an old-fashioned one hung to the wall, and doors have to be kept open at all times. I can lie on my bed and listen to one side of a conversation. Tonight, Robert is on the phone. He's getting very worked up. He's trying to keep his voice low, but he forgets about it every few words, so he's half whispering, half bellowing through the hallway. *No, no I'm not getting out TOMORROW, they're holding me another TWO WEEKS. I know. I KNOW! I HAVE tried, trust me, I HAVE TRIED EVERYTHING. I've physically threatened THE DOCTOR and even that didn't work!*

I am listening to Robert's wailing, lying on the hard single bed, staring at the ceiling, and no matter how much I try to imagine other moments, I can't leave here. I am stuck. One Mississippi. Two... I stop counting. It's futile. I am here. Until they decide I am not. I can't wish it away. I stare up. The ceiling is a murky shade of white. I imagine it falling down on me. It doesn't work. *Fuck, fuck, fuck,* I mutter, in place of the Mississippis. *I am not dead. I am glad I am not dead,* I think. *But this alive isn't it, either.* I hear Robert's soap opera, his ups and downs, as I stare at the ceiling. How the fuck did I end up here?

19

Eighteen hours in, I am in morning therapy. The thick scrambled eggs from breakfast are swirling around my stomach.

There is one new guy, replacing two who have left.

Robert is going around the room, taking cigarette orders in his notebook. He tells the room he has a contact dropping a shipment of cigarettes into the yard tomorrow, by drone, and who wants in? Everyone clamours to add their order. I look down at my journal. *Robert is fucking mental*, I write down, then underline. *Everyone else can't see how crazy he is, because they're nuts too. I am the only normal person in here.* I underline that sentence twice, as a reminder.

Right before the hour, just before Juan comes in to start therapy, Mercy turns to the schizophrenic guy. *Hey! Quit looking at me.* He touches his eyebrows. *I'm not, I have a lazy eye. It chooses where to look, not me.* Mercy spits on the floor in front of her. I look around the room as she does it, and catch eyes with another patient. I smile at her. I'm pretty sure she's the only other person in here who isn't crazy. I see her roll her eyes when Robert talks. I watch her smirk as Mercy spits. I can just tell she's normal. She's pretty, in a 'Girl, Interrupted' way. But Winona, not Angelina. Normal. Her long, blonde hair is stringy. She hasn't showered in a bit, but she's pretty. Unlike everyone else in here, she's quiet. She doesn't speak unless spoken to, and even then it's a minimal amount of syllables. I walk across the room and sit on the chair beside her. When I introduce myself to her, she whispers, *Jade*.

She arrived a few hours before me. She's young. When I ask her her age, she tells me seventeen. This is her third time in here. *You've tried to kill yourself three times already?* She shrugs. *Not really, but yea, I guess.* She's not allowed any sleeping pills, because her bloods came back elevated, because she's been doing a lot of drugs. When a seventeen-year-old says they've done a lot of drugs, your instinct is to laugh at them. But when the same seventeen-year-old's blood shows she's done a lot of drugs, and screams that she's destroying her body before she's even old enough to drink, you kind of have to listen. *I haven't slept in a week*, she says, and shrugs again.

Everyone likes her, because she shares her cigarettes, saying yes to anyone who asks. *Don't say yes to them, they're just taking advantage,* I warn her, with my older wisdom. *My parents will bring more*, she says, shrugging again. This girl is just one big shrug. Her parents visit each evening, bringing her Sweetgreen salads and Chick-fil-A nuggets and, most importantly, cigarettes. I can tell they are rich. I can tell they love her. I can tell by their eyes.

We become friends, as much as you can become friends in a psych ward in three days. We laugh at Robert, when he threatens to sue us for slander. We laugh at the schizophrenic, when he describes the aliens he met when he was living out of his car in Idaho, but can't tell us the secrets they told him because the government is listening. When Timothée Chalamet interrupts me in group therapy to tell everyone he's 95 per cent sure his dog wants to fuck him, we catch eyes and put our hands over our mouths, trying to suppress ourselves. She's my friend, because she gets it.

I am sad, because she gets it. She's too fucking young to get it. When I was seventeen, I was only beginning to get it. I suppose, at the time, I thought I fully got it too. But this seems worse. Maybe because I'm observing it. It's easy to see something clearly when you're outside of it. I want to fix her. I want to wash her hair, and comb it out. Clean her fingernails. I want to grab her by the shoulders and shake her until she lets all the sadness fall out. Instead, we sit together in the courtyard every two hours, sharing cigarettes as we talk shit about everyone around us. During the last smoke break before bed, I feel some mixture of affection and duty, and lean toward her. *It gets better, you know,* I say, *being seventeen is the fucking worst, but it does get better.* She smiles at me. *If that's true, why are you in here too?* I laugh. *Okay, well it gets better, and then worse again. Maybe it's that way forever. But can we promise not to give up until we're at least middle-aged?* I hold out my pinky to her. She smiles, but leaves me hanging. *I'm sorry, I just can't promise that.*

20

Twenty-four hours in. I am out of Tier 1. My reward: I get to go to the cafeteria for lunch. I line up with everyone at five minutes to twelve. We walk over in a single line. There are people in the cafeteria when we arrive. Skeletons of people, pushing their food around the plates. *The anorexics*, the schizophrenic announces. The building is in an L shape; the crazies in one part, the eating disorders in another, met in the middle by the nurses' station. The anorexics get an hour start on lunch before us, because it takes them so long. I grab a tray and wait in line. It's self-service. There are big spoons in every dish. There are two lunch ladies standing behind the food, monitoring the situation, making sure no one takes too much. I take a spoon of shredded pork, a spoon of unidentifiable green shit, a spoon of gravy. I walk over to the salad bar and take a heaping of wilted lettuce and tomatoes. I grab a box of juice and a bottle of water. Tier 2 is about options, baby!

I look around the room and sit down at an unoccupied table.

I take my first mouthful of food, and it tastes exactly like my first mouthful when I was in Tier 1. Sludge. They've tricked me with the plethora of options at Tier 2, but it still boils down to no choice.

I look around for Timothée Chalamet, but he's still on Tier 1, sitting in the recreation room with his tray on his lap, like he's at a spa. I walk back up and grab three bread rolls. I am hungry. When I get back to my table, it's full. The schizophrenic is here. I ask him his name. *Don't have one*, he says. He is shoving spoonfuls of food into him with an intensity that I can only admire. He is certainly alive. *If I am quick, I can go up for seconds*. Bits of green sludge spit out on the table as he talks. Without looking down, he scoops his hand and shoves the food back into his gob. He pushes his chair back, grabs his not-empty tray and runs to the buffet.

Left behind at the table are me and Jade, and a young skinny guy who has a face tattoo. *I skateboard*, he announces, like it was a burning question in our minds. We both stare down at our trays. *So, what are you guys in for?* he asks, licking his lips. We say nothing, swirling our plastic forks in the grey shite. *I bet it was suicide.* We look at each other. He's not wrong. He lets out a laugh. *I knew it! You pretty white girls, you're always trying to kill yourselves. Your lives are so dope you have to create bad shit in your brains. It's kinda hilarious.* He forgets about his fork, and sticks his fingers straight in the gravy jelly, letting out a moan as he tastes it. I have to look away, and my eye finds a skeleton pushing around a salad. I look back at the table, and the skateboarder is trying to floss with his plastic fork. *I am not these people*, I think for the fifteenth time today. And yet, here I am.

The schizophrenic rejoins the table, his tray spilling over. *The anorexics are here forever. Six months usually*, he says, spooning more dribble into his mouth. *I am a virgin. I've never had sex. But I've thought about it a lot. I want to fuck another virgin. Maybe a girl who is twelve years old. The Bible says that is okay. I've never done it, though, just thought about it.* I look at the skateboarder, and he's still flossing. I look at Jade, and she laughs, so I laugh. He is still talking about virgins when Sandra shouts, *TIME'S UP!*

We are lined up against the windows, beside the entrance. I can see the paint chipping off the door. *Code red*, Sandra yells. No one responds. I am beside the skateboarder, and I can see his fingers glistening with greasy oil, and I wish he'd drop dead right now, in front of me. *Someone is going crazy*, he says. *They have to subdue them. Probably with a shot to their ass. They'll be put in a straitjacket into a padded room. C'EST LA VIE.* He screams the last sentence. Like we're celebrating.

We find out at evening therapy who it was. Mercy. She attacked Juan. Tried to bite his ear off. He wears a bandage as he talks to us about the power of journaling, and I never see her again.

21

I am sitting at reception, waiting for my sleeping pill. It's only 8pm, but better to be ready. Mary the mute is in the corner. Her little helper is rubbing her head. Mary the mute, who has been assigned to our ward because her anorexia is a form of self-harm. She's trying to kill herself, through starvation. Because the rest of the anorexics are in the other end of the building, I only see them at lunchtime, or at the nurses' station to collect their sleeping pills. There's a group of them here tonight, sitting beside us crazies, but they're a few months into treatment, so they don't look like skeletons. A couple are even chubby. One is in a onesie, which makes me uncomfortable, because I hate when adults infantilize themselves. She went from wanting the body of a child to dressing like an infant. Baby steps, I suppose.

The onesie girl keeps talking about food. *It's French toast for breakfast tomorrow, which I'm so excited about because I'm a foodie, so I really love French toast.* She says more than this. She just goes on and on. Robert interrupts her. *It shows, how much you love food.* And he laughs. He bends over, howling. It's the funniest joke he's ever heard.

Fuck you, you fucking bastard! she screams, and I back her up. Robert might be crazy, but that doesn't mean he has to be a cunt. *Shut up, you fucking fool,* I tell him. Robert smiles. *You girls are so naughty.* I stare at him. He thinks we are flirting. *I'm sorry,* I say to the girl in the onesie, like I am a spokesman of the crazy people. She shrugs. *What he says about me says more about him than it does about me. I worked really hard to get here; I'm not going to let him push me off the ship.* I nod, and we all sit in silence, unsure of where to go from here.

Mary and her helper walk up to the nurses' station. All of us on the couches stare at her. Words are exchanged, assumedly not from Mary, because of her vow of silence. All we hear are whispers. Mary leans across the counter, as much as she can lean, maybe a ten-degree difference from her standing. Whatever the angle is, it's enough. Her jeans fall down from her. They slide down her bony hips, and her bony thighs, and her bony calves, so they are just a puddle at her bony ankles. She is wearing a diaper. *Oh God,* I hear someone whisper. Robert laughs, loudly, and someone else follows suit. The laughter vibrates through the room. I know, without looking, the people who are laughing. I know it's Robert and Chan. Mary glances back at us, and says nothing. Does nothing. I stare at her face, and can't pull out a single emotion from it. She is blank.

I keep staring, even after everyone else has turned their eyes away. And then I see. Water collecting at her eyes. Tears falling down her cheeks. A flicker of something across her face. That flicker pierces through me. There is someone trapped inside this mute body; someone who used to be. Who was a baby, and a child, and a teenager, and then a woman. What terrible things happened to her to make her give up? She's killing herself in the slowest way possible. She wants to suffer. They don't have this method on lostallhope.com. I wonder how deeply you have to hate yourself, to kill yourself that slowly? And what about her helper, who is watching her do it? Holding her hand during therapy, rolling her wheelchair down the hall, having a one-sided conversation with a person who won't talk back. What is more masochistic, the person doing the killing, or the one watching them die?

Her helper notices what has happened, and quickly pulls up her jeans. She rolls over her wheelchair, placing Mary in it, quickly wheeling her away. I see her hand on top of her shoulder, squeezing. As this is happening, the tears keep falling in silence. There is a Shakespearian play happening inside this woman, and it's starting to spill out.

And I do nothing. I just stare.

22

The next day is the same as the first two. Everything is already all melding into one. I lose sense of time, the only clock in the building being in my bedroom. My only gauge of continuum is breakfast, free time, therapy, snack, art class, lunch, therapy, doctor, dinner, recreation room, medications, sleep. By the third day, they all fall into each other, and I stare at the list in my notebook, unsure if each lasts ten minutes or eight hours. Confined to this building, the illusion of time simply fades away.

In morning therapy Robert tells us why he is in here. *See, my daughter, who I love dearly, is difficult. She's a cunt, so to speak. I would do anything for her, because I am a good person. She is very lucky in that regard. She was unhappy with me one day, so picked a fight. I don't like to argue, but I am good at it because of my years as a lawyer.*

Chan inexplicably starts clapping when he says lawyer, and Robert bows, before continuing. *She was upset I wouldn't give her money, because I do have millions. She called the police on me; said I was waving a gun around. I've never even touched a gun in my life! So, the cops came, she turned on the waterworks, said I threatened to kill her, blah de blah. I wouldn't mind, but I never even raised my voice. The police were in cahoots with her, of course. She promised them a slice of my money. The corruption of the police is a topic I will be exploring in my next book, but I can't say any more on that, so please do not ask.* He shoots Chan a pointed look, and Chan looks down at his feet. *Anyway, they took me away. Threw me in here. And the cherry on top, they took away all my guns!*

Juan tries to steer the conversation towards resolution. *Can you see it from your daughter's point of view? How she felt in that moment? How she might have seen things differently to what you saw?*

Robert ignores him. *I love my daughter, but I will never forgive her for this. I told her, you have to live with what you've done, and you will burn in Hell.* He smiles, and shrugs, in a 'What can ya do?' way. *That's her problem, though, not mine. History is not going to be kind to her betrayal.*

Juan says nothing in response, and the rest of the room are leaning forward, absorbing all of Robert's bullshit. For a second, I am leaning too, until I snap back to reality, realizing that you can't both have no guns and have the police take away your guns. I know Robert is lying, but I also know no one else can see that right now. To the rest of the room, he's a martyr. Robert scares me. He speaks in such a way that you believe him, until you listen to the words he says. That's a dangerous type of crazy. The ones who have bought into the reality they're pushing. I know that reality so vividly, it haunts me. I can see his future, and it ends at the bottom of a canal bed, with his daughter wondering for the rest of her life what she did wrong.

23

In art class, the schizophrenic draws up a plan to fix the economy. It consists of a spiral with a line through it. He spends the rest of the class asking people how he can get it to the President of the United States of America. He asks who the President is, so he can address the envelope right. There's a debate in the room, because Obama is still President, but Trump just won the election. Chan chimes in. *Obama is gonna be busy, packing and shit. He won't have time for this. You should address it to Trump.* The schizophrenic accepts this, nodding thoughtfully, writing on the top of his page FORE THE ATENSCHUN OF TRUMP in bright red marker.

He also has an idea for flying cars he's going to include in his plans. Not the execution to actually make the flying cars, just the idea, because he's an ideas man. He holds up the paper for everyone to see, and at the bottom of the page is a drawing of a car with aeroplane wings.

That's so stupid. You're not the first person in the world to have the idea of flying cars, I say, laughing. I'm pretty sure every schizophrenic homeless guy to exist has had that idea. He looks at me like I'm crazy, like I'm the one who drew a car with aeroplane wings to give to the President. *That's just not true. I invented it right now.* He points to the drawing for effect. *Please apologize to me, because it upsets me for you to call me a liar. This matters to me.* He spits out his words, because he's now crying.

I am sorry, I offer to him. He stops crying, smiles and takes a blue marker from the pile. *Where does the President live? I want to make sure he gets this.* I look down when he speaks, and draw a spiral on my paper too.

I tell Robert to shut up in afternoon therapy. He's talking too much and his words are giving me a headache. I get a warning, for aggressive behaviour. Apparently, I said more than just shut up. I corner Juan after therapy. *You know Robert is a fucking idiot, please don't try and make me crazy for identifying his bullshit.*

Juan gives me a restrained smile. *You need to focus on yourself. There will always be people worse than you, and if you use that as a measure, you'll never get better. You are here for a reason, and you'll only get out of here if you face up to that reality.*

I narrow my eyes. *Is that a threat? Because I was told I was only here for seventy-two hours, so don't try and add time to me. There is nothing wrong with me. I know you know that. Deep down, you know I'm not crazy, right?*

Juan shuffles the papers on his desk, avoiding my gaze. *I don't think you're crazy. I don't think most people in here are crazy. Life is hard, and it's harder for some of us, just because of how we're programmed. You don't choose the brain you get, but you choose what to do with it. I believe you'll choose the right path.*

I stare at him, confused. *I am not crazy*, I repeat, and walk out of the room.

At dinnertime, I shovel the food into me and go up to get seconds. *More sludge, please*, I announce, happily.

I listen to the schizophrenic as he harps on about virgins. *Go fuck one of them then*, I yell at him. *If you're so sure, go do it right now.* He looks down at his food. *I don't want to be rushed*, he whispers into his plate.

That night, I swallow my sleeping pill and lie on my bed. My heart beats against my chest, so loud I'm sure it could break right open, as I stare at the ceiling. I think of the tears falling down the mute's face: tiny molecules of her trying to escape. I think about all the different ways there are to kill yourself. How some don't even involve death.

I think about Robert, and his daughter, calling the police because he's waving a gun around again. I think about how bad things happen to normal people, and it ruins them, and they sometimes stay ruined. And the people surrounding them get to feel the shrapnel of that ruin, bystanders watching a car crash in slow motion and being unable to stop it. Seeing the time before the crash grow smaller and smaller as they move further away.

I think of the spiral on the piece of paper, and how it means so much more than just a squiggle to the schizophrenic.

I think about how much harder life is for some people, just because of how they are hardwired. How life stays hard for those people, unless they work their balls off to undo their genetic make-up. How exhausting it is to try, all the time. How even with all the trying, life can still stay hard, but maybe less so than it had been. Is that a success? To still fail, but not as much as before?

I think of all the people inside this building, and all the lives they've led that have brought them here. I think about where they'll go from this moment. I think of them, and how much of them is me, until I drift off to sleep.

24

Eighty-two hours after I first arrived in this dump, I am called into the little back office. Dr Cabera is sitting at the desk, his head bent down in a stack of papers, scribbling away. He asks me two questions.

Do you have any thoughts about harming others?
Do you have any thoughts about harming yourself?

I answer no to both. He looks up, smiles and signs some piece of paper. *You're free to go*, he says, handing me a prescription for antidepressants and sleeping pills.

I am free to go. I grab my belongings: denim shorts, shoelaces, my phone and a $20 bill. The locked door buzzes open. I walk outside and wait for the steel gates to part. I am a free man. It's hot, that dry heat of a desert, because LA is technically a desert after all, a desert full of Sweetgreen salads and insincerity and Juvéderm, but a desert nonetheless, and I am someone who sweats very easily, so I change into my shorts in the middle of the street. I know I have only been in the psych ward for three and a half days, and seven days in the hospital before that, but I feel like a prisoner being released after ten years. The world feels peculiar, just a tiny degree off. The grass looks a different shade of green, which is crazy because I am in LA so there's no grass anywhere.

In the gas station, I am rude to the attendant. *Have a nice day,* he says, after ringing up a pack of cigarettes and a Snapple. *Fuck you*, I reply, delighted with myself.

I have spent the past three days really seeing humanity, the true truth of people, and now everyone else is still playing pretend, but I can see through it all, and I am somehow better than everyone else for it.

I chain-smoke while waiting for the bus towards Conell's house. We're so far out of the city, it will take me a couple of hours. I hate the buses in LA. They move too slowly, meandering around the city, really taking their time. They are hot and stuffy and there's always a guarantee of someone smelling of piss. The people who take the buses in LA are the same people who end up in 5150s. They're all different degrees of crazy, but it's still crazy.

I have five hours to kill in Conell's neighbourhood until he's off work. I am starving. I walk into a hipster deli. I order the cheapest sandwich on the menu, a vegetarian half sub. I check my change; I have $5 left. I look at the drinks menu. Kombucha, homemade lemonade, coffee, craft beer. I count on my fingers. Eighteen days of sobriety. I look back at the menu. Eighteen days. I think of the AA meetings, and the overdose, and the seven days hooked up to wires in the hospital, and the three days after that hooked up to craziness. These eighteen days have been a black hole, and I don't know how to get out. I glance back at the menu. Maybe I do know. I order a beer. I take my first sip, feeling the cold liquid pour down my throat. It feels fucking good.

By the time Conell collects me from the deli, he has to hand over $30 to pay my outstanding bill. *I'm free!* I scream at him. *We must celebrate.*

We pick up a case of beer on our walk back to his apartment. We sit in his living room, drinking and laughing, as I tell him about everyone inside the ward.

Where's Timothy? I ask at one stage. Conell's boyfriend is missing. *He's not answering me*, Conell says, looking down at his phone.

Timothy avoids the apartment the entire night. I know he's avoiding me. *What's his fucking problem?* I slur. *I didn't catch a disease just because I got committed.* That's what I decide his problem is. Timothy hates depression. *Fuck you*, I text him. I get a response fifteen minutes later. *You are one of my best friends. And you never told me any of what was going on. I had no idea. Then you tried to kill yourself, and it hurt me. You could have died. And now you and Conell are laughing and drinking like nothing has happened. Something has happened, Marise.*

There's a cause and effect to everything we do. I understood that when I was the effect, but I forgot it when I was the cause. When you hurt yourself, you're not just hurting yourself. You're hurting everyone who loves you: the people who have tacos with you when you're hungry, and pick out your outfits before a date, and fight with you, and go on road trips with you through the desert. The people who blend your blush when you've put it on terribly, and buy you beers when you have thirty cents in your account, and give you Christmas presents of sexy lingerie so you can take really good nude photos. You forget those people when you do it, but they don't. They don't forget what you've done. No person is an island; no matter how alone you feel in that moment, there are people who care about you, whose hearts you are breaking because of what you've decided to do. You don't get absolved from that reality.

When I read his text, I shove my phone in my bag, ignoring that reality. *He's a dick*, I say to Conell, and we open another beer.

By midnight, we are bananas drunk, dancing in the sweaty box of Akbar, our favourite gay bar. We are downing shots, and scream when Britney comes on the speaker. We take breaks outside when we overheat, sitting on the sidewalk outside the bar, smoking rings into each other's faces, laughing about Robert. A car drives by, and hurls something at us. Not specifically at us, but it lands on us. I feel a hard whack against my shoulder. For a second, I think I have been shot. The gays smoking cigarettes around us scream.

I've been egged, at twenty-five, wearing the real leather jacket an old man bought me so I'd continue to fuck him, the fucking day I'm released from a psychiatric hospital, outside my favourite gay bar in LA. I cannot believe it.

I fall down, clutching my shoulder. *A hate crime* is repeated multiple times. I nod. *They shouted TRUMP when they threw the eggs*, I add to the tale at some stage during the night. This leads to more gasps, more shrieking, more outrage. Conell leans over to me. *I don't remember them yelling Trump.* I shrug. *Well, no, but they definitely thought it.* He eyes me suspiciously, then shrugs. *Fuck Trump.* We're both sipping our complimentary drinks, revelling in the commotion we've caused.

Trump, Trump, hate crime, homophobic, Trump, spreads around the bar. I raise my beer in a toast, delighting in the bedlam I've stirred up. *Trump, trumpets, a trump card, The Truman Show.* Words fold into each other, creating something else, until the origin is so far removed, I forget exactly what we're angry about. The chaos zipping around the room is so familiar it sobers me up. I am trying to make a distinction, between yesterday and tonight, but the line seems made up. Maybe we're all crazy, and some of us just hide it better than others.

25

I wake up the next morning on Conell's couch, with a pounding headache. I get an Uber back to my place, stopping to throw up on the side of the 401, the heat of the 4am jalapeño pizza burning my throat. I walk into an empty house, and when I reach my room I notice the door is missing from its frame.

I collapse on my bed and take out my phone, scrolling through my recent calls, thinking I'll call Gal and bother him, demand he comes home, and the attention he'll surely give me will spur me out of my hangover. I see a call to a number I don't have saved, from eleven days ago. The night I overdosed. I click into it, and see it lasted twenty minutes. I see a further two missed calls from the same number, a day after I placed the call. I type the digits into Google. The website for a suicide prevention line flashes up on my screen. I sit up on my bed and call them back. *Hey, I am a bit confused, but I think I called this number eleven days ago, and I don't remember it, but...* They ask for my full name, and then transfer me. A warm voice picks up.

Thank you for calling me back, she says. *I was so worried when I didn't hear from you. I thought the worst, so I am really happy to hear your voice.*

I clear my throat. *Um, I am sorry. I don't remember calling you, or what I said. I overdosed that night, and I can't really piece it all back together.*

Her voice radiates through my phone. *That's okay, I can help you with the missing pieces. You called us, and sounded very distressed. You said you were afraid you were going to kill yourself. You had just taken some pills. You told me you had taken them only a few minutes ago. You said you didn't see any other way for yourself, but this. You got very upset, and asked me to help you. You said you don't really want to die. You said that, over and over again. I tried to get you to call 911, and you seemed receptive to doing that. Then you hung up on me.*

I cringe as she speaks. *I'm so sorry, that I did that to you. That's really unfair. Trying to drag you into my mess.*

She inhales. *No, no! You can't look at it like that. You asked for help when you needed it. Don't ever apologize for that.*

I stare at the ceiling as she talks. *I was so weak,* I tell her.

No, no, you were brave, Marise. I really hope you believe me when I tell you, you are brave. Tears fall down my face when she says that. *Thank you,* is all I can mutter back. We end the call once I've given her my medical details, and promised her I'll call if I feel this way again. *Life is hard,* she tells me, *but you are here right now, and that isn't a failure, okay?*

I hang up the phone and close my eyes, my cheeks still wet. I see a future where I keep running. I see bottles of booze, and bottles of pills, and maybe not death, but definitely not much aliveness either. I see the schizophrenic, and Robert. I know they are not so different to me really. Not so much that I can't understand them, even if I wish I can't. They are like me, but they just kept running, all their lives. I see Mercy, and the mute. Opposite sides of broken. I see myself in all of them. I also see another me, a woman the Samaritan described, someone who made the choice to save herself. I see the me who begged, *Please, I don't really want to die.* I see all these different strands of me, dancing together in my eyelids, and I wonder who will win.

FIVE

THERE WILL BE BLOOD

1

I cycle through the streets of Dublin, weaving in and out of traffic, my breath fogging in the cold air. I look around at the buildings as I wait for the light to turn green. Everything looks exactly as I left it four years ago. Nothing in this city has changed. I can't decide if that is comforting, or suffocating. When the light changes, I stick my feet into the pedals and furiously cycle along the quays, until a stitch burns into my side and I have to pull over. *Jesus Christ,* I pant, *since when is Dublin so uphill?* I stare at the very level road in front of me, turning my head to give it more of an incline. *Just fucking do it,* I will myself, and begin cycling again.

Despite the three different pit stops I make on my two-mile journey, I still arrive at my new therapist's office ten minutes early, which is very out of character for me, but I am desperate to get the ball rolling; I don't want to miss out on even a minute of my new beginning. I tear off my jacket and scarf and jumper, fanning my t-shirt against my sticky body to generate some cold air. The receptionist ignores the sweat dripping down my face as he hands me a new patient form to fill out.

Under previous treatments, I write *Lots*. Under current medication, I scribble *Lexapro – not a fan*. I sit in the waiting area, my leg shaking, counting down the minutes to my absolution.

A woman with blonde wiry hair and thick glasses pokes her head out of the door to my left and calls my name. I follow her down the corridor, repeating the words I am going to say in my head. This is too important to stumble on. Once inside her office, I plonk down in the armchair by her desk. *I am here today to…* I begin, at the exact same time she says, *No!*

I look at her outstretched arm, paused in the air. *Sorry, no, that's my chair.* She points at the much less comfy chair beside the door. *That is your one.* I stand up, embarrassed, and slink over to my chair, the awkwardness hanging in the room. This is not how I wanted to start my new beginning. *Look, sorry about the chair. Maybe you should have a sign making it clear, because it's an easy mistake to make when you have two chairs in your office, it's a 50/50 guess…*

I look up at her, and a poker face stares back at me. I wish I hadn't said so much about the stupid chair. It wasn't part of the speech I had spent hours reciting in my bedroom. I hope she's not judging me for my verbal diarrhoea. *Okay, anyway, fuck the chair. I just need you to know I am serious about this. I've had a lot of false starts, but this time, I am ready to help myself. I am so fucking ready.*

She smiles. *That's exactly the attitude I want a patient to have! So, my name is Aine and I…*

I lean forward. *Let's not waste any more time. Take out your notebook please; there's a lot to get through. I'm pretty sure it's all textbook stuff, so this should be your bread and butter, but the sooner we get through what happened before now, the sooner you can fix me.* I laugh self-consciously at that. *I mean, I know you can't fix me, but, you know, we can fix me together, or whatever...* I trail off, mortified at how stupid I sound.

At the end of the session, she opens her diary. *I think you should meet with me twice a week, to begin with, and the psychiatrist once a month. Does that sound like a plan?* I nod. She hands me a slip of paper with the dates and times.

So, you're telling me there's a chance?

She stares at me blankly. My face grows hot.

It's a 'Dumb and Dumber' quote, sorry, forget it. I was just trying to be funny. But I'm very serious about this. I'll see you on Wednesday.

When I get back to my apartment, my roommate Kevin is sitting on the couch. *So how did it go?* he asks, looking up from the TV, where 'There Will Be Blood' is playing, a film he's watched nine hundred times before.

I collapse on the couch beside him. *Oh God, it was awful! I made a stupid joke, and sat on the wrong chair.* I shake my head. *It was really fucking grim.*

He pauses the film. *I'm sure it wasn't as bad as you think it was. And the first step is always the hardest to take. It's good you took that first step. I'm proud of you.*

I throw an empty Pringles can at his head. *Oh God, shut up!* He laughs. *I don't know what came over me there. It felt weird as soon as I said it. Let me submit an official recant, please. I'm not proud of you. In fact, I'm deeply ashamed of you. And furious that you're interrupting my film.*

I laugh. *Oil, hard men, money, greed, softening of men, hardening of them again, more greed, death, credits roll. There you go, you're welcome.*

He shoots me a filthy look. *You know it's more nuanced*

*than that! Anyway, want to get some food? I'm in the mood
for a burger.*

Kevin is my best friend, but he wasn't always my best friend.
The first night we met, we had a big argument, screaming in
each other's faces. I thought he was an egotistical dick, and he
thought I was an up-myself bitch. And then we were forced
together through circumstance, and he kept making me laugh,
more than anyone else I had ever met. So, my hardened stance
on him softened. We became friends. I hated him, then I liked
him and now I love him. That's often how it goes.

We bite into our burgers. *I'm not sure about this woman,*
I tell him. He laughs. *I know you think you're the Nostradamus
of our time, but sometimes your first impressions are wrong.
Look at us. So just give her a chance.*

I look across the table at him, at the person who makes
me happier than anyone else, and give in. *Okay, that's a good
point, I guess. I suppose I can give her a chance. And if you end
up being wrong, you owe me a burger.*

He rolls his eyes. *Deal.*

2

I show up to Aine's office twice a week, and sit for an hour
each time, unpacking who I am. I don't leave anything on the
table; I give her all of it. I tell her everything about my dad, and
the old men, and the depression that never seems to leave me.
In between the talking, she gives me tests: pages of questions
that she promises there's no right answers to. When she hands
me the results, words on a page that mean nothing to me,
I read 'destructiveness', 'attention seeking' and 'entitlement',

with little paragraphs underneath to explain how they apply to me. She says other words I can't make sense of. She mentions a personality disorder. *Disorder sounds bad, but it's really not that absolute. I think it would be good for the psychiatrist to follow this up, and see if there's a diagnosis*, she explains.

No! I shout, gripping my chair.

I had met with the psychiatrist the first week of my treatment, and he listened to ten minutes of my monologue on how Lexapro wasn't helping, and that there were still times I wanted to kill myself, before cutting me off. *How recently?* he asked, not looking up from his stack of papers. *How recently did you want to die?*

I did the quick maths. *Maybe a month ago?*

He nodded. *That's fine, that's not immediate.* He wrote a prescription for Lexapro.

I threw my bag at the wall, hot with anger. *You're not listening to me! You people never really listen.* He checked his watch as I spoke, ignoring the missile I had just launched across his desk.

The Lexapro is fine, and I have another appointment now, so…

I tell Aine what he said when she brings up the personality disorder. I assume she'll dismiss me, just like he did, so I am aggressive with my words, expecting her to combat them. *Hmm, that's not right,* she tells me, looking right into my eyes. *You know, these guys come in on placement, they're only here for six months, so I don't know how committed they are. That doctor did his studies in America, and it's different there. It's either you're crazy, or you're not. They don't have the grey area there, of what mental health can often be, so I think he could have ignored you based on that.*

I stare at her, waiting for the catch; the swerve of words that will invalidate everything she's just said, that of course he is actually right and I am wrong. But they don't come. I pinch my arm to make sure this is real life, that this is really happening. I can't believe that after all this time a professional is actually listening to what I say, and we are having a two-way conversation. That is not me trying to shite talk the mental-health industry. Some doctors didn't listen to the words I told them, and instead plopped me into a predetermined box, one that didn't fit me. Others wanted to help me, and either I wasn't willing to accept the help, or their help was in a language I didn't understand. There's no one at fault in this, or else we're all at fault, because there's no easy answer to mental illness. Everyone is just guessing. And up until now, no one has guessed right with me. I knew there was something wrong with me when I was fourteen years old, and now, thirteen years later, I finally feel heard. Therapy is like a much more time-consuming and expensive type of dating. You have to try a lot of different people, before you find the one who fits you. And I feel such a fucking relief, that Aine really hears me.

I just want to talk to you, I tell her softly. *I've never trusted any of you people, but I think I could trust you.* She writes into her little notebook. *That's okay, I won't make you see him if you don't want to. We can just keep talking.*

So, we keep talking. The hours pile on top of each other, and the pieces start to form a blurry picture. I talk and talk and talk, and when I'm not sure of things, she offers up an answer, not forcing something down my throat, but just a suggestion. *Maybe you found your ex crying about his son pathetic, because the first time you saw a man's vulnerability was your father, drunk?*

I nod. *Oh shit, yea, that makes perfect sense!*

Some days I am tired of talking, so we just sit in silence. And even though nothing is being said, I still feel like something is happening.

3

When I bring up the old men I have fucked for money, or getting fired from my job, Aine always brings it back to my father. *You love getting attention, even if it's bad attention, because your father taught you that was the most valuable part of you. That having eyes on you meant you were worthwhile.* I roll my eyes when she does this, when she reduces everything I am to some part of him, but I also get it; an addict father who killed himself – that's a therapist's Olympics. They live for that shit. Still, it does annoy me, that no matter what I tell her, she always brings it back to him. *You know everything isn't related to him, right? I exist away from him. I am not just my father's daughter.*

Of course, she says, readjusting her glasses. *But until you accept everything he was, and everything that happened to you, you can't move forward from it. That is true for anyone: until we fully accept our childhood, we'll keep repeating the mistakes of it; trying to rectify what happened to our child self, the person who didn't have autonomy over their own life.*

If I played a drinking game during therapy, downing a shot every time Aine said, 'Child self', I'd need my stomach pumped. *You know, sometimes you're such a stereotype of a therapist. I like you a lot, but sometimes you are such a fucking cliché.*

She laughs when I say this, never offended. *Oh God, I know! It's very therapy by the numbers. But some clichés are such because they're the truth.* I reluctantly nod. Even though I don't like what she is saying, I trust her enough to believe it's true. I hold up my hands in surrender. *Fine! You win!* And we keep digging.

4

In the spring, or it might have been the summer, I tell Aine about the psych ward. *That was my rock bottom,* I earnestly say, regurgitating words I've heard from Dr Phil and other hack shows. *I don't like the term rock bottom,* Aine responds, *it implies a linear nature to depression, when the reality is that really it ebbs and flows.* I ignore her, annoyed she's trying to wreck my buzz with her therapist logic. I have read enough memoirs, about people in terrible trouble, and then getting themselves out of it, to know the drill. If it was written in a book, it has to be true. So that was my bloody rock bottom! And I have come out the other side; I am making progress, and so, deducing from that, the only way forward is up.

I am better now, I tell myself, as I unchain my bike after our session. But this turns out to be a lie.

I leave a coke-fuelled after-party, in a part of Dublin I don't know, and my phone dies. I am lost, and spend hours walking the streets, growing more frantic with each passing minute. For the past month, I have been slipping. I have let myself slip. Staying out every night until 6am, drinking. Sleeping most days until 5pm. No yoga, or vegetables, or daylight. My bones have become heavy again. Being awake is exhausting. I have lost my grip. And to arrive back here, after believing it was behind me, comes as a shock. But a very familiar shock. Of course, if I am honest with myself, I knew it would always come back to this.

I finally get back to my apartment and, unable to find my key, climb in the window to my room. I lie on my bed, staring at the ceiling. I can't get to sleep. The bad thoughts are back.

I'd forgotten how bad they are. They come into my head with a strength that overwhelms me. Despite all my good work in the previous months, I have spent the past five weeks undoing everything, so here I am, yet again, wanting to die.

I text Kevin: *Come home, I need you.* My phone buzzes a minute later: *I can't.* I throw my phone on the floor and take four Xanax, hoping I don't wake up for a week.

When he comes into my room the next morning, I turn away from him. *I'm not talking to you.* Within an hour, I have relented, and he sits by my bed, his hungover head resting on my duvet, eating Pringles. I go to make a joke, but he interrupts. *If I have to hear another gag, I will get up and leave. I need you to have an honest conversation with me. I can't do this otherwise.* I look at him, and start talking. He doesn't have answers, neither of us do, but he is there, at the end of my bed, listening to me. Handing me Pringles while I search for the words.

When I get dressed, I tell him I am okay. And I believe the words I'm saying. I am okay. By 4pm, I am drunk, throwing a glass at the wall because I've gotten an answer on 'Countdown' wrong. By midnight, I am back to where I was the night before. Wanting to die. I still convince myself I am okay. If I admit to myself I am not, that means I have to do something about it. And I'd rather just let myself sink.

Five nights later, Kevin and I are both at a stand-off, on opposite sides of the living room. I kick the flatscreen TV off the stand. My mind has lost control again. It doesn't really matter what the catalyst is this time – what matters is that I always end up back here.

I lift up the TV and try to throw it at the window. Kevin

quickly slams it out of my hands, and we stand in the quietness for a moment, staring down at it, a deep crack across the screen. I shrug. I run into the kitchen, ignoring the shredded cheese on the countertop, the remnants of a meal I rustled up out-of-my-mind drunk last night, and grab a knife from the drawer. Without thinking, I stick the silver blade into my thighs, over and over again, watching the blood pour from me. I feel nothing.

I walk back to the living room, blood trickling down my legs, and watch Kevin's face as he takes it all in. I laugh. I charge forward with the knife, positioning it towards him now. And then his body slams against mine, hitting the kitchen knife out of my hand. I stand up, like someone possessed, and lunge for the knife again. When I get my hands around it, I slice it against my thigh. If I can't hurt someone else, I can use myself as the punching bag instead. Then I feel his grasp around me, and I fight it. I kick and punch him, but he's stronger than me. It will take hours, but he won't give up, eventually getting the knife from my hand.

He will stay up with me all night, until the sun comes up, lying beside me on the couch, the broken furniture strewn around us. *I want to die*, I will sob. He will hold my crying body, and I'll feel his own tears fall onto my face. *Well, tough luck, because I'm not going to let you do that.*

As the dawn cracks through the curtains, I will try a different strategy. I will climb atop him and stick my hand down his pants. He will whisper, *No, no, this is a bad idea*, and try to push me away, but then his dick will grow hard and he'll flip me over on the couch. *You know I've always loved you*, he'll say, and I'll pretend I haven't heard him. We will fuck, frantically, like animals, and when I wake up the next day, he won't be able to look at me, so ashamed of what I made him do. The cold autumn sun will pierce through the living-room window, and my head will be pounding bloody murder, but I'll feel satisfied, looking at his head buried beneath the cushion. That I was able to destroy something that had meant everything to me.

5

I continue to let myself slip. I keep drinking, and skipping therapy. I stop responding to all the messages that flash up on my phone.

I am fine, I tell myself, knowing I'm not. *Who cares?* another part of me asks, and I nod. If it always comes back to this, at least it's something familiar. A thing I can recognize.

I leave my apartment at night and walk across a busy road with my eyes shut. I hear the tyre screeches and a horn blare. *Hey, lady, watch where you're going! I almost knocked you down.* I give the finger. I walk down to the methadone clinic on the quays, to where addicts congregate outside. *I'll give one of you €20 to punch me in the face. At least three times.* Someone accepts, taking the note from my hand, giving me a light slap. *Harder*, I demand, and they run off.

One night, I stick a plastic bag over my head. I suck in air, until there's nothing left but me and the bag clinging to my face. I cut through it when I start to get lightheaded. *You are destined to die by your own hand*, I tell myself. *So why can't you pull the fucking trigger?*

I walk down my street, to the Liffey. I grip the metal rail, looking down at the river. I listen to the water hitting the banks. I lean over, so my feet leave the ground. *Do it,* I tell myself, *just fall in.*

I keep leaning further over the bar. The sound of the water gets so close, I can feel it inside my body. Almost there. My head dangles over the rail, so it is meeting the river face-first. I can almost taste the water. I loosen my grip on the metal rail. *Fucking do it*, I will myself.

 I pull myself back, until my feet meet the concrete. There's some part of me that wants to live, and it's what stops me falling in – I can't wrangle out that piece of me. It stays buried deep within myself. Strong enough to keep me going, but not strong enough to stop me wanting to die.

Most nights, I drink a bottle and a half of wine. By not finishing the second one, I convince myself I am still in control. *Someone with a real problem would drink this dry*, I reason, as I pour the remaining chardonnay down the sink.

I take a Xanax when my drunk thoughts turn negative, and another if the first doesn't work, until I am splayed out on my bed, giggling at all the different images my ceiling is creating.

And still, I can't always stick to the flimsy boundaries I've set myself. One night, when I have drunk two full bottles of wine, and taken three Xanax, and still can't shake the bad thoughts, I fill up a bath. The hot water instantly relaxes me, and I sink down, my eyes growing heavy. Then I slip under, letting myself fall in, and only wake up when I am coughing up water. I use all the strength I can muster to grab the edge of the tub and roll my body over, on to the cold tiles. I am still gasping for breath as I reach for my phone, calling up the one person I know who won't judge me.

Harvey answers on the third ring. *I need help*, I tell him. *If I keep going like this, I'm going to die. Just please tell me how to save myself.*

He begins his AA sales pitch, just like he does every time I call him.

Alcohol isn't my problem! It's a solution to my problem.

Please, can we just have a conversation that doesn't centre around my drinking?

I hear him smile on the other end of the phone, thousands of miles away. *We can. But you need to really be honest with yourself. You need to talk about him.*

I laugh. *I'm in therapy. I talk about this stuff every week. I make jokes about it to my friends. I don't have a problem talking about him.*

It's one thing to make jokes about it. To talk about it, detached. But have you ever talked about him with emotion?

That question does something to me, brings me to a place I've never allowed myself to go. The knot in my throat tightens. The tears fall, hard and fast. *I miss him*, I choke out. When he doesn't respond, I keep talking. *I miss my father in ways I don't have words for. I miss him like an amputee misses a limb. The phantom pain of what should be there. He always said I was a part of him, and without him here, I don't feel complete. And that doesn't make any fucking sense! It's so fucking stupid. Because if we're lucky, if life plays out fairly, we will all bury our parents. I know so many people who have done it, and are fine. So why does his absence burn a hole in my stomach? Why do I feel so incomplete without him here?*

I wait for an answer I know he can't give me.

This is so fucking dumb, to talk about something you can't change, I say.

Don't do that. Don't pull back from how you feel.

I sit in silence, holding the phone to my ear, hearing both of us breathe in and out. *I'm so fucking angry at him*, I finally admit.

It's okay to be angry he killed himself. That is normal.

That's not why I'm angry. I'm angry he tried to kill himself, when I was fourteen, and blamed me for it. I'm angry I let nine years pass, without us really addressing it, and then he actually fucking killed himself. I'm angry we'll never have a resolution to my pain. That we were robbed of the opportunity to forgive each other. That we didn't get that big Hollywood moment, when he told me how sorry he was for hurting me, and I was allowed forgive him.

I can barely make out the words I am saying. Snot is pouring down my face.

Keep going, Harvey tells me.

And I'm so fucking angry at myself, for being angry at a dead person, at a person who decided to die, because he felt so alone he didn't see any other way out than death. I know my father like I know my own body. He wouldn't have given up if he thought I hadn't already. I let my father die, I sob. *And there's no way to forgive myself for that.*

Your father hurt you in a way a parent isn't supposed to.

He also loved me more than anyone.

He can be both things.

I feel my heart beat through my mouth. *I let him die, okay? And if someone can let the person who loved them most in the world die, they don't deserve to live either. I let him die, alone on that canal bank, and I'll never forgive myself for that. I don't deserve to be forgiven for that.*

Harvey lets me pant and heave. He lets my heart beat against my chest. He lets me suck in air, breathing it out slowly. *I am still here*, he says every few seconds. *Don't worry, I am still here.*

When I have calmed down, when my breathing is back to a regular pace, he speaks again. *So, can you see how the destructive choices you keep making are directly linked to that? That self-hatred you feel, you can see it's the cause of every bad thing you're doing? Tell me you can see that.*

I can see it, Harvey. But he is still dead. And I still let him die. There are no words that exist that can change that.

That shame that you feel, I understand it, because I've felt it too, but it's going to kill you. If you can't meet it head first, it's going to destroy you. And I know you are strong enough to meet it head first. Please, Marise, please meet it head first.

6

When the autumn turns into a too-early winter, I sit back in front of Aine, dejected. I am only here because she threatened to cut me off; if I didn't show up to my next appointment, after missing the past two months, she'd have to release me from the programme.

We sit in silence for what feels like an hour, but when I check the clock, less than a minute has passed. *You know, I was really worried*, she begins softly.

I nod, and interrupt her inevitable sentence. What she is about to say are words I have heard before. How many times can you hear the same sentiment, without getting bored? *I get it, I get it, I am a fucking drain*, I think to myself.

You know, when I was sixteen, I thought if I got to live to be an adult, this would all go away, and I'd laugh at the juvenility of wanting to die, I tell her. *Well, I've lived to be an adult, and time has only confirmed my inability to exist. It wasn't growing pains; it's who I am.*

Aine shakes her head. *You're attached to this idea of who you are, and that is the biggest threat to you. You need to let it go. It's paralysing you.*

You're wrong, I tell her, shrugging. *I am sorry, but you are wrong. You can't overwrite your DNA. You know, when I really think about it, I know my dad wasn't a tragedy because he killed himself; he was a tragedy because he was always going to kill himself. He was a person who did not have the tools to get himself out of bad situations, especially when the bad situations were inside his head. If I had answered his call to me the day before he killed himself, I might have stopped him doing it that day. What about all the other days after that?*

Aine says nothing. I sit back in my chair, digesting what I've just spit out. Sometimes I like the sound of my own voice so much I just pour out sentences without letting my brain inspect them. And then afterwards, when I'm listening to them, I'll think, *What a load of horse crap!* But this isn't one of those times. I consider the words, rolling them around my mind, and decide they're true.

Someone else can save you in a moment. Maybe they're your daughter, going into your room when you call her. Maybe they're your taxi driver, telling you a silly story once they've turned off the meter. Maybe they're your best friend, wrestling a knife from you. Maybe they're a do-gooder on the Samaritans hotline, repeating back at you everything you just said, so you can hear how fucking stupid you sound. So you can hear they're not really your words at all. But that is just one moment. What about all the other moments after that? There are not enough people in existence to save us from every moment. You save yourself, or you die. That's the reality. Another reality is that you can try and save yourself, and still die. There are no guarantees of happy endings for any of us.

I stare down at my hands, peeling away skin from my thumb. *When I was nine, I went to the dentist and he told me I had weak teeth. And I thought, what a piece of shit I am, or whatever the nine-year-old equivalent of that thought is. And then he asked my mum if she had eaten well when she was pregnant with me. She admitted she hadn't. She had been sick all the time, unable to keep down the food she knew she was supposed to digest. I was vindicated! I don't know what felt better, that it wasn't my fault or that it was hers, but I sang the whole car ride home. You did this to me! You caused this! The glee.*

I keep pulling the skin, until blood forms and my thumb starts to throb. *I was predisposed to have bad teeth, because my mother didn't eat right. My mother gave me weak teeth, and my father gave me a weak mind.*

You may be inclined towards certain things because of your dad, but that isn't set in stone. Your father didn't give you a weak mind. Your mind is your own to...

You're not fucking listening to me! I feel the heat rising in my body. I push it back, kick it down. I take a deep breath, determined not to get upset. I detach myself from my voice. *I am sorry for cursing, but just listen to me, please. What I am saying is that I can try and try and try, and things will go very well for a period of time, and I will smugly think I have beaten it, but all it takes is one day off, one day for the madness to seep back in, and suddenly I'm sitting by a canal, wanting to throw myself in. And that's a metaphor, but also sometimes literal. It's sometimes an actual canal, but other times it's a knife, or a bottle of pills. The point is that the force of it still takes me by surprise, every time. It happens so quickly my mind has to catch up with my body.*

The heat builds again. I feel it caught in my throat. My voice starts to crack. *Look, you can give me every test under the sun, and throw all your therapist lingo at me, and that other dude can pump me full of antidepressants, until I'm shitting out live-laugh-love quotes, but the horrible reality is that there might be a day I do not save myself. And then – then I will die.*

That's a fatalist attitude, Aine tells me, but I don't hear her. Tears are falling down my cheeks, creating wet patches on the collar of my t-shirt, not that I notice them. I am focused on the wall behind Aine, the bland cream melting into my brain. Words are pouring out of me more quickly than I can keep up with. I know if I look away from this wall, I'll suddenly become self-conscious and swallow them back down, and I know they need to be said, so I keep my focus.

Some people don't have happy endings. We don't all get ourselves out of bad situations. Maybe we don't try to save ourselves. Or maybe we do, and it haunts us all the same. You can try so fucking hard, and you can still lose. How long am I supposed to fight for, before I can just hold up my hands and admit defeat?

I am shaking on adrenaline, at finally saying out loud what I've always known was the truth. I look up at her, breaking away from the wall and myself, suddenly desperate for an answer.

You fight until you can't, she tells me, fixing me in the eye. *I wish I had a better answer, something more concrete, but that is all there is. You fight until you can't. And, from knowing you, I know you are able to fight. Your mind isn't weak, Marise. Your mind is so strong. It got you to here. Do you realize how hard that was, just to get to here? You think this is stronger than you, but I promise you, if you keep fighting, you will win. That win might not look how you think it should. It probably won't be neatly packaged, with an obvious label you can read and know, oh this is it. I can't promise you a clear answer, and you might struggle for the rest of your life. But if you are alive to see it, to see any of it, well, in my book, that's a fucking win.*

An instinctive, guttural laugh escapes from my mouth. *Are you allowed to curse?*

She laughs back. *Oh, I probably shouldn't. Don't report me.*

I wipe my tears with my hoodie sleeve, still laughing, my body relaxing down. *Is this what you guys call a breakthrough?*

It might be something. But a breakthrough is the same trite language as rock bottom. Nothing is really that clear-cut. Whatever happens from now, happens because you decided on it. There's no one moment of resolution for this. It is a continued effort. You have to wake up every morning, and pick back up where you left off. It's a slog. But it's the most worthwhile slog I know.

I look down at my bloody thumb, and raise it to my lips, giving it a light kiss. *I think I want to keep trying.*

She smiles. *There are no right or wrong answers in therapy, but let me break the rules, just for a second, and tell you: you've just given me the right answer.*

7

In my mother's house, I am rooting through old photos, trying to find a picture of me at my graduation. I stop at one. A photo of my brother, maybe five or six, playing dress-up in my pink clothes, and my dad smiling in the background. I smile at his smile. He was always so accepting, of whatever we wanted to be. How lucky I was, to have a father who didn't try to make me into something I wasn't. *You were a good dad*, I tell the photograph. *That's why it hurts so much now you're gone.*

I keep sifting. I come across a photo I've never seen before, of my dad when he was a teenager. He is smirking, his eyes shining. I don't recognize him at first. I see myself before I see him. I outline his face with my finger. In a way, it's like looking in the mirror. *We are made from each other*, I remember him telling me.

Seeing my father at this age, fifteen years before I was even born, I know there was no way I could have saved him. His story started much before mine. I came in mid-way, not knowing all the chapters that existed before me, and there's no way to save someone that late. In that same vein, he couldn't have saved himself. This smiling teenager didn't know what was in store for him. He was as much of a victim as anyone that he hurt. Maybe, if he had been born a decade later, the help he needed might have been available to him. But it wasn't. I look at the teenager staring up at me. I know I have to stop punishing him for what neither of us could control.

I kiss the grainy photo. *I forgive you*, I say out loud, knowing I'm not just talking to him.

I hold the photo of my father in my hand. I text Harvey: *What if I try, and fail?* My phone buzzes a few minutes later: *That's okay. Actually, that's to be expected. But you fail, and you try again. And again and again. As long as you keep trying, there will be people there to support you. And I'm one of them.*

I place the photo back in the pile, and slide the box back into my mother's wardrobe.

When I walk into the kitchen, my mother is standing by the stove, swirling a curry round with a wooden spoon. *Did you get what you were looking for?* she asks me, her back still turned.

Don't be so bloody nosy, I tease, and peer over her shoulder into the pot. *You've cooked that to oblivion!*

She laughs. *Oh shut up! I read a recipe that adds some mango chutney, so I've put some in. I'm basically Gordon Ramsay now.* I reach under her arms to pinch her. She elbows me away. *Get off me.*

She flicks her wooden spoon at me. I grab my face and laugh. *Ow, Mum, that was hot!*

We continue to argue as our laughter echoes through the kitchen.

8

I am twenty-eight, in a hotel room with my mother. We are lying in single beds. She wanted to go out to a bar after dinner, but I could barely keep my eyes open, so we are back in the room. I can feel her annoyance, having a daughter who isn't what she hoped for. I can't pretend to care that I'm less than she wants. I am tired. I am just so tired.

Mum, I begin, and cut myself off. I never know the next part of this sentence. I am skirting around the problem that has danced between us for years. I don't know how to talk to her, but maybe I can try.

I've been feeling low again.

Why? You are doing something you like. You have a stable job, and friends who you love. You should be happy. Why are you not?

I know all those things, and I also know they don't matter. I know they should, but they don't matter when I feel this.

What do you feel when you're low?

Tired, mostly. And sometimes I think I don't want to live. It's a thought that attacks me over and over.

She comes over to my bed. *I love you so much*, she tells me, and I start to cry.

You're so brave.

How am I brave?

I don't know, but you are.

She starts to tell me a story, about my cousin pretending it was his birthday when he was little, and having thirty kids show up at the house with presents, and his mother, furious with him, sending them all away. It has no relation to what is happening, and it makes me laugh. This is the same tactic she used when I was a kid and had skinned my knee, or gotten a bee sting: tell me a funny story to distract me from the pain. It doesn't have to make sense; it just has to work. And I laugh, because it has worked.

On the drive back to Dublin, an ad for Pieta House comes on the radio. *At Christmas time, people are more likely to commit suicide...* I feel her eyes on me.

Stop looking at me.

I'm not, I'm looking out the window.

You're looking at me!

I'm looking at the cows!

We laugh, and she squeezes my hand. *I really am trying,* I tell her.

I know, she says back to me. *I know. Thank you for trying.*

I look at my mother as she changes gear, and I feel her silent love pumping through the car. She doesn't understand, but she is here. She will always be here. And that is enough.

9

I am twenty-nine years old, living in the south of France. And this is now. This is now. I dance in my apartment by myself, moving my hips out of rhythm to some French jazz music my neighbour is blaring. I am still in my bikini, the salt from the sea crystallizing on my body, making my nipples itch. I smell the basil as I chop it up for a gazpacho recipe I found on the internet. *A cold soup!* I think to myself. *How fucking Mediterranean of me.* I crack open a cherry Coke and watch the opening credits to my favourite reality show as I slurp on my civilized soup. *What has Ramona done now?* I gleefully wonder.

I am twenty-nine, and I haven't felt depressed in a year, a full 365 days and counting, but I know it could come back. I could go back down the rabbit hole and not resurface. Mental illness is a slippery, rocky terrain that pulls and pushes with a nuance we can never truly understand until we're reading the eulogy. I know the timer could be reset in the blink of an eye, without me even realizing, and that everything I've worked so hard to get could be thrown out the window. But, when that happens, and I know with depression it's a when, not an if, so when it happens, I am ready to rebuild myself. No matter how many times it takes, I am here to piece together the ash into a stepping stone. I'm no phoenix rising, because real life isn't as grand as mystical ideas. It is boring and mundane. I am not a phoenix rising, but maybe I can be a cockroach, crawling out from the explosion, my shell still intact.

I am drizzling enough olive oil on my tomatoes that Greta Thunberg's nose is surely itching. I am googling 'mozzarella to basil ratio', just so I don't overdo it on the cheese. And I'm laughing. I love this new life I am living, full of knotty hair and sandy crotches and Caprese salads. Swimming in the sea during the day and sitting out in the courtyard afterwards, spraying every inch of my body with mosquito repellent, settling in for an evening of writing.

Bad days keep happening, of course. Sometimes I sleep for too long, and when I wake up, the sun is already setting. *Oh, God damn it,* I scream into my pillow. I drag myself up, and guzzle down a beer before I eat anything. That evening, as I stumble along the empty streets, I think about everything wrong I've done in my life up until this moment. *I don't want to exist,* I think, and the words pump through my body. I hate how easily they infiltrate me. But I let them collect in my stomach, knowing they have no power if they just remain there.

On those days when I don't love life, and there's a lot of those days, I just let myself not love it. It's not an ending. I remind myself it's just a pause. It's okay to be a person that sometimes wants to die. It's not ideal, but there are so many of us who feel this way, and just because we haven't figured out our happy ending doesn't mean we won't claw our way out of it. I close my eyes when this feeling seeps into me. *It's just a pause*, I remind myself.

I know I am my father's daughter, and I know I will carry the weight of him for the rest of my life. But I also know I am not him. My fate isn't decided in stone because of my DNA. I have his lips, and the same freckle on my nose, and his mental-health tendencies, but I am not him. He is just a piece of my story. As much as I am made from him, I am also half my mother. The quieter half, the boring half, the forgotten half. Yet, it's the stronger half. And that part survives.

Still, when I combine my father and my mother, it doesn't total the sum of my parts. There is something else, something that is just me, and that part slaps me awake each day. I am here. I am fucking here. And I am here because I want to be here. That decision is all my own. I finally understand, after all this time, that I belong only to myself.

I am twenty-nine years old now, dancing, the sweat dripping down my back as I move through the tiny room, and I exist. I exist, because I choose to exist. And I will keep choosing it, even when it gets so hard I can't see any other path but an exit sign. I will choose to live, in spite of everything I am. But maybe, too, because of it.

ACKNOWLEDGEMENTS

Thank you to my agent Katie McKay at Avalon. Her name is just Katie McKay, not Katie McKay at Avalon, but that's showbiz baby! Thanks for being a maverick and signing someone after seeing a five-minute stand-up set. Thanks for answering all my off the clock texts, buying me drinks on the company card, and telling me I am amazing when I ask you, *am I even good?* In our very first meeting I told you I had a book in me. And you said, *so, write it.* Sometimes it is that simple. You championed my writing from the very beginning, when I was just scribbling down wild essays about the fucked-up dreams I was having. You gave me the confidence to explore something I thought was beyond my grasp. If you hadn't said, *keep going, this is good*, I wouldn't have. And now a fucking book exists because of it. How wild is that?

Thank you to my publisher and editor, Jake Lingwood. You have challenged me, and pushed me, and made me a writer when I was just a person writing a book. This book would exist without you, but it wouldn't be nearly as good.

Thank you to everyone at Monoray, and especially to Sybella Stephens for correcting my grammar and syntax but never making me feel like an idiot for getting both so insanely wrong.

Thanks to Jon Gray, for the cover of my dreams. Don't judge a book by it's cover, but if it's by Jon, then please do.

Thank you to my most casual best friend, Fiona Carroll. When I met you at 17, I knew you were someone I wanted in my life. Thanks for always believing in me, in your very laid back way. Thanks for making me laugh, and letting me stay at your place, and eating cheeseboards with me when you were on a diet. There's no one else I would rather dissect Nobravok with, or watch '90 Day Fiancé' with. I love you beyond words, but those are the words that will make you the most uncomfortable, so I'll repeat them: I love you.

Thank you to Ray Badran Entertainment, for always making me laugh when I called you up depressed out of my mind about this book. This is a power move!

Thank you to my friend Jim Norton, for talking me down from a ledge when neither of us knew how high it really was. You understand the worst parts of me, and never judge me for them. Your patience and encouragement has helped me more than you'll ever know.

Thank you to my mother, an intensely private person. My thanks is pre-emptive; thank you for not reading this book. You'll hate it, but you love me, so you'll have to get over it. I am made from you, and even if we don't always understand each other, you will always be home to me. And what a fucking home that is.

Thank you to Mike Rice. A lot happened in between the drafts of this book that isn't included on the page, but you're still my favourite person I've ever gotten to know. There's a lot of thanks I could send your way, but the most pertinent here is this: thank you for pushing me forward when I wanted to stay still.

And finally, thank you to my past self. Thanks for writing this book when you could have done a million other things, like watch reality shows or sleep until noon. It's hard to do something, but you did something, and even if nothing else comes from it, even if this is all you do, you still did this.

This **monoray** book was crafted and published by Jake Lingwood, Sybella Stephens, Caroline Taggart, Juliette Norsworthy, Ed Pickford and Peter Hunt.